MW00770812

DIRT PERSUASION

DIRT
PERSUASION

Civic Environmental Populism
and the Heartland's Pipeline Fight

DEREK MOSCATO

University of Nebraska Press | Lincoln

© 2022 by the Board of Regents of
the University of Nebraska

Chapter 3 first appeared as "The Metanarrative of
Rural Environmentalism: Rhetorical Activism in
Bold Nebraska's Harvest the Hope," *Public Relations
Inquiry* 8, no. 1 (2019): 23–47. Copyright © 2019 SAGE.
Reprinted by permission of SAGE Publications,
https://doi.org/10.1177/2046147X18810733.

All rights reserved.

The University of Nebraska Press is part of a land-
grant institution with campuses and programs on the
past, present, and future homelands of the Pawnee,
Ponca, Otoe-Missouria, Omaha, Dakota, Lakota, Kaw,
Cheyenne, and Arapaho Peoples, as well as those of the
relocated Ho-Chunk, Sac and Fox, and Iowa Peoples.

∞

Library of Congress Cataloging-in-Publication Data
Names: Moscato, Derek, author.
Title: Dirt persuasion: civic environmental populism
and the heartland's pipeline fight / Derek Moscato.
Description: Lincoln: University of Nebraska Press,
[2022] | Includes bibliographical references and index.
Identifiers: LCCN 2021061670
ISBN 9781496208392 (Hardback: acid-free paper)
ISBN 9781496232106 (ePub)
ISBN 9781496232113 (PDF)
Subjects: LCSH: Environmentalism—Political
aspects—United States. | Communication in the
environmental sciences. | Political participation—
Nebraska. | Keystone XL Project. | BISAC: NATURE /
Environmental Conservation & Protection |
POLITICAL SCIENCE / Public
Policy / Environmental Policy
Classification: LCC GE197 .M67 2022 |
DDC 320.58—dc23/eng20220215
LC record available at https://lccn.loc.gov/2021061670

Set in Minion Pro by Laura Buis.
Designed by L. Auten.

This book is dedicated to my grandfather's hometown of Lac-Mégantic, Quebec, where a tragic 2013 oil train derailment took forty-seven lives and devasted a community. I also dedicate this book to the victims of the 1999 Olympic Pipeline Explosion in Bellingham, Washington, and the families they left behind.

CONTENTS

ILLUSTRATIONS

TABLES

ACKNOWLEDGMENTS

I am grateful to a number of special people and supportive organizations who have helped make this project possible as it moved
from academic concept to a fully developed book project. At Western
Washington University, the Office of Research and Sponsored Programs funded research that led to the development of critical parts
of this work. Overall moral and logistical support for this endeavor
also came from WWU's College of Humanities and Social Sciences
and the Department of Journalism, including college dean Paqui
Paredes Méndez and department chair Jennifer Keller. At the University of Oregon, where this project found its start when I was a
doctoral student at the School of Journalism and Communication,
I owe thanks to a number of university community members past
and present who were instrumental in providing significant scholarly
guidance and research inputs at various points along this journey.
First and foremost, I owe a debt of gratitude to my adviser and men-
tor Kim Sheehan, who provided theoretical inspiration and major
moral support during the early days of this project. I would also
like to thank Marsha Weisiger, Endalkachew Chala, Tiffany Gallicano, Gretchen Soderlund, Chris Chavez, Dean Mundy, Patrick
Jones, Charlie Deitz, and David Staton. At Bold Nebraska, I would
like to thank Jane Kleeb for her assistance at various points in this
research and Mark Hefflinger for his extensive help with securing
and identifying photographs and graphics. Similarly, I thank *Omaha
Magazine* for generously sharing their creative output. At the Uni-

versity of Nebraska Press, I owe a debt of gratitude to Bridget Barry, Emily Casillas, Elizabeth Zaleski, and the entire UNP team for their enthusiasm and support of this project. And finally, a big thank you to Miho, Cody, and Nelson for their patience, good cheer, and positive vibes throughout this process.

DIRT PERSUASION

1   A Pipeline Runs through It

Nearly three hours west of Omaha, in the heart of Nebraska's Antelope County, lies the farmland of Art and Helen Tanderup. The rural property's bountiful corn fields, sitting atop the Great Plains water source of the Ogallala Aquifer, are the very picture of idyllic Nebraska prairie. Yet this land has also been the scene of conflict, past and present. The Ponca Trail of Tears, memorializing the state's Native Americans who were forced to walk to a reservation in Oklahoma in 1877, passes through here. Such history gives the land a sacred dimension. More than a century later, oil and gas executives earmarked these same grounds for a different kind of route for one of North America's largest petroleum pipelines. In response, activists from an organization called Bold Nebraska descended upon these fields to challenge the encroaching infrastructure of petroleum-bearing steel tubes. With an unlikely coalition of environmentalists, Indigenous groups, ranchers, and farmers—a "Cowboy and Indian Alliance"—they unveiled a symbol fitting for the location: a massive crop art display, the size of eighty football fields, and best viewed from the air. The image, dug by the Tanderups' tractor into the farm's sandy soils, depicted facial silhouettes of a cowboy and an Indian warrior united atop giant letters spelling out the rallying cry of "Heartland." Beside it was a call to action to stop the Keystone XL Pipeline: #NoKXL.

Multi-billion-dollar oil and gas projects—including pipeline infrastructure projects such as Keystone XL—continue to be proposed and built around the world, contributing to a global oil and gas market worth roughly $3 to $4 trillion annually (IBIS World 2020). In North

America alone, this private and public investment has transformed the North American oil economy, leaving the United States and Canada as two of the world's top five oil-producing nations. In strictly economic terms, the stakes are high for industry and government. But the stakes are significant also for environmental activists and their allies, who have resisted projects such as Keystone XL on account of their ecological and societal impacts. As a result of their opposition, the environmental debate over Keystone XL became one of the most contentious environmental topics in U.S. memory (Wolfgang 2015). In the early 2020s, that polarization between two paradigms showed no signs of going away.

Environmental movements have proven they can effectively deploy and amplify strategic communication within contemporary environmental disputes to build support for their mission and cause. What is less understood, however, is how and why their messages succeed or fail. Why do some green messages resonate with policymakers and mass audiences when others are rejected? Bold Nebraska's environmental campaign against TransCanada's Keystone XL Pipeline provides an important view into the evolving role of environmentalism in a United States that is polarized like never before. Contemporary configurations of green activism such as pipeline opposition inform climate politics and energy policy, but they also offer key lessons about media advocacy and public interest communication. Nebraska's eco-activists in particular have gone against conventional environmental wisdom by embracing a gritty and populist approach that remains embedded within regional culture and hyperlocal ecology. Their story offers a compelling but sometimes controversial way forward for environmentalism at a time when the battle for hearts and minds in ecological protection and climate policy is paramount.

Prairie Petroleum

Traversing a broad expanse of North America's Great Plains, the Keystone Pipeline System transports Canadian and U.S. crude oil across a vast 2,639-mile network. When seen on a map, it appears to snake its way across physical and political geographies. One might be tempted to compare its path to that of a continental railway, or a geological entity such as a river and its tributaries. Originating in Hardisty, Alberta, the original Keystone pipeline travels east across the Canadian prairie—through Saskatchewan and a section of Manitoba—before it changes course and heads due south across the U.S. border: First to North Dakota, and then South Dakota, Nebraska, Kansas, and Oklahoma, finally arriving at refineries in Texas along the Gulf of Mexico. An easterly branch of the network also transports oil through Missouri to the Wood River Refinery in Roxana, Illinois, and the Patoka Oil Terminal Hub. Since it began operations in 2010, a decade after the pipeline project was originally proposed, the network has moved more than one billion barrels of crude oil to U.S. refineries. Designed using high-strength carbon steel and featuring thousands of data points along its route sending information to a central data center, the pipeline moves oil at the speed of the average person's walking pace (Keystone-XL.com 2017).

"One of the most modern and technologically advanced pipeline systems in the world" is how TransCanada, the company behind Keystone, described its energy infrastructure (Keystone-XL.com 2015, para. 2). Based in Calgary, Alberta, TransCanada (which was renamed as TC Energy in 2019) is an energy company with a focus on oil pipelines and power generation stations. It is a publicly traded corporation, with shares listed in New York and Toronto under the ticker symbol TRP. In addition to its Keystone assets, it operates more than fifty-seven thousand miles of natural gas pipeline, numerous power plants, and stakes in nuclear, wind power, and natural gas power generation projects (TransCanada 2017). It also maintains the TransCanada pipeline network, a system of natural gas pipelines connecting Western Canada to the provinces of Ontario and Quebec. The company's market capitalization is roughly $50 billion, making it one of Canada's largest public companies.

Central to the Keystone XL project is the development of Alberta's oil sands, which represents one of Canada's, if not the world's, most ambitious yet contentious undertakings in the petroleum sector. These oil sands, also known as tar sands, represent 97 percent of proven oil

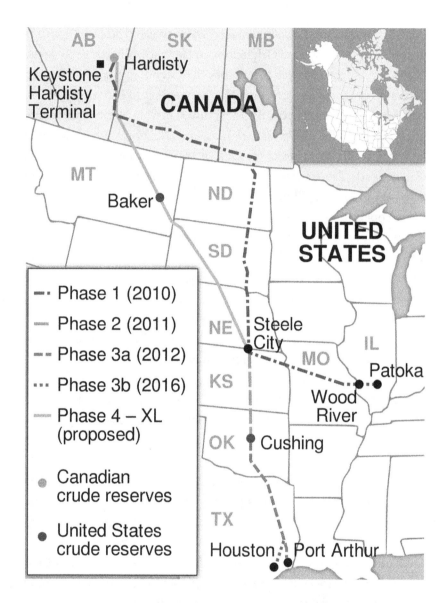

Fig. 1. Keystone XL's proposed route between Hardisty, Alberta, and Steele City, Nebraska. The proposed pipeline travels through Alberta and Saskatchewan before routing southward to Montana, South Dakota, and Nebraska. The dotted lines on the map depict completed pipelines in TransCanada's network. Image by cmglee, Meclee, Flappiefh, Lokal_Profil et al. via Wikimedia Commons.

reserves in the country, leaving Canada with the third-largest amount of oil reserves in the world, trailing only Saudi Arabia and Venezuela (U.S. Energy Information Administration 2020). The role of a continental pipeline in transporting this petroleum to markets in the United States and internationally has therefore been paramount in moving the product to markets both efficiently and safely. A 2014 State Department assessment determined that the proposed Keystone XL pipeline would be a better choice for moving petroleum in terms of safety, cost, and environmental factors over other options such as rail (Biello 2014).

Construction of the Keystone network has comprised four phases, with the first three completed between 2010 and 2016. The first connects the Keystone Hardisty Oil Terminal in east-central Alberta to Illinois; the second extends the first phase south to Cushing, Oklahoma, a major oil trading hub. The third continues the southern trajectory to the Gulf refineries in southeastern Texas. It is the fourth, however, the proposed Keystone XL pipeline, that held up TransCanada's bid to bolster its continental oil network for well over a decade. This proposed segment of the pipeline, estimated to cost more than $8 billion to build, would again originate in Alberta, run through the Bakken Formation oil reservoir of Montana and North Dakota, and transport crude oil to Steele City, Nebraska. Here, it would rejoin the extended Keystone network carrying oil to refineries. It is also here, in Nebraska, where the Keystone XL project ultimately became bogged down in an unlikely and years-long fight with environmental activists opposed to the 1,179-mile extension of the original Keystone project.

The Opposition

A number of groups and individuals along the new pipeline's path, as well as across the United States, long opposed the construction of the Keystone XL pipeline. Opposition to the project revolved around five issues historically (National Resource Defense Council 2015). The first: the safety of oil and gas pipelines, given that leakages or spills from them are destructive to local wildlife, geology, and human populations. A second, related issue was the long-term health and environmental impacts of human and wildlife populations living along the pipeline, particularly individuals near the source of the Canadian oil sands in Alberta. Third, opposition groups cited the questionable economics of oil pipelines, particularly their positioning by corporate and political backers as national job generators. They have argued that the project primarily serves offshore oil demands and the interests of the oil sector. A fourth, related argument by pipeline opponents is based on the reliance of the United States and other industrial economies on oil as a source of energy instead of clean energy alternatives. Finally—and this is critical to the evolution of environmental debates—over the years the construction of Keystone XL has become a symbolic battleground in the global debate over climate change. In a now-famous op-ed for the *New York Times*, James Hansen, an expert on climate science, warned of an apocalyptic future stemming from the extraction of Alberta's "dirty oil" (tar sands oil produces more greenhouse gas emissions than regular oil)—including an expanding dust bowl in the central United States, drought and water shortages in California, spiking food prices across the country, and rising sea levels globally. "If Canada proceeds, and we do nothing, it will be game over for the climate," he wrote (Hansen 2012, para. 2).

Since 2010 high-profile national organizations publicly opposed TransCanada's pipeline bid, including groups with national and sometimes even international profiles, such as the Natural Resources Defense Council, the Indigenous Environmental Network, the Sierra Club, and Greenpeace. At the forefront of opposition to the Keystone XL pipeline, however, emerged a state-based organization with a message aimed at local, national, and even international constituencies: Bold Nebraska.

The growing prominence of the environment as a focal point for public debate at levels regional and global underscores the importance of activists who leverage their resources and support to campaign against projects like Keystone XL. As a state-based organization that drew from grassroots support—including environmentalists, farmers, ranchers, and Indigenous communities—the case of Bold Nebraska offers new insights into the changing faces of environmental persuasion and activism.

Table 1. Organizational opposition to Keystone XL Pipeline, 2010–21

ORGANIZATION	FOCUS OF OPPOSITION
350.org	Climate change
American Rivers	River conservation
Bold Nebraska	Environmental protection/justice
EarthJustice	Legal/environmental
Environment America	State-based environmentalism
Friends of the Earth	Global environmentalism
Greenpeace	Global/national environmentalism
Hip Hop Caucus	Social justice/equality
Indigenous Environmental Network	Environmental protection/justice
League of Conservation Voters	Environmental politics
League of Women Voters	Democratic participation
National Resource Defense Council	Environmental protection
National Wildlife Fund	Wildlife conservation
Oglala Sioux Tribe	Environmental justice
Sierra Club	Conservation/environmental policy
Tar Sands Blockade	Energy/oil sands policy
The Other 98%	Economic injustice

The Rise of Bold Nebraska

In 2010 Bold Nebraska was founded with a mission of mobilizing "new energy to restore political balance" (Bold Nebraska 2015, para. 1). In its early days, as a Nebraska affiliate of the national online advocacy organization ProgressNow, Bold Nebraska cited state politics both lacking balance and being heavily influenced by right-of-center policies in close alignment with big business: "Our state is currently dominated by one political voice—conservative, and it's not the conservative voice many of us grew up with in our families. The conservative voice in our state is now dominated by far-right ideas and policies that are more about protecting big business, not fighting for our families" (Bold Nebraska 2015, para. 1). This political scenario was seen as adversely impacting environmental, economic, and social policy in the state. Not surprisingly, Bold Nebraska's initial focus was on health-care reform, a theoretically bipartisan issue that crossed party boundaries and resonated with a wide swath of Nebraskans. A key goal was highlighting the virtues and benefits of the Affordable Care Act, better known as Obamacare, after the federal statute was signed into law in March of 2010.

As the Obamacare era got under way, Bold Nebraska's trajectory appeared to be set—until the pipeline proposal came along. During the same month Obamacare was passed, the National Energy Board, a federal body with oversight of Canada's international oil, gas, and electricity projects, approved TransCanada's application for Keystone XL. One month later, the U.S. State Department released a draft environmental impact statement declaring that the pipeline would have minimal impacts on the environment.

Bold Nebraska pounced on the pipeline issue. This was a perfect political storm for Nebraska, but also an optimal venue for bridging political divides in the state. The initial Keystone proposal highlighted the economic and social challenges facing local heartland populations, such as farmers, ranchers, and Indigenous peoples. It also marked the beginning of Bold Nebraska's long-standing fight against the pipeline and, by extension, the traditional energy sector. Bold Nebraska named its opponents in the Keystone saga as "the Provincial Government of Alberta, the Government of Canada, the most powerful industry on earth, and in the United States, the Republican Party and half the Democratic Party" (Bold Nebraska 2016, para. 9). But perhaps a more apt description at the time would have been "the political and economic status quo."

The overriding goal of Bold Nebraska, in their words, was to "put the brakes on this pipeline" (Bold Nebraska 2010, para. 21) and by doing so to transform the political landscape of Nebraska. In the decade that followed, the group's activism was marked by a steady stream of coverage in publications such as the *New York Times* and *Time* magazine, alongside demonstrations and rallies from Lincoln, Nebraska, to Washington DC. There were public community events devoted to pipeline education, the planting of sacred Ponca corn, and even the construction of a clean energy barn. There were website missives, Twitter hashtags, and Flickr photo sets, plus press conferences and publicity photo opportunities galore. And in the middle of all of this arose a high-profile music festival featuring musical acts of international repute from the United States and Canada, a cultural event that conjured up the storied cultural legacies of Farm Aid, Live Aid, and Woodstock. The pipeline was no longer mere material infrastructure but rather the catalyst for a larger conversation about the expansion of the global economy, the erosion of American rural life, and the planet's ecological future. As *Rolling Stone* magazine described it, activists from Bold Nebraska helped "turn the pipeline into a symbolic crossroads, a chance to make a national decision about what form our long-term relationship to energy will take" (Jarvis 2013, para. 8).

Jane Fleming Kleeb, who lives in the small but vibrant city of Hastings, Nebraska, is the founder of Bold Nebraska. In taking up the pipeline fight in 2010, the longtime organizer initially thought she was looking at a one-year ordeal—if that. She had no idea that, more than a decade later, the battle between TransCanada and prairie environmentalists would continue to be waged, with Bold Nebraska in the middle of an increasingly contentious battle. While pipeline infrastructure and policy were new to Kleeb, she was stranger to neither politics nor the public spotlight. She was formerly a national executive director of the Young Democrats of America as well as a reporter for the cable television music channel MTV. Having been chosen by MTV from among hundreds of competitors from across the United States in 2008 to be a street reporter, she was responsible for submitting weekly reports to the channel's website and covering a wide range of political topics.

Kleeb was not always linked to the Democratic Party or progressive politics, however. Growing up in south Florida, her parents were staunchly Republican. She often watched her mother lead rallies for the Broward County Right to Life movement (Elbein 2014). Until taking a

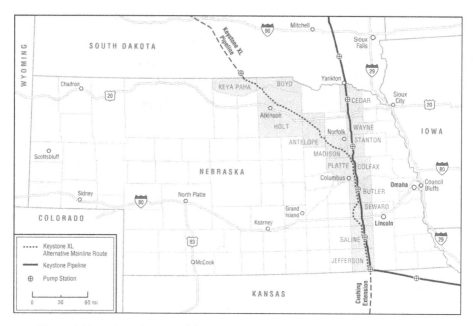

Fig. 2. A TransCanada map of the Keystone pipelines' route through Nebraska. The north–south line in eastern Nebraska is the existing Keystone pipeline. To the west is the proposed Keystone XL route. Map created by Erin Greb.

job with the Young Democrats of America, Kleeb claims to have been a Republican herself. Her connection to the state of Nebraska was initially a result of her marriage to energy entrepreneur Scott Kleeb, at the time also an aspiring politician. The two met at the 2005 Democratic Convention in Phoenix. Running as a Democratic candidate, he would eventually run (and lose) in a 2007 bid for Nebraska's third congressional seat, as well as a 2008 bid for the Senate. Notably, he was also a cattle rancher in Nebraska's Sandhills region, a designated National Natural Landmark known for its rolling, grass-covered sand dunes on the high plains. While many newcomers to Nebraska experience larger cities like Omaha or Lincoln as their first point of reference, the Sandhills' landscape of ranches and rolling hills was Jane Kleeb's first point of geographic and cultural reference in the state, one that was strikingly different from south Florida. Experiencing this world with fresh eyes as an outsider would significantly influence her future politics and activism.

Kleeb's media and communication background also had a significant impact on her work with Bold Nebraska; she was listed for the better part of a decade as the organization's "editor and founder." In 2014 she helped organize a benefit rock concert, which hearkened back to MTV's Rock the Vote concerts in support of youth voting. Bold Nebraska's Harvest the Hope concert was staged in a cornfield near the pipeline route in the town of Neligh and featured folk rock musicians and noted activists Willie Nelson and Neil Young, drawing 8,500 spectators. In a statement connecting the performances to the pipeline issue, she explained that "ranchers, farmers and tribes that have been standing up to TransCanada are rock stars in my eyes" (Saldana 2014, para. 4).

This confluence of popular culture and activism extended into Bold Nebraska's online communication. The organization's website featured petitions, guidelines for writing to government leaders, and calls for fundraising. It also drew from music festival culture and commercial appeals with the Bold Store, where supporters could buy the "No Permit, No Pipeline" T-shirt, a "Pipeline Fighter" trucker hat or armband, and a Cowboy and Indian Alliance bracelet. Even Nelson and Young, as celebrity anti-pipeline advocates, were featured in Harvest the Hope concert apparel available for purchase.

These symbolic artifacts have served as reminders that this activism was located within Nebraska, a relatively sparsely populated Great Plains state (ranked forty-third of fifty U.S. states for population density) with a heritage of agricultural industries, including livestock and dairy production, and farming of crops such as corn, wheat, soybeans, and sugar beets. The state is also a long-standing stronghold for Republican politics (Mahtesian 2020; The Hill 2014). Having voted for a Republican candidate in the last fourteen presidential elections (not including the Second Congressional District), Nebraska is better identified with conservative politics rather than a liberal political climate where contemporary environmentalism is more likely to be embraced. Of course, this political and economic heritage exists within or alongside the state's Indigenous peoples' legacy. Tribal nations have called this area home for thousands of years, and well over a dozen tribes or bands are connected to the area. Six are federally recognized within the state: the Iowa Tribe, the Omaha Tribe, the Ponca Tribe, Sac and Fox Nation, Santee Sioux Nation, and the Winnebago Tribe.

With this backdrop, Bold Nebraska's deployment of strategic communication proved to be extensive and ambitious. The organization's website included a resources page specifically for press that also included pipeline pictures, videos, and Nebraska contacts and resources. Kleeb herself was listed as a primary press contact. Some news releases and campaign materials even embedded entire legislative bills. The group's account on the microblogging platform Twitter, established in 2010, claims nearly ten thousand followers and has broadcast about eleven thousand tweets.

Between 2011 and 2021, Kleeb's leadership team included Digital and Communications Director Mark Hefflinger, a former journalist who also worked as an online organizer for progressive causes, including the 2008 campaign to stop California's Proposition 8, which eliminated the right of same-sex couples to marry in California. Her team has also included Ben Gotschall, a cattle rancher and Nebraska Farmers Union representative, who served as the movement's Energy Director. Both Hefflinger and Gotschall regularly contributed to Bold Nebraska's public- and media-facing website communication, along with Kleeb herself. Bold Nebraska also had two members serving on its board of directors during this timeframe: Rick Poore, a small business owner from Lincoln, Nebraska, and Amanda McKinney, a doctor from rural Nebraska who advocated for President Obama's health-care reforms. In spite of its relatively small organizational size and its limited impact outside of its home state, Bold Nebraska drew from extensive, national-level communication and political expertise.

Grassroots Activism and the Media

Opposition to TransCanada's Keystone XL proposal, and the ensuing debates in mainstream and social media, emphasized the outsized role of media within environmental activism. For example, pipeline opponents from Bold Nebraska provided commentary or op-ed articles for national media outlets such as the *New York Times*. Their stories, sometimes emerging from news releases and media advisories, were (and continue to be) disseminated through social, local, and national media channels. At the same time, TransCanada attempted to garner the trust and goodwill of the public in North America with large-scale public relations efforts. For a period, this included representation from the Washington DC and Calgary offices of U.S.-based Edelman, the largest public relations firm in the world (Edelman.com 2015, para. 1). While polling during 2014, an especially high-profile period for the anti-pipeline activism, showed that 61 percent of Americans supported the construction of the pipeline, those numbers dropped for specific groups. Among Democratic voters, only 49 percent were supportive. For Democratic women, support dropped even further, at 43 percent. Conversely, support for Keystone XL was much higher with Republican males and females (90 percent and 78 percent, respectively).

Thus, the quest for sympathetic public opinion was a constant driver of communication for both TransCanada and Bold Nebraska. It also highlighted the increasingly prominent role of North American energy politics in the United States, marking a potential divide between the economic interests of Canadians and the social and environmental interests of Americans. To date, the United States imports more crude oil from Canada than any other country, and by a wide margin. However, Canada's embrace of its petroleum industry has garnered the wrath of some pundits. A "climate villain" is how one liberal American magazine described the United States' northerly neighbor in light of its oil agenda and growing carbon footprint (Leber 2015). Since the rise of Canada as an energy power, environmental activists in the United States have engaged not only with policymakers, companies, citizens, and media in the United States, but also with political actors in a foreign jurisdiction. Even when the threats of climate change and oil spills hit close to home, the network of involved parties in these debates is increasingly dispersed and globalized.

For Americans living in the path of pipelines carrying Alberta oil, Canadian politicians, lobbyists, and media outlets are now part of the debate about America's energy future. This new macroeconomic and political reality has also fostered necessary linkages between environmentalists and tribal communities on both sides of the U.S.-Canada border. In addition to Keystone XL, potential additions to Canada's energy pipeline interests include the Kinder Morgan Trans Mountain Pipeline Expansion Project, which carries Alberta oil through British Columbia to the West Coast (where it will be shipped to Asia), and Enbridge's Line 3 pipeline expansion project, carrying crude oil from Alberta and Saskatchewan to Superior, Wisconsin.

The complex interplay of resources extraction industries with grassroots environmentalism and advocacy has fostered new discussions in communication scholarship about the growing role of activists in the public sphere. For many years, social movements were understood by scholars from the disciplines of sociology and political science, where activities such as organizing, direct action, and collective psychology have been emphasized. Within the public relations and management communications literature, much analysis has considered the role of activism from the perspective of the companies it opposes. Often missing, however, is an understanding of how activists might attempt to persuade media and publics through a hybrid of traditional or institutional communication tactics, regional mythology-making, and populist appeals. That is, environmentalists not only have the ability to provide successful, surface-level opposition to specific issues measured by short-term results such as public opinion and policy outcomes; they can also create a broader metanarrative in which these issues are consumed and understood by the public for decades to come. In doing so, they redefine environmentalism as a mode of individual and social existence.

Bold Nebraska's years-long fight against TransCanada provides a compelling case study: a contemporary state-level organization that simultaneously challenged political and business leaders in its home state of Nebraska, at the national level in the United States, and in the foreign jurisdiction of Canada. Such a focus sheds light not only on the activism practices of social movements but also the changing environments in which such actions are deployed. The Keystone XL saga, then, represents a watershed moment not only in energy politics and public policy but also in the communication of environmental activism. Given that Bold Nebraska joined international environmental groups such as the Sierra Club, Greenpeace, and other national advocates in providing media leadership on this issue, it is clear there are new lessons to be learned from this prairie pipeline fight.

Critical to this book is the rural dimension of this green controversy and the evolving leadership of prairie environmentalism. Traditional environmental groups have struggled to gain the same kind of foothold in the rural United States that they have enjoyed in the country's coastal and metropolitan regions. This rift becomes apparent in how the environment is often communicated by politicians, by journalists, and by other cultural elites. To put it another way, ecological challenges are rarely mediated by our cultural institutions through an agrarian lens. A fundamental premise of this book is that environmentalism needs to be understood through the eyes of rural Americans who coexist with one of the planet's most delicate ecologies. In middle America, that demographic includes Native Americans, farmers, ranchers, and other agricultural workers. For many reasons, including the fundamental rift between Great Plains and coastal politics, this rural demographic does not hold particular sway in national environmental efforts. As a case in point, farmers and ranchers have not historically enjoyed leadership positions with organizations like Greenpeace or the Sierra Club.

This becomes a problem when a certain form of cultural capital is perceived to be requisite to involvement with the environmental movement. When it refuses to transcend party politics or class polarization or even commercial interests, public environmentalism risks becoming a moral badge to be worn only by those who meet certain demographic and psychographic profiles. When this is the case, environmental movements—and the way they are understood by journalists and media audiences—move toward an idealism that transforms ecological matters into strict abstraction or religiosity. Green activists at the national level tend to be highly educated with degrees from some of the country's most prestigious institutions. Many environmental opinion leaders in political and media circles, including national journalists and NGO senior executives, similarly hold qualifications from such institutions.

Conversely, understanding environmental politics from the perspectives of farmers, ranchers, and Native Americans helps to bridge this imbalance and provides new means to conceptualizing environmental problems. But this is also about confronting the immediacy of environmental crises in every part of the United States. The green movement is doomed in red states like Nebraska unless it can shed its country-club sensibilities, understand the paradoxes inherent in prairie politics, and ground itself in the issues closest to middle America. When environmentalism is shaped through the exclusive lenses of national politics, coastal media outlets, and international NGOs, it is vulnerable to missing the heart of the environmental matter: matter itself. Contemporary environmental controversies, including pipeline developments, are at their very core driven by concerns of materiality. Their debates hinge upon issues of nature, labor, property rights, and direct ecological threats to lakes, rivers, and land. While a long-standing and usually deserved religiosity embedded in green controversies provides a signal to journalists and policymakers that they are worthy of attention, it is their material underpinnings that are most important to local constituencies. This is a worldview shared by the Canadian political economist and geographer Harold Innis, who connected social and community institutions to natural resources commodities. In developing his "staples theory," Innis situated resources such as timber, fur, fisheries, and wheat as catalysts not only for economic and technological growth but also as the underpinning of cultural activity, political ideology, and even international communication (Rotstein 1977). This obsession with the materiality of the social world, coupled with his sprawling research activities in remote regions across the North American continent, earned his scholarship the moniker of "dirt research." Following in the Innis tradition, this project tracks what I refer to here as a "dirt persuasion": a hinterland environmentalism at the crossroads of the material and the discursive. Along with its specific agricultural staples, Nebraska's anthropogenic ecology of farms, ranches, rivers, floodplains, and grasslands is situated not merely as backdrop to the Keystone XL saga but indeed as the central protagonist in pipeline communication and activism.

Also central to this book is the question of when and how a pragmatic and decidedly strategic communication strategy can enable a social movement to make significant gains, where other movements without such acumen have failed (Bob 2001). In other words, how does this emergent environmental activism go beyond movement purity or moral indignation and deploy decidedly strategic appeals to sway public opinion amid critical debates over global energy politics and climate change? Such an analysis builds upon but also informs existing understandings of environmental advocacy, social movements, and ecological media.

To answer these questions and better understand this confluence of environmentalism and communication in a regional context, this book draws from three research methodologies, which are described in subsequent chapters: quantitative content analysis, rhetorical (narrative) analysis, and the case study method. This mixed methodology captures various elements of the pipeline activism story in Nebraska, including communication and media production, news media coverage, and seminal cultural events. In turn, this approach provides an avenue for highlighting various media texts related to this saga, including news stories and press releases but also artifacts such as images, promotional materials, and music.

Layered onto this mixed-methods approach are long-form qualitative interviews with pipeline activists in Nebraska, which I conducted at various locations in the state during the fall of 2018. In explaining the value of the qualitative interview, McCracken (1998) describes it as "one of the most powerful methods in the qualitative armory. . . . The method can take us into the mental world of the individual, to glimpse the categories and logic by which he or she sees the world." These interviews should follow the "less is more" rule (McCracken 1988), asserting that it is more important to work longer and with greater care with fewer people than more superficially with too many. These interviews helped to inform multiple areas of research focus throughout this book and provide further clarification of quantitative or qualitative analysis of texts.

Though pipeline battles continue to rage across North America, lessons from the Keystone XL proposal in Nebraska offer insights into how activists and marginalized publics are able to level the playing field against much better-funded corporations, lobbyists, and government bodies. Looking back at the pipeline drama starts to fill in gaps for understanding the interplay of social movements, public interest communication, and ecology. Populism, rhetorical appeals, strategic advocacy framing, and media framing approaches all factor prominently here—leading to a civic environmental persuasion built upon the attributes of narrative, engagement, hyperlocalization, and bipartisanship in order to build broad support and influence public policy.

2   Plains Spoken

In its decade-long fight against the Keystone XL pipeline, Bold Nebraska wore the sometimes-controversial label of "populist." The description was applied in magazine features and newspaper reports, but it was also embraced by the organization itself in media interviews, press releases, and digital communication. Populism describes a political process that typically exists outside of the conventional party system or societal institutions, a historic force to be reckoned with on the Great Plains and a catalyst for citizen-driven democratic engagement. Yet it is often viewed with suspicion by observers from the media, business, national politics, and academia. Many scholars have reduced populism to pejorative understandings or have sidestepped the topic altogether (Jansen 2011). In his book about contemporary American populism and the societal institutions working furiously against it, author Thomas Frank (2020, 48) describes with humor a "showdown between peer-reviewed expertise and mass ignorance" and "the horror of populist anti-intellectualism. . . . Populism is the mob running wild in the streets of Washington, bellowing for beer and cheap gasoline." One reason disapproving scholarly understandings flourish is because populism is often conflated or tangled up with regressive developments in global and national politics, including nativism and xenophobia. That challenging paradox—of a process that fosters citizen engagement and agency while simultaneously blaming outsiders or an institutional status quo—also underpins the complex interplay of populism and ecology.

To understand the role of populism as an environmental communication process in the Great Plains' pipeline saga, it is helpful to follow

Bold Nebraska to the western reaches of the North American continent, and specifically the remote Cortes Island. Situated halfway between Vancouver Island and the British Columbia mainland in the northerly reaches of the Salish Sea, Cortes is geographically and culturally a world away from the state of Nebraska. Its landscape of old-growth rainforest and secluded beaches makes it without question one of western Canada's more beautiful landscapes. The remote island's opportunities for fishing, boating, and hiking, not to mention its backdrop of blue ocean waters and British Columbia's snow-capped Coast Mountains, more than make up for the challenge of getting to the place from virtually anywhere else on the continent. From most American cities, Omaha or Lincoln included, finding this utopian enclave would require some combination of ferry, float plane, commercial airline, and automobile— plus an international border crossing. One of the key draws that keeps tourism dollars flowing into this remote island oasis is an educational institute called Hollyhock. The teaching center is home to programs dedicated to the arts, writing, yoga, and social ventures. It also hosts conferences and leadership events with themes such as "digital leadership," "advocacy training," and "tools for thriving in the climate era." Its Social Change Institute in particular has attracted climate activists and environmental leaders from across the continent. Not surprisingly, political progressives have an affinity for the place. Others aren't quite as enamored; Hollyhock tends to attract suspicion from political conservatives in Canada, particularly in oil-friendly Alberta. Nor would old-school Nebraska ranchers necessarily feel at home here. Hollyhock's beef-free menu features "healthy, organic, vegetarian fare . . . from our abundant French-Intensive garden."

All of these variables help situate Hollyhock as a symbolic meeting place for North America's progressive environmentalists but also well-connected political and cultural elites. Jane Kleeb found herself at one such Hollyhock event—perhaps unwisely, in retrospect—along with other green activists focused on mitigating the construction of oil sands pipelines (including TransCanada's Keystone XL) across North America. Kleeb would have come a long distance for such an event—nearly

1,900 miles from her home in south-central Nebraska. That geographic distance pales in comparison to the stark cultural divide between British Columbia's West Coast and Nebraska's prairie. It would have been a key takeaway from her time at Hollyhock. And while Kleeb's endgame of stopping Keystone XL resonated with other pipeline fighters gathered at Hollyhock, an interesting rift emerged—one concerned more with process and strategy than the final outcome of the oil sands pipeline proposal. Other environmentalists at Hollyhock had asked Kleeb to tone down her rhetoric against Canada—especially the kind of anti-pipeline language that demonized Canada as a whole. Their belief was that Bold Nebraska should take aim at specific corporate and political leaders who were responsible for TransCanada's actions—but not the entire country. Besides, Cortes Island itself was far both geographically and politically from the oil sands epicenter of Fort McMurray, Alberta. To paint the entire country with such a broad brush would be a disservice to environmentalists north of the border, and in particular the green idealists who converged on this island paradise. It was time for Bold Nebraska to stop channeling the spirit of "Blame Canada," the chorus made famous by animators Trey Parker and Matt Stone in their movie *South Park: Bigger, Longer and Uncut*.

Despite the pushback from the Hollyhock crowd, Kleeb didn't back down. "Blame Canada" it was and would be. And back in the United States, she also caught flak from one of the highest-profile climate action organizations in the world: 350.org. The criticism—which focused on Bold Nebraska's use of the word *foreign*—argued that it was negative and carried more than a whiff of right-wing political rhetoric. While the complaints came from 350.org staffers and not 350.org founder and high-profile climate activist Bill McKibben (who is a personal friend of Kleeb's), the exchange between the two organizations revealed the different philosophies about how to navigate transnational pipeline politics within media and communication. Not everybody was pleased that Bold Nebraska was attacking Canada in press releases and newspaper headlines, and that included fellow environmentalists and progressives. Yet Bold Nebraska continued to forge ahead with an us-versus-them,

Nebraska-versus-the-world strategy that emphasized a struggle by the ordinary citizens of the state against non-rural outsiders who represented elite or foreign institutions and corporate interests. This was just one example of Bold Nebraska's embrace of populism.

Unlike the coastal oasis of Cortes, Nebraska is not an island. It is, of course, landlocked. Depending on one's worldview, the state lies either at the heart of the nation or the center of flyover country. Yet most visitors to Nebraska's farm and ranching country will arrive from the east, owing to the location of vibrant, denser population centers on the state's east side and by extension across the Upper Midwest. Some travelers will arrive at airports in the bustling cities of Omaha and Lincoln—urban centers that have not only survived the ups and downs of the global economy but by official demographic and economic growth figures have thrived.

That's not necessarily the case as one fans out from the major metropolitan areas, particularly in Nebraska's westerly reaches. Yet visitors would be hard-pressed to find a better way to experience the state than by first arriving from the hinterlands of eastern Wyoming, northeastern Colorado, or southwestern South Dakota. This is the heart of the high plains, characterized by semi-arid climate, foothills, and a striking but mostly treeless prairie that gives way to the state's beloved Sandhills and the heart of cattle country. The geological landmarks in this part of the state, particularly in the southwest, are an essential part of the state narrative. Scotts Bluff National Monument, with its unearthly rock formations looming over the North Platte River, reminds visitors of Nebraska's crucial place in America's pioneering story—and in particular the westward migration history of the Oregon and Mormon Trails.

Further east, Chimney Rock National Historic Site, which is featured on Nebraska's state quarter, further highlights the state's impressive confluence of geology and history. Yet mere minutes from this iconic landmark, in the small town of Bayard, history also provides a necessary lesson about global economics. A century ago, the town boomed—in great part due to the nearby establishment of the Great Western Sugar Company factory, which refined sugar from locally grown sugar beets.

Banks, hotels, and shops sprung up close by, and the population boomed around prolific job creation. But the closure of the factory in the 1980s put the town into a permanent decline from which it has never recovered. Today, the community's downtown is eerily quiet—a sharp contrast from the vibrant community shown in photos on display at the Bayard Depot Museum. Bayard, like countless other small towns dotting the American hinterland, was always vulnerable to seismic shifts in the global marketplace for resources and commodities—in this case, sugar. Bayard has also suffered from another economic and sociological trend over the past several decades: the transitioning of the family farm to large-scale industrial agriculture.

Civic life in Bayard has suffered as the population has stagnated and young people have migrated to urban centers—even as economic activity continues. Boarded-up storefronts and vacant lots are noticeable, in spite of well-intentioned beautification efforts by community volunteers and civic leaders. Bayard is located several hours west from the heart of the pipeline fight in Nebraska, but its story is one that resonates across the state, and helps to explain why economic globalization has not been embraced universally. Market forces at the national and international level have made independent farmers and ranchers especially vulnerable. Company mergers, national trade agreements, and volatile price swings for agricultural commodities leave rural dwellers unprotected from job loss or bankruptcy. They also fuel over a century's worth of populist anger in the state.

In his 2009 book *Nature's Metropolis*, the environmental historian William Cronon demonstrated how the city of Chicago became one of the world's most dynamic and economically robust cities due to how it drew from its adjacent hinterland—one that sprawled out across the Great Lakes region and the Great Plains. Well over a century ago, the city's evolving infrastructure for commercial activity and commodities exchange—stockyards, lumberyards, railway hubs, and markets for trading futures—ensured the city's centrality to resources extraction across large swaths of the United States. Grain was brought in from farmers in Iowa, Illinois, Indiana. Old-growth forests across the Upper

Midwest were logged for shipment to the Lake Michigan metropolis. Cattle farmers from Nebraska and across the high plains also found a market for their livestock in Chicago. Rail lines out of the city ensured efficient subsequent transport of raw and refined materials to the East Coast.

Thus, the American hinterland transformed Chicago into the modern metropolis. In turn, Chicago's economic institutions enjoyed an outsized influence over the everyday lives of rural peoples across the American heartland. That urban-rural dynamic remains in play today for multiple cities and resource towns, although globalization has amplified these concerns. The prices for commodities are set not only in Chicago and New York but also in London, Frankfurt, Sydney, and Osaka. All of this leaves agricultural communities vulnerable to not only national but also international market forces and politics. This aligns with the understanding of contemporary populism described by Katz and Nowak (2017) in which regional or local groups resist national or global systems based on economic self-interest alongside cultural and historic interests. This is nothing new for rural Nebraska—but the cycle of boom and bust perpetuated by economic and regulatory activity fostered an environment perfectly rife for anti-pipeline populism.

From its inception, Bold Nebraska embraced ecological populism as a means for mobilizing support and discrediting its opponents. The organization's website constantly referenced giving voice to "the populist and independent roots of Nebraskans" (Bold Nebraska 2019, para. 6). Its Twitter account also included the word "populist" in its bio, alongside the words "progressive," "independent," and "moderate." Bold Nebraska even referenced the historic legacy of Nebraska's populist Democrat William Jennings Bryan for his rousing speeches, reform proposals, and embrace of rural interests at the turn of the last century. It was Bryan who blamed industrialists and Wall Street leaders for the plight of workers and farmers—a disruptive and yet electrifying message that almost carried him to the presidency. Clearly, Bold Nebraska was playing to a statewide tradition, one steeped in the agrarian politics of the American prairie.

Yet recent history has seen populism take a drubbing in press stories and public deliberation, especially when taken out of its rural context. While the term was equated with the popularity of Democratic reformer Bernie Sanders during the run-up to the 2016 U.S. presidential election, it was used most frequently in relation to Republican candidate (and ultimately president-elect) Donald Trump. Both politicians promised to confront economic and government institutions and disrupt accepted political norms. Yet populism was also seen as fueling Trump's confrontational political rhetoric during and after the 2016 campaign. Frank (2020, 241) argued that beyond specific politicians the liberal establishment's anti-populism rests on a "contemporary culture of constant moral scolding . . . a new iteration of the old elitist fantasy." Meanwhile, the rise of anti-globalization sentiments in Europe and South America (and the election of world leaders who ultimately echoed these sentiments) were also viewed as proof of populism's dangers. In some cases, media outlets and their political pundits conflated populism with nationalist or ethnonationalist ideologies. Despite this backdrop of confusing and sometimes dark politics, Bold Nebraska—wisely or not—chose to forge on in the agrarian populist tradition.

As a contemporary vehicle for political communication and action, populism is described as a form of movement that lies outside of traditional party politics (Krämer 2014). The presentation and rhetoric of populism is argued to be of equal or greater importance than the political content itself: "The style is ostentatiously intelligible and plainspoken while complexity is represented as interest-led obfuscation. As populism is at odds with political routine and bureaucracy, it tries to raise moral sentiments and a need to restore morality and the nation" (Krämer 2014, 45). However, there is little evidence of common ideological purpose among populists (Stanley 2008). Rather, the icons and appeals of populism are local rather than universal. To this end, they also serve as storytelling variables. As Laycock (1990, 18) noted, "the success of any populist project depends on the widespread acceptance of a system of narration or distinctive ideological ordering of political and social facts."

Even as scholarly discussions of populism appear disjointed or confusing, the process is usually recognized as inherently rhetorical and persuasive and is connected to a multitude of motivations, themes, and outcomes. It is associated with anti-globalization (Tsatsanis 2011); digital politics (Rolfe 2016); right-wing discourses (Wodak 2015; Wodak et al. 2013; Rohler 1999); and political mobilization (Jansen 2011). Populism as a form of civic communication and collective action in agricultural communities is a historically known quantity in Nebraska and the Great Plains. To further understand it in the context of anti-pipeline activism, it helps to revisit the pivotal role the region has played in fostering its popularity in the United States. In the late 1800s, populism enjoyed a strong appeal in Nebraska because of its agrarian traditions and strong public sentiment against banks, railroads, and other powerful institutions seen as working against farmers' economic interests. In Nebraska and neighboring Kansas, populist appeals offered a remedying of political and economic problems outside of the existing political system (Ostler 1992). During the 1880s, wheat farmers from the two states, facing a bleak economic environment driven by transportation costs and a deflationary market for their agricultural output, joined forces with other wheat farmers from plains states and cotton farmers from the south. The People's Party, also known as the Populist Party, became a force in American politics, taking aim at Wall Street, railroad barons, banks, the gold standard, cities, and other institutions from the East. The party's formative convention in 1892, held in Omaha, called for sweeping changes to the electoral and taxation systems, the nationalization of railroad and telecommunication networks, stabilization of the national currency, and assistance for farmers.

Nebraska's agrarian culture helped grow populist sentiment on account of three identification variables: its association with the western frontier, its strong rural identity, and finally, a regional focus on the collective in light of the hardships farmers have traditionally faced through macro- and micro-economic events. Larson (1974), who looked at historical rural discontent in New Mexico, noted that frontier conditions are typically rife for populist movements. That's because semi-collective movements in the populist mode tend to polarize against the forces of "extraordinary opportunities for individual aggrandizement." History also bears out the repeated success of populist enterprises across the United States. In the Upper Midwest, for example, populism served as an agent for political change or vacillation—even bringing unconscious attitudes and beliefs to the fore (Youngdale 1975). In Minnesota, aspirations of "paradigm revolution" during the 1890s resulted in populism's giving way to necessary progressive reforms or lofty-minded socialist ideas subsequently being absorbed into mainstream politics (Youngdale 1975).

Historical prairie populism also points to broader alignment of regional and rural state interests. The growth of the Kansas and Nebraska Farmers' Alliance in 1889 and 1890 grew out of a frustration with two-party politics in the United States when neither of the traditional parties responded to the pleas of farmers facing economic hardship. Tens of thousands of farmers were mobilized in an effort to control their political destiny through the identification of an outside political entity. "Through hearing the words of their leaders and by discussing and debating various proposals among themselves, they could arrive at a solution to economic injustice. United farmers could then assert their democratic right to choose representatives and to restore government to the hands of the people; a responsive government would regulate economic affairs and recreate equality of opportunity" (Ostler 1993, 110).

The demand for such equality—equality of economic circumstances and of human rights—helped ultimately usher in the formation of the People's Party. Yet this worldview was not influenced by market and political forces exclusively. The party's populist doctrine announced an environmental creed early on, declaring that the earth belonged to humankind and that wealth belonged to those who created it. Such a platform was predicated on four overriding themes—land, labor, transportation, and capital. Here, populism emphasized the rights of the collective over the individual, and the primacy of citizens steering government programs such as railways over the private monopoly (Ostler 1992). It also made explicit the material underpinnings of a political cause. The People's Party enjoyed mixed success in the decades ahead of its founding, and more than a century later its platform continues to be broadly relevant in contemporary politics. Independent farmers have found themselves susceptible to shifts in global and national economic policies but also to the agricultural economy's shift to industrial farming. Farm owners and rural workers must contend with commodity price swings, shifting regulatory and transportation environments, and increasing foreign competition.

It is when populism is taken out of its prairie context that more contentious debate emerges over the aims and approaches of this process. To date, studies of populism bear out recurring themes: anti-elitism, dissatisfaction with institutions, and the primacy of the interests of "the people." Building on this, measurements of populism consider the presence of two key attributes: people-centrism and anti-elitism (Rooduijn and Pauwels 2011). But at the heart of discussions about populism is the lingering question of whether the process delivers a net benefit for citizens and society. Some scholars have defended populism as politically transformative. Yet within environmental politics, these movements are sometimes unfairly (and perhaps ironically) discredited on account of their success (Poli 2015). This criticism comes not only from politicians, journalists, and other political and cultural elites but also from academia. To describe a movement as "populist" is, for some scholars, a means to avoiding grappling with its greater meaning. Incumbent politicians can just as easily use the term to ignore or overlook an opponent (Poli 2015). Ardent defenders of populism might conclude that these disparaging perspectives prove their point exactly. At the same time, critics of populism have accused it of more sinister attributes: demagogic leadership and practices, creating an atmosphere of distrust toward political elites, and playing on individuals' emotions (Stanley 2008). This is the populism that comes to mind for some in a contemporary political context. An emergent challenge, then, is to identify the political or social movement corresponding to the broader concepts of populism and to understand "context-specific ideation resources" that drive this political phenomenon, given that it can start from anywhere and adjoin itself to wide-ranging political ideologies (Stanley 2008, 108).

In environmental activism, this process is often overlooked as an agent of change. That is because pro-environmental action, whether it comes in the form of climate emissions mitigation or green taxes, is often the target of politically organized populists in the Americas and Europe (Arias-Maldonado 2020; Bogojević 2019). Thus, populism and environmentalism are situated rhetorically as inevitably at odds with one another. A notable exception comes from the study of activisms against toxic waste in communities across the United States, showing how they permeated American popular consciousness and influenced national lawmakers (Szasz 1994). The media populism of Canadian journalist and activist Naomi Klein provides another useful example. In a 2013 article for *The Nation*, she lumped some environmentalists together with other so-called elites, such as corporate executives and politicians, in promoting market-driven environmental schemes like carbon offsets:

> Some of the most powerful and wealthiest environmental organizations have long behaved as if they had a stake in the oil and gas industry. They led the climate movement down various dead ends: carbon trading, carbon offsets, natural gas as a "bridge fuel"—what these policies all held in common is that they created the illusion of progress while allowing the fossil fuel companies to keep mining, drilling and fracking with abandon. We always knew that the groups pushing hardest for these false solutions took donations from, and formed corporate partnerships with, the big emitters. (Klein 2013, para. 4)

Her suspicion of elites—including those moderates *within* the environmental movement—is echoed by other activists and scholars. According to Foster and Clark (2015), a shortcoming within the environmental movement is its continued reliance on technology- and market-based solutions and discourses. Thus, the penalty for journalists like Klein going "off script" from conventional liberal thought about the environment is "excommunication from the mainstream, to be enforced by the corporate media" (Foster and Clark 2015, para. 27). From this critical ecological modernization perspective, some within the environmental movement have erred seriously in their approach to addressing climate change through market solutions, and they should be viewed with the same suspicion reserved for establishment politicians and corporations.

While Klein's brand of populism attacked the status quo from the progressive left, other environmental movements fueled by populism have perhaps counterintuitively emerged from the right. The 1970s anti-nuclear movement in California's Central Valley provided a case in point, as described in Thomas Wellock's (1998) book *Critical Masses*. Led by a "disgruntled used car salesman" tapping into egalitarian and anti-authoritarian sentiments, the movement against nuclear power in the Central Valley was infused with the spirit of Oklahoma transplants, Nixonian politics, and the so-called Bakersfield sound produced by the likes of country musician Merle Haggard (Wellock 1998). The Central Valley's residents rhetorically attacked political elites from the California coast with the slogan of "Stick it in L.A."—the "it" referring to the federal nuclear waste disposal facility originally destined for their community. This anti-nuclear movement—steeped in regional culture and suspicion of institutional elites including the federal government—represented the dawn of an emergent populist era in California politics spawning the prolific usage of petitions and recalls (Wellock 1998). As this example from the West Coast demonstrates, environmental populism is most effective in state, regional, and localized contexts. This emphasis on place naturally continues in related areas of contention such as land disputes. In more recent times, conflicts between Nevada ranchers and federal agencies fueled by populism-infused discourses were at the fore during the Sagebrush Rebellions (Merrill 2002) and standoffs during 2014 and 2016 that pitted armed ranchers against federal government agencies in Nevada and Oregon.

The wildlife protection movement in Alabama during the mid-2000s was steeped equally in regional culture. The adoption of populist wilderness frames by groups such as the Alabama Wildlife Association and Wild Alabama represented a major departure from the rational, scientific discourses used by many wilderness organizations (Walton and Bailey 2006). These activists framed wilderness not in terms of endangered species or pristine natural landscapes but rather using regional populist sentiments, incorporating wilderness as part of a broader cultural heritage for Alabama residents. Reaching out to this demographic required a different tack:

> By recognizing that the Deep South is one of the most culturally, socially, and politically conservative regions of the country, these activists have realized that any preservation efforts that put them in the mold of "environmental radicals" will threaten their success. To many Alabamians, concern over endangered species is an eco-liberal and elitist preoccupation, and one unlikely to win widespread support. The mainstream environmental movement can promote an endangered species agenda and attract support from middle- and upper-middle-class citizens. The wilderness advocates that are our focus here target an entirely different public—the rural and working class people of Alabama who have never viewed themselves as part of any environmental movement but who have a strong attachment to the land and a deep distrust of both big government and big industry. (Walton and Bailey 2006, 128)

With this strategy, environmentalism and wildlife were framed to be part of a broader cultural realm that included what Helvarg (1998, 15) described as "barbeque, beer, and firearms" alongside southern traditions like college football and prayer meetings. This is region-specific populism—a so-called populist culture framing—that leverages cultural traditions and symbols, as well as dissatisfaction with ruling elites (Walton and Bailey 2006). Like other circumstantial properties, it demonstrates the importance of focusing on issues that are common to groups at the community, regional, and national levels and go beyond individual-level problems. And the focus on such issues provides a venue for civic service in which participants feel more invested in their communities through personal engagement and agency (Hilton 2018).

To further understand this political discourse in a Great Plains context, Nelson (2018) provides the explanation of "cowboy politics," which situates the American West as an arena for environmental rhetorical appeals through popular culture. Westerns, including movies, television program, and novels, situate the frontier as a "place for fresh starts and freedoms by individuals, families, even peoples" which in turn regenerate larger societies and civilizations (Nelson 2018). These individual and societal resets are imbued with nostalgia as they seek to ward off the advances of the industrial economy: "The green valleys, golden plains, and steep passes yield to the iron rails and rites of an encroaching civilization" (83).

This enduring populist tension—between the local and international, rural and urban, agrarian and industrial, frontier and metropolitan—lies at the heart of the Keystone XL fight. To what degree did Bold Nebraska live up to its billing as a purveyor of populist discourses? To gauge how prolific such populism was, the author conducted a quantitative measurement of Bold Nebraska texts published between January 1, 2011, and December 31, 2015. This measurement of populism's frequency accounted for discourses generated by Bold Nebraska (website articles) and national media articles dealing with Bold Nebraska's pipeline activism in the United States and Canada (the *New York Times* and *Washington Post* newspapers in the United States and the *Globe and Mail* and *National Post* newspapers in Canada). More than one thousand articles were identified by the author in the organization's news section during the five-year timeframe. The news section includes all blog posts, media releases, information updates, opinion articles, and other public-facing strategic communication and editorial materials. Once their metadata was gathered, these articles—1,032 of them, to be precise—were documented by the author in a Microsoft Excel spreadsheet. From this list, a total of 236 articles were randomly sampled using Microsoft Excel's randomizer function. With a second coder independently coding website articles, the author established intercoder reliability of the content analysis. Furthermore, potential statistical associations with environmental issue frames produced by the organization were analyzed by the author (these issue frames are fully described in chapter 4). These seven issue frames were farming/ranching, land rights/eminent domain, Indigenous rights, climate change, clean/alternative energy, threats to land and water, and globalization.

Within Bold Nebraska's self-generated website communication, 87 percent of all articles included populist appeals of some kind. In other words, the vast majority of the organization's strategic communication featured populist variables or narratives. And the populist appeals often carried over into media coverage, with more than 70 percent of the national stories in the U.S. and Canadian media outlets featuring populism attributes. In order to assess the association between populism and environmental issue frames, the author undertook chi-square tests, comparing expected and actual usages of populist communication across the seven issue frames. It should come as no surprise that stories featuring globalization were most likely to integrate populism (χ^2=17.6, df=1, p<0.01). Localized environmental threats, featuring impacts to water and land, also carried populist framing elements (χ^2=10.16, df=1, p<0.05). Significant associations using Pearson's chi-square test were also found with the issue frames of land rights/eminent domain (χ^2=9.43, df=1, p<0.05) and farming/ranching, an issue frame that recalls the populist traditions within the state of Nebraska (χ^2=9.94, df=1, p<0.05).

In order to further assess the type of populism deployed, Bold Nebraska articles were assessed for the two previously mentioned types of populism measurements in content analysis (Rooduijn and Pauwels 2011): (1) the presence of *people-centrism*, indicated by language such as "citizens," "our country," and "we the people," and (2) the presence of *anti-elitism*, indicated by criticisms of political/economic elites. Stories analyzed were drawn from those already containing populism as a strategic framing element (87 percent of all stories). Within Bold Nebraska's communication, 72 percent of all stories featured people-centrism, while 68 percent contained criticism of political and business elites. Figure 3 shows that 52 percent of the articles featured both attributes.

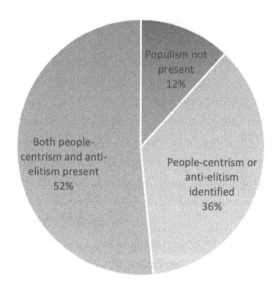

Fig. 3. Populism as people-centrism or opposition to elites (percentage of all articles). Created by author.

We the People: Prairie Populism Reborn

Among the framing elements analyzed in Bold Nebraska's website activism, populism emerged as a dominant communication process. Phrases like "we the people," "victory for the people," and "the people's voice" were a mainstay of the organization's communication. So too were criticisms of TransCanada officials and politicians at the state and national levels that emphasized a Nebraska-versus-outsiders narrative—in tones ranging from mockery to dismissal to anger. The association between the usage of populism and the issue framing of farming/ranching provides a critical reminder that Nebraska's people-centric appeals were embedded in (and likely made more palatable by) the state's agricultural traditions. Populism was also linked to two other issue frames directly impacting the prosperity of American farmers: ownership of agricultural property free of government or corporate interference (land rights) and the availability of a clean water source (environmental threats).

Bold Nebraska's rhetoric drew directly from historic plains populism, featuring criticisms of elites in combination with the rising of the people:

"For self-proclaimed outsiders, the image of the enemy took on particular importance. A persuasive rendering of political evil could transform radical dissenters into legitimate contenders for power, reversing the natural advantages possessed by those who already held it. . . . Champions of the people described the elite as being everything that devout producers, thankfully, were not: condescending profligate, artificial, effete, manipulative, given to intellectual instead of practical thinking, and dependent on the labor of others" (Kazin 1998, 15).

This conflation of hyperlocalization with distrust of political and economic elites leads to the regional populist sentiment (Walton and Bailey 2006) discussed earlier in this chapter. Just as wildlife protection advocates from Alabama framed the wilderness of the Deep South in an emotionally resonant matter in order to broaden support for environmental preservation and protection, so too did Bold Nebraska: "Successful adoption of populist and cultural frames poses a challenge to those who seek to characterize wilderness advocates as elitist liberal tree-huggers. These gun-toting, beer-drinking, football-loving activists claim kindred spirit status with their neighbors and can effectively label individual, corporate, and government actors who threaten wilderness as outsiders not to be trusted" (Walton and Bailey 2006).

The use of specific cultural artifacts and signifiers within communication (such as references to beer, football, hunting, and prayer meetings) was not part of the five years of anti-pipeline communication analyzed for this book. However, a simple keyword search of all Bold Nebraska website articles over a five-year period reveals that a populist cultural symbol such as beer was a central appeal to bolster support and dialogue. For example, the group invited U.S. president Barack Obama to a Tarsands Free Beer and Beef Summit featuring "the best water from the (Nebraska) Sandhills that makes great beer and lots of ranchers with tarsands-free beef" (Bold Nebraska 2012, para. 12). A related activity during the summer of 2011, "a beer-cooler talk," provided Bold Nebraska supporters with talking points for their July 4 parties in order to build support for several protest actions, including the I Stand with Randy events across the state in support of aggrieved landowners. Finally, to mark the occasion of the first meeting between Obama and Canadian Prime Minister Justin Trudeau, Bold Nebraska hosted a Politics and Pints: Bold State Dinner event, which included a "pub quiz" comprised of topics such as climate change, oil sands, and the North American Free Trade Agreement. Public actions and events such as Politics and Pints and the "beer-cooler talk" conjure up classic mass-communication theories emphasizing the role of individuals and groups in mediating issues and messages to each other. These include Katz and Lazarsfeld's (2017) two-step flow, which explains the role of interpersonal communication in message transmission as it moves from mass media to group and interpersonal settings; and Rogers's (2010) argument for the diffusion of ideas by opinion leaders. Both theories situate social structures inside the larger communication process, and hearken back to nineteenth-century French philosopher Gabriel Tarde, who argued for a public opinion process that traveled from the pages of newspapers to conversations in coffeehouses and salons, before finally merging into one or two primary public positions (Katz 2006).

So what was Nebraska's version of Tarde's Parisian coffeehouse? Memorial Stadium in Lincoln, home of the beloved University of Nebraska Cornhuskers football team, certainly fit the bill. Football, it turns out, was layered into the years-long campaign against the pipeline. Though some of the references to the popular team were part of conversational blogs and not central to pipeline politics, at least one moment ensnared the flagship college team into the Keystone XL debate. During the 2011 football season, TransCanada paid for pro-pipeline video advertisements aired inside the team's iconic Memorial Stadium in Lincoln. One ad, dubbed "Husker Pipeline," attempted to adjoin TransCanada's corporate brand to the University of Nebraska's storied football legacy, including its 1995 national championship. It was met with a chorus of spontaneous boos in the stadium, and Kleeb believed the promotion ultimately backfired on TransCanada—even if Memorial Stadium was an influential venue appropriate for a battle over winning hearts and minds.

Kleeb wasn't at the football game herself, but she recalls receiving phone calls and texts about TransCanada's running the advertisements. Subsequently, Bold Nebraska ran radio spots to counter TransCanada's gameday promotion. And at a subsequent Cornhuskers game, Bold Nebraska gathered signatures from parking lot tailgaters and football fans in the stadium to urge the team to take down the ads. The organization also handed out a variation of the Cornhuskers foam finger popular with fans—two thousand of them in total—with a slogan of "No Oil in Our Soil" on one side and "Stop the Keystone XL Pipeline" on the other. TransCanada's quick lead in this sports marketing battle had given way to the equivalent of a fourth-quarter comeback. By the next game, the Keystone XL advertisements were canceled. The university ended the sponsorship arrangement because of pushback from agitated fans, which included spectators actively booing the ads during the games (Abourezk 2011). The university's athletic director Tom Osborne, the legendary former Cornhuskers coach, told media that TransCanada in its own way had fumbled the ball: the spots were just too political for gameday. For opponents of Keystone XL, this was a victory as significant as the Huskers' beating a rival like the University of Oklahoma. Nebraska's usually apolitical football fans served as a proxy for the mood of the state. "In Nebraska, if you don't eat steak, corn, and cheer for Nebraska football, you might as well not live here or at least stay home on Saturdays," said Kleeb, who savored this cultural win in her adopted home state. Yet, she said, the Husker Pipeline campaign was a bust for TransCanada and "a strategic mistake on their part."

Bold Nebraska was quick to pounce on TransCanada's public relations mishap. Kleeb provided comment to local media, explaining how she "worked with an advertising agency to estimate how much TransCanada had spent on (football) advertising and discovered the company had spent about $200,000 over a recent two-week period" (Abourezk 2011, para. 24). Later, in a story headlined "Huskers Sack TransCanada," Bold Nebraska declared on its website that "when college football's best fans start booing your ads (not even the other team), well, the actions speak for themselves" (Bold Nebraska 2011, para. 6). Here, Bold Nebraska had successfully situated its environmental rhetorical appeals within the state's cultural heritage.

To an outsider, this integration of populist American imagery—the Cornhuskers football team, the Fourth of July beer-cooler talks, the "tarsands-free beef" served up by local ranchers—might clash with some key dimensions of Bold Nebraska's activism: its ability to navigate mainstream and social media channels, its alliances with green organizations like 350.org and the Sierra Club, and its effective lobbying of state legislators and national leaders. Given this political savvy and sophistication of networking, it would be easy to dismiss Kleeb and her leadership team as cultural elites themselves—and their appeals to local heritage as less than genuine. Yet previous studies have shown such a tension within a populist movement to be essential to its success: "This symbiosis was intrinsic to the political process. Without strong movements to rally around and mobilize grievances at the grassroots, elite reformers stood naked before their stand-pat adversaries. Yet, without the aid of insiders able to speak to a national constituency and work the levers of government, movements withered away or became impotent, bitter shells. . . . Movements usually have to shear off their radical edges and demonstrate that, if necessary, they can march to the rhetorical beat of an influential set of allies" (Kazin 1998, 25).

Populist appeals were a natural fit for Bold Nebraska's activism because they synchronized with topical environmental frames. American populism is rooted in the experience of the Nebraskan independent farmer. Bold Nebraska's narrative of disenfranchised farmers' and ranchers' fighting big business and government officials resonated because it was built upon a story that has already been told—through historical texts, popular culture accounts in films and novels, and even oral histories passed down from family members.

There is also the performative dimension of populism that aligned with Bold Nebraska's efforts. The organization's struggle in many ways took the form of a cinematic Western, with its appeals premised on state heritage and emphasis on morality, honor, and anger. The Western narrative—which very much explains the Nebraska pipeline struggle—

Fig. 4. This image of Bold Nebraska supporters (*left to right*) Suz Luebbe, Susan Dunavan, and Randy Thompson accompanied the organization's statement about the pipeline's routing. On May 23, 2012, the three landowners sued the State of Nebraska over the pipeline law passed in Nebraska's legislature. Graphic design by Justin Kemerling (justinkemerling.com). Image courtesy Bold Nebraska.

rhetorically made prominent what is understood as a medieval code of chivalry that rewards direct, brutally honest confrontation (Nelson 2018). Inherent in Bold Nebraska's populist appeals, therefore, was the unwritten code of its larger community, which sought to shield the interests of citizens and a broader regional collective from state- and national-level politics along with encroaching corporatization. These same appeals provided a venue for civic service in which local community members, through personal interactions, gained newfound agency related to the environment.

With that said, it is prudent here to return to populism in the 2020s. Contemporary populist activism does not exist in a regional or national vacuum. Populism in recent decades has reached beyond the United States to find a new enemy recognizable to the original Populist Party of a century ago: "Banks and corporations who routinely moved capital, goods, and services around the globe and could shrug off the once potent restraints of national governments and labor movements" (Kazin 1998, 281). As shown through the statistical association between usage of the populism element and the issue frame of globalization, Bold Nebraska's activism was predicated on villainizing not only U.S. elites but also those from outside the country's borders. Canada, in the form of the TransCanada corporation, emerged as a convenient and easy target. It held the distinction of being both foreign and a for-profit corporation—an aggressive purveyor of "dirty oil" and a serious threat to the prairie farm. However, the sentiment that drove this newer form of populism also generated some of its most impassioned criticism. It's part of the reason why other environmentalists at 350.org and the Hollyhock retreat asked Kleeb to reign in her pipeline version of the "Blame Canada" refrain. As a powerful process, populism has been associated with more dangerous appeals to isolationism, nationalism, and even ethnicity and race. Kleeb recognized this reality. When the author spoke with her in her hometown of Hastings, she acknowledged that populism as a broad political concept has come under scrutiny from the media, politicians, and other public voices—especially since the 2016 election of Donald Trump—for unleashing a more polarizing political climate. Not mentioned by Kleeb was the antagonism toward populism generated by academics.

In fairness, populism is interpreted through multiple worldviews in media and the academy to describe a wide range of political circumstances that don't always match up with basic definition of the term. Yet there is a growing chorus of voices calling for a true confluence of ecological leadership and populist thought. In particular, anthropogenic understandings of climate change have necessitated a populist style in politics to mobilize citizens and rescue humankind from its urgent existential crisis (Davies 2020; Beeson 2019). Furthermore, Bold Nebraska's coalition-building politics and its progressive-leaning stances on non-environmental issues like the provision of health care for undocumented immigrants helped define a larger populism that was both hopeful and tolerant. But the question remains: Did Bold Nebraska engage in nationalism during its years-long fight with TransCanada?

Definitions of nationalism have included themes of anticolonial sentiment, class ideology within capitalism, and mythological, irrational, and extreme ideas of nationhood (Gellner 2008). For this discussion I focus on the latter interpretation of extreme patriotism. Bold Nebraska's communication held up TransCanada as a foreign corporation, a merchandiser and conduit for foreign oil, and a Canadian interloper devoid of any sense of social responsibility to Nebraskans. Yet the criticism was specifically targeted at the company's leadership and occasionally Canada's political leadership class. Otherwise, Bold Nebraska communicated the threat of "tar sands oil" to Canadian citizens and its First Nations groups, engaged with Canadian media through the provision of media commentary, and even took an active interest in Canadian policy decisions as they related to the oil and gas sector, including proposed pipeline developments *within* Canada, such as TransCanada's Energy East pipeline. Kleeb went so far as to express her fondness for the Canadian rock band the Barenaked Ladies as proof that she liked Canadians (though not all would recognize this sentiment as genuine). But by walking this line—between rhetorically infused criticisms of foreign (primarily Canadian) elites and active interest in the well-being of Canadian citizens and Canada's environment—Bold Nebraska successfully leveraged the power of populist, anti-globalization communication without devolving into any of its darkest attributes.

Further insight here comes from understandings of nationalism and patriotism as features of culture imbued with history and communal life. Forms of organization based on personal relationships are bolstered by communication-driven "imagined communities"—fostering commitment to patriotism and national life while cementing an in-group dynamic (Anderson 2006). This imagined fraternal or community life plays a central role in establishing, or at least influencing, identities for groups and individuals. Patriotism emerges here as a form of cultural expression—more closely aligned with the attributes of religion or community life than a specific political ideology. It is also a catalyst for community in contemporary American life (Brubaker 2004). Patri-

Fig. 5. Nebraska landowners along the route of the Keystone XL pipeline, including Rock County's Steve Coble, sent #NoKXL messages to TransCanada and the White House. The billboards were painted by volunteers during the Build Our Energy Barn event. Photo by Mary Anne Andrei. Photo courtesy of Bold Nebraska.

otic appeals can foster more engaged citizenship, better integration for newcomers and immigrants, and advocacy for social justice positions.

Seen through these perspectives, Bold Nebraska's focus on the interests of local community members helped align its state and national appeals with inward-looking civic engagement, while reasonably distancing the organization from dangerous exploitation of in-group/out-group dynamics. But translating populist appeals into authentic, longer-term coalition-building across a diverse audience would require more than just one-off grassroots discourses and dramatic media narratives that pitted ordinary citizens against corporate and government elites. It would require the kind of real-time and interpersonal engagement that could change the way these pipeline fighters viewed their collective history and their relationship to the natural world.

3 Harvesting a Rural Metanarrative

During the early fall of 2014, a crowd of thousands descended upon a sprawling corn field just a few miles north of the Elkhorn River, in the country where Nebraska's easterly Sandhills finally relent to a gentler prairie farmland, to witness a morphing of environmental activism and popular culture. The Harvest the Hope benefit concert, a large-scale music event headlined by Neil Young and Willie Nelson, brought a coalition of ranchers, farmers, Indigenous leaders, and environmentalists together to take a stance against the intrusion of an oil and gas project slated for construction over ecologically sensitive lands and water. Joining the headliners were Lukas and Micah Nelson, Willie's sons, and Lukas's band The Promise of the Real; Frank Waln, the Sicangu Lakota hip-hop artist from the Rosebud Reservation in South Dakota; and Lincoln- and Omaha-based musical acts such as Jack Hotel, The Bottle Tops, Dr. John Walker, and McCarthy Trenching. The tapestry of images and sounds from the event—conveying Nebraska's wider ecology, including historical symbols of rural and Indigenous America—provided a form of persuasion that hearkened back to wilderness conservation campaigns from more than a century ago. And what would become a signature moment for Bold Nebraska highlighted the important role of environmental rhetoric as a form of ecological communication.

It also showed how the social movement organization communicated to its members and mass audiences through the symbolic and cultural levers of a nontraditional vehicle such as the benefit rock concert. The music festival drew from mainstream, alternative, and Indigenous cultural artifacts, symbols, and traditions in contesting an existing paradigm of inevitable natural resources extraction. Here, strategic narrative appeals emerged within an environmental advocacy to advance organizational identification, in-person coalition-building, and the alignment of messaging with contextual and cultural factors.

Underpinning the communicative strategies of activists, and specifically their usage of tactics, is the importance of rhetorical device. The calls of persuasion—such as symbols, metaphors, and specific messengers—help drive meaning-making within strategic communication and environmental advocacy. Visual artifacts and symbols, for example, represent a major part of the rhetorical environment and have significant impacts on contemporary culture (Foss 2004). Understanding rhetorical appeals thus provides an effective way to explore how activists situate issues for publics (Kuypers 2010). This is because rhetoric involves the creation of persuasive discourse to alter modes of thought and mediate a message of change (Bitzer 1968). The conscious crafting of messages for public consumption thus becomes a strategic act: "rhetoric is persuasive. It seeks to influence our personal and collective behaviors by having us voluntarily agree with the communicator that a certain value, action, or policy is better than another" (Kuypers 2010, 288).

These appeals stand on their own as a means for activists to identify and position themselves within broader societal discourses and to set direction and meaning for the collective. Such persuasion is reliant on the communicator's credibility and charisma, the mood or tonality of the appeal for the audience, and the advancement of appeals to reason or intellect (Demirdöğen 2010). A confluence of variables therefore dictates the success or lack thereof for such communication. These historic, political, moral, and psychological dimensions are emphasized by the rhetorical theorist and philosopher Kenneth Burke. Holding up motivations of groups and individuals as the central object of inquiry puts a spotlight on the "resources, limitations, and paradoxes of terminology" (Burke 1989). Drawing from this perspective, contemporary rhetorical analysis "assumes that opposing actors in a context of social change adopt genres of speech and writing that subconsciously reflect and deliberately manipulate the values and ideology of a particular discourse community" (Suddaby and Greenwood 2005; Berkenkotter and Huckin 1995). This rhetorical perspective—what Burke (1969, 43) refers to as a "symbolic means of inducing cooperation"—positions environmental controversies as the site for emotional appeals, tropes, narrations, and argumentation, whether they are featured on websites or in speeches, banners, campaigns, or events (Cox 2012). Persuasive appeals and attention-grabbing tropes can subvert institutional messages and support alternative discourses, evidenced in explanations such as "pranking rhetoric" or "carnivalesque activism" (Harold 2004; Weaver 2010).

It is not surprising, then, to find celebrities from entertainment, the arts, and the sporting world recruited into a variety of activist campaigns. Even if they are ill equipped to solve social and political problems by themselves (Dieter and Kumar 2008), they can bolster advocacy and public relations programs by appealing to key constituencies and attracting widespread media attention (Smith 2013). To this end, Willie Nelson and Neil Young are not the first high-profile musicians to serve as celebrity advocates. Environmental groups in New Zealand campaigning against genetic engineering, for example, recruited members of the 1980s British pop band the Thompson Twins to relay their message members of the media and the public (Henderson 2005). In turn, the musicians attracted other well-known celebrities, such as fashion designers and television stars, to their cause. By the very nature of their celebrity, famous artists bring extra publicity and media attention to their causes. In spite of some skepticism on the part of both the public and scholars, celebrities can therefore play a significant role in moving the public toward a particular ideological point of view.

Building on Burke's notions of dramatism and the "philosophy of myth" to explain the phenomena of public and mass consciousness, McGee (1980) describes the language terms that build political consciousness in collectives as "ideographs." As linkages of rhetoric and ideology, constructed symbols provide explanations of the power of a dominant ideology or state, help propagate common beliefs, and create a sense of "the people" or a broader collective: "Each member of the community is socialized, conditioned, to the vocabulary of ideographs as a prerequisite for 'belonging' to the society" (McGee 1980, 15). Used in political discourse to develop support for political positions, such a rhetorical approach establishes the value system of a community, guiding future behavior and beliefs: "The important fact about ideographs is that they exist in real discourse, functioning clearly and evidently as agents of political consciousness. They are not invented by observers; they come to be as a part of the real lives of the people whose motives they articulate" (7).

Conceptualizing the powerful role of ideographs such as nature, technology, and economic progress in contemporary environmental battles, strategically produced image events emerge as a rhetorical means to shifting existing discourses (DeLuca 2005). Powerful visual moments that depict humanity's connection to nature or community members banding together to stop ecologically harmful projects not only mitigate the counter-imagery of an industrial status quo, they reverse it to foster collective thinking and social movement activation. The example of Greenpeace's 1975 Save the Whales effort, with its visualization of a whale rescue mission on the North Pacific, provides a case in point. The success of this campaign and others like it relied upon the reduction of complex ecological issues to understandable symbols that served as a wake-up call for audiences (DeLuca 2005). In Greenpeace's case, even when protest tactics failed as direct action, they leveraged mass media dissemination—in particular the possibilities of television broadcasts— for radical change. Another example comes from the civil rights movement. The Children's Crusade in Birmingham, Alabama, provided "an exercise in cross-racial vision" and a triumph for visual communication thanks to the emotional photographs of fire hoses and police dogs turned against black youth (Johnson 2007). Images are powerful resources in the public sphere and should be studied and understood in terms of their production, reproduction, and circulation. Such an approach "accounts for both the history of images as rhetorical events and the rhetoric of images as historical events" (Finnegan 2004, 211).

The fusing of rhetorical performance and political ideology in movements also emphasizes the constitutive or group-building ramifications of narratives within ideological discourse, forming the basis for appeals to collective action (Charland 1987). Such constitutive rhetoric answers the call for scholars to understand the potential of public communication to rhetorically form identifiable norms and influence how audiences engage with social issues (Stokes 2005). Along with other group-building strategies such as investment in local relationships and task sharing, constitutive rhetoric emerges as a key means to membership recruitment and retention with grassroots organizations (Gallicano 2009). Those alternative movements that push back against dominant narratives need to tell a persuasive story—or counternarrative—that compels audiences to adopt a different vision of the future. Building this political identification for broader audiences requires both earnestness and a constitutive approach that forgoes an "us-versus-them" strategy in favor of constitutive public communication that is palatable across different groups (Stokes 2013).

This focus on the creation of broader identities and coalitions through a deliberate communication parallels the view that strategic dialogue and engagement exist as a vehicles for collectivist collaboration and communal relationships within activism at the expense of individual or group-level competition (J. Grunig 2000). Seen through the lens of rhetorical public discourse, such communication allows multiple groups in a society to reach consensus on public policy issues (Heath 2000). However, in its more polarizing or oppositional forms, this approach to activism often finds itself at odds with existing understandings of public interest communication as a site for mutual compromise and understanding between activists and institutions (Stokes and Rubin 2009). This approach also highlights the complex but significant role persuasion and engagement can play in deliberative democratic systems (Edwards 2016).

Metanarrative and the Master Frame

To this end, rhetorically developed representations such as cultural or heritage narratives help members of a collective make sense of their organization, set boundaries for public discourse, and create an audience for subsequent appeals (Bridger 1996). These narratives in combination provide a larger metanarrative—a global or totalizing cultural narrative schema—for groups, fostering sense-making of the world for the collective and its audience (McKee 2003; Stephens and McCallum 1998). The metanarrative in turn underlies and gives sense to the stories of various narrators (Zilber et al. 2008).

From this sociological perspective, the rhetorically infused metanarrative can also be understood as a master frame (Koenig 2004). For social movements, master frames both "punctuate and encode reality but also function as modes of attribution and articulation" (Snow and Benford 1992, 146). Therefore, the master frame emerges as both a means to both interpret a situation and a vehicle for confronting it.

For activist organizations without access to traditional political or economic resources, specific applications of collaboration are vital to the collective's success or lack thereof. Where the master frame emphasizes socio-psychological conditions necessary for a perceived reality to exist for the collective, the metanarrative considers the crafting and content of the group's story. Within the latter, specific appeals are selected or excluded based on their relevance to the collective's reason for being. Group formation becomes weaker when the symbols and events are not coordinated, asynchronous, and narratively incoherent (Steinmetz 1992). Previous studies of social movement and activist organizations have considered how appeals are extended to larger audiences through public discourse, thus pointing to the potential role of rhetorical appeals within persuasive activist communication. Rhetorical narratives embedded in this discourse help groups to define themselves within a metanarrative or master frame and establish an audience for subsequent appeals.

At Harvest the Hope, Bold Nebraska found its opportunity to develop a powerful metanarrative and simultaneously strengthen the Cowboy and Indian Alliance. But within this approach, distinct appeals were used to build a coalition and establish a wider audience. Furthermore, relative to other forms of communication this persuasion played a unique role in mobilizing the organization's audience and constructing meaning for the anti-pipeline movement. In blunt terms, it provided the perfect vehicle for disseminating an overarching story.

One approach to grappling with the interplay of activism and storytelling is Walter Fisher's (1987) narrative paradigm. Emerging from the pervasiveness of stories as a mode of discourse throughout human history, the narrative paradigm has been applied to a variety of communicative events in order to understand them (Foss et al. 1991). A focus on the tensions between technical and rhetorical communication is important in the environmental context. The narrative paradigm represents a rebuttal of scientific discourse, emphasizing instead the power of story development in persuasion (Fisher 1987). Several factors come together to make for successful narrative rhetoric. These include performance, historicity, and cohesiveness. An ability to succeed in these realms can even offset other significant shortcomings such as a lack of technical knowledge or even fidelity (Fisher 1987). This approach also affords the researcher the ability to understand the full array of rhetorical tactics that comprise environmental narrative, including textual but also visual appeals.

The 2014 Harvest the Hope rock festival, held at the Tanderup farm in the central Nebraska community of Neligh, represented the pique of Bold Nebraska in terms of public visibility—singlehandedly driving more searches on Google than any other activity or milestone by the organization. Proceeds from the concert were directed toward Bold Nebraska as well as the Cowboy and Indian Alliance and the Indigenous Environmental Network. The event gathered Bold Nebraska's leadership, its grassroots membership from Nebraska and neighboring states, members from local tribal communities, and other environmental organizations to participate in a cultural event that conflated popular and traditional cultures to create a landmark activism moment. Activist and nongovernmental organizations frequently find themselves working with multiple publics, though these networks are often cultivated virtually. Additionally, the event brought together almost all of the appeals, symbols, and spokespersons featured in anti-pipeline activism from the four years previous. Archived, publicly available media documentation

Fig. 6. More than eight thousand people attended the Harvest the Hope concert and fundraiser organized by Bold Nebraska on September 27, 2014. Environmental advocates, Indigenous leaders, ranchers, and farmers were present for the event, which was headlined by musical performers Neil Young and Willie Nelson. Photo credit: Arto Saari. Photo courtesy of Bold Nebraska.

provided by the organizers allowed for rhetorical analysis of this live event discourse and production.

Harvest the Hope brought these various stakeholders together in the same physical environment, providing valuable insight into the narrative devices used by Bold Nebraska, including characters, audiences, and appeals. Central to understanding how Harvest the Hope worked as a metanarrative builder was the identifying of appeals used by Bold Nebraska, both logical and emotional; the organizational spokespersons; the different narratives deployed broadly across the event; the audience engagement; and the paratext within the performative aspect of the event itself, including songs, signs, artifacts, and other visual imagery and symbols.

People collectively can participate in a public narrative that places values alongside reason (Fisher 1987). To this end, the event sought to establish a coherence between the argument against the pipeline and the lived experiences of rural Nebraskans. The concert site, situated in the path of the sacred Ponca Trail of Tears, was a key part of this metanarrative: it was also located on the route of the proposed Keystone XL pipeline.

The media artifacts for narrative analysis were (1) the music video for Neil Young's "Who's Gonna Stand Up," featuring footage from the Harvest the Hope #NoKXL Benefit, and (2) images from Bold Nebraska's Harvest the Hope Flickr (photo sharing) set, which contained 168 images of the event (accessible from http://boldnebraska.org/concert/). "Who's Gonna Stand Up?" was written by Young in 2014 and promoted by Bold Nebraska as an "anti-pipeline anthem" (Bold Nebraska 2014). The resulting Harvest the Hope video was released on Bold Nebraska's website, as well as its YouTube channel, in October of 2014, in an effort to raise voter awareness in the leadup to November 4 national elections in the United States. On the YouTube channel, prospective voters from Nebraska who "give a damn about protecting our land and water" were also encouraged to visit the New Energy Voter Guide, a project of Bold Nebraska's that seeks to influence elected positions in the state by recommending candidates based on their stance on Keystone XL and related energy topics.

The beginning of the video itself, however, is more direct about its political leanings: "We ask President Obama to STAND UP to protect our land and water. #NoKXL." This message, composed on white letters against a black backdrop, then fades away to the close-up image of the sun setting on a Nebraska cornfield. The cheering of a crowd can be heard, and a sign with the words "Pipeline Fighter Village" is shown hanging from a lamppost. As an electric guitar is strummed, the scene moves toward a row of traditional Native American teepees. Three of the cone-shaped tents, identified by their animal hide composition and wooden poles jutting from smoke flaps at the top, represent the strong presence of Nebraska's Indigenous peoples at Harvest the Hope. The support of tribal leaders also provides the impetus for the Cowboy and Indian Alliance, a Bold Nebraska initiative that sees ranchers, farmers,

Fig. 7. A promotional poster for Harvest the Hope features an aerial image
of a #NoKXL crop art installation in Neligh, Nebraska. Artist John Quigley
partnered with the Cowboy and Indian Alliance to create the world's largest
crop art installation on land located on the Ponca Trail of Tears that would
be traversed by the Keystone XL pipeline. The installation was based on
the original logo by tribal artist Richard Vollaire. Aerial photograph by Lou
Dematteis/Spectral Q. Photo courtesy of Bold Nebraska.

and other non-Native rural dwellers partnering with Native communities to stop the pipeline.

The diversity of visuals, symbols, and messages is noteworthy at
Harvest the Hope because it shows that Bold Nebraska has different
audiences that it needs to engage in order to win support from the
public and policymakers. These audiences include rural Nebraskans

engaged in farming and ranching, tribal community members, environmental advocates, and a broader swath of Nebraskans who are not traditionally engaged in environmental activism. This audience can also be extended to a much larger audience beyond the event itself. The artifacts of Harvest the Hope were widely circulated to thousands on social media, including YouTube, Twitter, and Facebook, and received attention in state and national press, including the *Omaha World Herald* and *Rolling Stone*. The event also established the organization's peak of search-based Internet traffic. Through this collage of images, symbols, and words represented in both the Harvest the Hope music video and the Flickr photo set, a typology of narrative appeals emerges. The criteria for determining these thematic areas included frequency of appearance within the event's paratexts of photos and music video, saliency of the themes in terms of their representation within the media artifacts, and an interpretation of how these themes align with audience interest and reception. The narrative appeals that emerge reflect the way the Bold Nebraska campaign, manifested through Harvest the Hope, wove broader stories and mythologies into the fight against the Keystone XL pipeline.

Narrative 1: We the People

As a conflation of environmental issues, Bold Nebraska's opposition to the Keystone XL pipeline also requires a melding of audiences. It speaks to agricultural landowners, Indigenous communities, environmentalists, the citizens of Nebraska, and the American public. This outreach helps establish a coalition of pipeline proponents while bridging political, cultural, and historical gaps between groups. To this end, the imagery of Harvest the Hope promotes a democratic pluralism imbued with patriotism, one featuring marginalized Nebraska groups (farmers, Native Americans, rural dwellers) united against a multinational corporation and layers of government from two countries. The character of the movement is established as simultaneously open to different groups, but decidedly confrontational against the established, pro-pipeline antagonists from the business and public sector camps. Symbolically this is revealed through a combination of event-day sloganeering, visual imagery, and Young's rock anthem lyrics. Young's concert video lingers on the image of a homemade sign propped up against a wooden barn that reads "Whisky is for drinking. Water is for fighting. #NoKXL." The scene pans to motorcyclists arriving at the concert. The message is clear: these Keystone XL opponents are salt-of-the-earth Nebraskans, not fair-weather protesters—and they are united in their disdain and fear of what the pipeline represents.

Lyrically, this grassroots appeal is made readily apparent in Young's chorus, imploring Nebraskans to fight Canada's pipeline industry in order to save the planet: "Who's gonna take on the big machine?" Here, he articulates a populism that incorporates both empowered citizens and a special contempt for the elites responsible for encroaching industrialization and environmental degradation. This conflict-laden narrative gives way to a moral conceptualization of pipeline opponents as religious crusaders with a special charge to redeem the earth: "Damn the dams, save the rivers."

Young's musical religiosity within the video is synchronized with the visual of a small child holding a marker and filling in the lettering for a Harvest the Hope sign. The child's efforts transition to a collage of signs along a fence marking the messages of the movement: promoting clean energy, protecting landowners, and saving the Ogallala Aquifer water supply. The latter geological entity takes on a particular urgency. One of the largest shallow water tables in the world, the aquifer underlies 174,000 square miles of the Great Plains and is essential to drinking water and agricultural irrigation in the region (U.S. Geological Survey 2009). Here, the significance of the Tanderup farmland as concert venue is elevated further. The Ponca trail and the proposed pipeline route both cross the farm, but the property also exists directly above the Ogallala water table. Like the attendees of Harvest the Hope, the land itself stands in for different histories and lives impacted by the pipeline. Another scene from the music video shows a Nebraska building with the American flag painted on one side, and the words "Freedom isn't free" sprawling across the top of another. This is followed with Bold

Nebraska's directive to the White House, encapsulated in another sign, propped up with wire fencing in a hay field: "President Obama: Protect Our Sacred Land."

Narrative 2: The Heartland

Starting with its name, the Harvest the Hope festival is built upon the activist communication emanating from rural symbols, imagery, and language. The word *harvest* is imbued with meaning directly relevant to Bold Nebraska's activism. It is defined by the *Oxford English Dictionary* as both "the process or period of gathering in crops" and "the collection (or obtaining) of a resource for future usage." Notably, it is also the namesake of Neil Young's best-selling 1972 album (*Harvest*) and his 1992 album (*Harvest Moon*). The language of Bold Nebraska thus evokes the values of environmentalism but also the traditional agricultural society—evidenced in the event's photographs. Underneath the event's own Jumbotron, on a large red banner, the silhouettes of the cowboy and Indian are seen, representing the Cowboy and Indian Alliance. Underneath this powerful image reads the words "Protect the Heartland." The word *heartland* evokes the heart, the central organ of life. The *Oxford English Dictionary* defines the word as "the central or most important part of a country, area, or field of activity." *Merriam-Webster* defines it as "a central area of land," "the central area of the U.S. which is known for traditional values," or "an area that is the center of an industry or activity."

This confluence of traditional values and economic activity is signified by the symbols of rural America featured in both the video and photographs. Art Tanderup, the Neligh corn farmer, is shown several times in "Who's Gonna Stand Up" backdropped by his John Deere tractor. John Deere is an American corporation that manufactures farm equipment, but its logo, which originated in 1876 and shows the iconic bounding deer—has become a stand-in symbol for rural life and Americana. In the same way that Coca-Cola signs and T-shirts have transcended a strictly utilitarian marketing function for the soft drink's brand, John Deere T-shirts, signs, and bumper stickers abound at county fairs and antique shops. The Deere brand exerts a "magnetic influence" over its audience through rural aesthetics but also, like Apple or Coca-Cola, a language of feeling more than information (Neumeier 2005, 18).

The company's logo and products feature prominently throughout the video, including a scene where a young woman dressed in a checkered plaid shirt and bright red dress (emblazoned with the letters "NoKXL") curtsies in front a bright green John Deere row crop tractor. Promoted here is the conflation of traditional American values with protest and anti-authoritarianism. In another black and white image within the video, a middle-aged couple stands in front of what appears to be a small-town market, backdropped by a weathered, vintage sign reading "Peter Pan Fresh Bread: Makes Tastier Meals." The scene evokes an idealized Main Street scene from a small prairie town, before the advent of big-box retailing and industrial farming.

Tanderup embodies this spirit. One of the Nebraska farmers who refused to sign land easements with TransCanada, his connection to the land—and his farm—is also shown in multiple images. He is back-dropped by symbols of the campaign, including his John Deere tractor but also his acreage of corn stalks and hay bales. As rhetorical appeals, this imagery embeds a sense of strong morality and small-town rural values, evoking a civic life enriched by rural work, small business, family life, and friendly neighbors. Such values are in stark contrast to depictions of modern life—the flight of young Americans from rural areas to cities, the growing disengagement of working people from civic life, and the intrusion of global and corporate entities into everyday life. Here, Bold Nebraska suggests to its audience that solving environmental problems is a natural extension of traditional prairie values. Harvest the Hope's mediation is also intent on juxtaposing age-old values of the prairie against contemporary realities of both globalism and global warming. Bumper-sticker-style slogans with agrarian and ecological themes appear on different signs highlighted in the music video: "Vote New Energy," "Stop the TransCanada Pipeline," "Save Our Land and Your Water."

These populist environmental sentiments are softened with a nod to Nebraska's families. In a later scene from "Who's Gonna Stand Up," a young boy wearing a cowboy hat stands in front of the concert crowd and gives the camera his nod of approval. Neil Young's voice joins the guitar fray: "Protect the wild, tomorrow's child." The inclusion of children as both messengers of and protagonists within these ecological narratives creates a universality to Bold Nebraska's message, and a reminder that preserving Nebraska's natural assets for future generations serves a collective good. It also deepens Bold Nebraska's environmental persuasion, extending it from the societal level to the family unit.

Narrative 3: The Ecological Indian

Indigenous communities represent an integral dimension to Harvest the Hope. Along with Bold Nebraska, the Cowboy and Indian Alliance and the Indigenous Environmental Network were the key partners for the event. The Tanderup farm and the Ponca Trail of Tears is pivotal to the narrative setting. As the venue of the festival, the farm lies directly on the proposed route of the Keystone XL pipeline, but it is also situated along the historic trail. In 1877 members of the Ponca Tribe of northeast Nebraska were forced by the federal government to march five hundred miles across the states of Nebraska and Kansas to an Oklahoma reservation. Harsh travel conditions during this journey led to the death of nine tribal members. One of those travelers, a young woman named White Buffalo Girl, is memorialized at a cemetery in the community of Neligh.

That legacy provides a key subtext to the festival. Nebraska's relatively young history includes a legacy of Native American communities historically disenfranchised and damaged by the actions of government and private business interests. Their presence at Harvest the Hope is especially important because it highlights the notion of a pan-Nebraskan pluralism as advertised in the Cowboy and Indian Alliance name. It also legitimizes the decision to situate the symbols of American Indigenous cultures alongside the symbols of non-Native America. Within the photographs, leaders from the Oglala, Ponca, Rosebud, and Omaha Nations are present. They honor musicians Young and Nelson for their dedication to Nebraskans and Native families. Both of the performers

Fig. 8. Shane Red Hawk of the Rosebud Sioux Nation traveled from Rosebud, South Dakota, to attend Harvest the Hope. Photo credit: Arto Saari. Photo courtesy of Bold Nebraska.

are shown wrapped in ceremonial blankets given to them by the tribal leaders—a key expression of Indigenous artistry and diplomacy.

Within the video footage and photos examined, it is the ceremonial that is put forth as Indigenous identity. A tribal elder, covered in a white gown with a blue, red, and yellow pattern headdress, is seen dancing in front of a large white teepee. In another scene, a young man from South Dakota rides a horse in full headdress and carries a traditional wood-carved hunting spear fletched with feathers. These visually elaborate images depict the richness of Native American culture and history on the plains. Simultaneously, they play into a broader depiction of what could be described as the "ecologically noble Indian" (Nadasdy 2005).

While such scenes convey a sense of respect of Indigenous cultures, they also position Native Americans almost exclusively in harmony with nature, at the expense of more nuanced or contemporary representations. Redford (1991, 46) connects these depictions to the myth of *the noble savage*, a term describing the idealized European vision of

Indigenous peoples: "The idealized figure of centuries past has been reborn," though accumulated historical evidence "refutes this concept of ecological nobility." Yet these depictions persist—in part because they cater to audiences already conditioned to accept these representations. Such scenes by their nature attract attention, sometimes driven by what anthropologist Renato Rosaldo calls "imperialist nostalgia" (Willow 2010), a reminiscing for a colonized culture as it was when first encountered by European settlers. A fascination of Native American culture based upon exaggerated mythology and misrepresentation, perpetuated by governments, academics, and popular media (Bataille 2001, 4) can also drive this communication. Black (2002, 616) refers to these appropriations or misrepresentations of Indigenous culture as "a conquering of Native America" that contributes to white hegemony while simultaneously commodifying Indigenous culture.

Even when motivated by good intentions, such representations risk masking the everyday lives of Indigenous peoples, and the current challenges they face in navigating modern societal, economic, and environmental realities. They hearken back to painter and writer George Catlin, who both celebrated and exploited Native Americans during the nineteenth century with artwork and staged performances. The well-traveled Catlin was the first white American to depict Plains Indians in their native territories, and he synchronized his artistry with a championing of Indigenous peoples' way of life (Watson 2002). Yet Catlin's paintings and other mediations, while well intentioned, merely accelerated the losses of many American tribal communities, by emphasizing the inevitability of their demise at the hands of colonial settlement and by positioning Indigenous cultures as other (Hausdoerffer 2009).

Given some of these scholarly perspectives, it is important to consider and contextualize the motivations of the Bold Nebraska coalition, including tribal members. Because this activism was calling for the survival of tribal and rural lands, it required specific forms of strategy and performance in order to foster policy and public opinion shift. At the same time, Bold Nebraska's Indigenous participants represented themselves in the way they deemed appropriate. Their presence was not merely mediated by others; they were active participants at Harvest the Hope. Landsman's (1987) analysis of ten years of coverage of a Mohawk-white conflict in upstate New York provides some insight here. During the 1970s, national media stories about Mohawk activists fighting for tribal rights used historical depictions of Native Americans while simultaneously providing coverage that was sympathetic to their cause. In turn, Mohawk organizers embraced this irony and chose to represent themselves to the media using discourses—such as romanticized views of Native Americans—that resonated with non-Indigenous readers, even if these selective representations did not match current Native American lifestyles or priorities (Landsman 1987). Writing about Cree Indians living in western Canada, Braroe (1975, 26) refers to this tension within mediated performance as impression management, the importance of which lies in the necessity for participants to exert "a degree of control over what is communicated about themselves, since information that conflicts with one's intended self-image should not be allowed to slip by." Bold Nebraska navigates this potential tension by empowering self-representation and impression management to produce a broader rhetorical coherence within its environmental metanarrative.

Given Bold Nebraska's attitudes about the ecological impacts of a petroleum pipeline passing through Nebraska land—Native or non-Native—we can infer that the organization would disapprove of depictions that reduce Indigenous peoples to simple caricatures or "the other." At the same time, the focus on ceremonial symbols and clothing in the video and photos, including their rich historical context, can come at the expense of more realistic portrayals of Native Americans in non-ceremonial contexts. There are exceptions here: In one video image, a younger Indigenous male handling a horse wears a decidedly more contemporary form of attire, a baseball cap with Nike's Air Jordan logo. Other members of the tribal communities are depicted within the video and photographs participating as musicians or as audience members—lending a credibility to the choice of Young and Nelson, themselves non-Natives, as the headline performers.

Narrative 4: The Celebrity Activist

The celebrity performers at Harvest the Hope not only serve as logical conduits between Bold Nebraska's message and a mass audience—they also lend their own symbols as rock stars to the organization's mission. Unlike the tribal members whose presence is mediated as grassroots but also performative, the involvement of musical celebrities is overt rather than implied. They are at the Neligh Farm ostensibly to help sell tickets and provide a focal point of entertainment. At the same time, they provide a set of ready-made symbols for the cause, honed over decades of recording, touring, and interfacing with the media and fans. This is underscored by their centrality to the event's paratexts of video and photographs. The twosome of Neil Young and Willie Nelson are a major reason why the audience for Bold Nebraska's activism on this day was in the thousands rather than dozens. (That only a sporting event could otherwise attract such a crowd in this state is reflected in the Nebraska Cornhuskers football attire worn by some members in the concert audience.)

Collectively, Young (from Canada) and Nelson (an American) embody as celebrities the binational nature of the fight against Keystone XL. Nelson is often referred to as a "national treasure" in the United States, and in 2015 was awarded the Library of Congress's Gershwin Prize for Popular Song. Young is considered a national icon in his home country and received the Order of Canada, the nation's highest civilian honor, in 2009. Both are international-caliber musical performers who have built their reputations on catalogs of hits from decades gone by but also have won over younger demographics because of their influence on contemporary musicians and their public activism in realms of politics and the environment.

On stage at Harvest the Hope, Young is photographed wearing a black T-shirt adorned with the hashtag #IdleNoMore and the image of a clenched fist holding a lone feather. This is the rallying cry for the Idle No More protest movement. Founded in 2012 by Canadian Indigenous leaders, Idle No More represents ongoing resistance by tribal communities to historically contested economic and environmental policies in Canada and internationally. The endorsement of the movement is important here because Young, as a Canadian, is communicating his criticism of the same Canadian policymakers who have given rise to the country's oil sands industry and by extension a demand for petroleum pipelines. Second, it provides him, as a non-Indigenous person, with political legitimacy and a degree of cultural congruency as he performs with and for the Native American audience members at Harvest the Hope.

In terms of conveying a grassroots aesthetic and sound, Young is arguably only outdone by his colleague Nelson. Joining Young on stage, Nelson plays a weathered six-string guitar that is slung around his neck with a red, white, and blue guitar strap. His attire choices also speak to the commercial sophistication of the concert organizers. He is wearing the official Harvest the Hope concert T-shirt, available at the Bold Nebraska online store for thirty-five dollars. The front of the T-shirt shows two guitars superimposed by the words "These Machines Stop Pipelines." The back, along with the names of the feature and opening acts, carries many symbols of the event: the silhouette of the cowboy and Indian and images of cows, forest, and tractors. Nelson is also wearing a "Pipeline Fighter" mesh cap, also known as a trucker hat and also available from Bold Nebraska's online store. Nelson helps construct a storyline that fosters the interplay of patriotism and protest, as well as grassroots spirit with commercial appeal.

Assessing the Narrative Fidelity of Harvest the Hope

Multiple elements converged at Harvest the Hope to convey an environmental message and cultivate a dynamic audience through synchronous persuasion. These appeals were propped up by culture—heartland values, Indigenous history, rock stars—but they were also supported by mediating the natural world. The notion of land as sacred was a recurring theme that bridged the values of Indigenous nations with their non-Indigenous Nebraska neighbors. The event's title, Harvest the Hope, implied a future for Nebraskans that was connected to the earth's metabolic processes. The bounty of Nebraska's farm crops—corn, wheat, hay—stood in for both individual and community sustenance. In one black and white image, a wooden barn was flanked by a sign reading "Reject and Protect: Protect Sacred Land and Water." The emphasis here was the role of land and water in growing food, raising livestock, and sustaining a way of life. This was exemplified by event images where the camera's focus homed in on the ground itself—corns stalks, haystacks, dirt fields—which in turn visually framed the attendees at Harvest the Hope. Seen from afar in one particularly telling photograph, the 8,500 attendees, the makeshift concert stage, the portable toilets, the tepees, and the parked vehicles seemed enveloped in corn and wheat fields that stretched for miles before meeting the horizon.

An ambitious pluralism helped bolster the fidelity of Harvest the Hope's storytelling. The festival united rural Nebraskans, Native Americans, and environmental activists in solidarity against a multinational corporation and against different levels of government. Bold Nebraska was able to make the case that their form of activism, imbued with symbols of patriotism and the American West, as well as Native American identity, positively impacted stakeholders with very different backgrounds and agendas. For environmentalists, Keystone XL represented simultaneous threats of global climate change and local threats to land, water, and wildlife. For rural Nebraskans, Keystone XL represented the intrusion of national-level and foreign elites into an agrarian way of life that was centuries old. These "sophisticates" were linked to the stagnation of small towns, the lack of economic viability of the family farm, and the vulnerability of land ownership in marginalized regions, including rural "flyover" states like Nebraska. For Native Americans, TransCanada's actions represented merely the latest in a long line of altercations with government and business over treaty violations and environmental degradations. Yet Bold Nebraska's appeals helped to weave these perspectives together.

Perhaps counterintuitively, the involvement of celebrity activists only served to further cement this fidelity. In Neil Young, Bold Nebraska recruited a singer-songwriter whose activism aligned with the plights of both farmers and Native Americans for several decades. Similarly, Willie

Fig. 9. At Harvest the Hope, musicians Willie Nelson and Neil Young (*center*) are flanked by (*left to right*) Russell Eagle Bear, President Cyril Scott (Rosebud Nation), President Bryan Brewer (Oglala Nation), and Mekasi Camp (Ponca Nation). Photo by Michael Friberg for Bold Nebraska. Photo courtesy of Bold Nebraska.

Nelson's well-publicized endorsement of marijuana, his taxpayer struggles with the Internal Revenue Service, and his advocacy for struggling American farmers ultimately affirmed his existence at the margins of mainstream culture—thus situating him outside of the "establishment" of elites. Narrative fidelity was also assured by Young and Nelson's historic involvement with a much larger cultural event, that of Farm Aid. Started as a benefit concert by the twosome three decades ago along with John Mellencamp, the event was inspired by fellow musician Bob Dylan's assertion that some funds from the 1985 Live Aid concert go to American farmers. Taken holistically, the rhetorical appeals of Bold Nebraska's activism embedded within Harvest the Hope's paratextual materials created a story about the state and the country that was more aspirational than real—a suitable reflection of the visionary politics of this environmental activism.

The inclusion of celebrities, however, does raise questions about the potential role of commercialization or commodification of protest. For example, Harvest the Hope merchandise was available for concert attendees to purchase, emulating commercial offerings from stadium rock concerts or athletic events: T-shirts, hats, and other trinkets and souvenirs such as pens and coffee mugs. These for-sale items include the official Harvest the Hope shirt (retail price $20); the Pipeline Fighter Trucker Hat ($15); a Bold Nebraska and Cowboy and Indian Alliance travel coffee mug ($6), and a pen engraved with the words "President Obama: This Machine Stops Pipelines. #NoKXL" ($3). This commercialization of grassroots appeals is also evidenced with the "I Stand with Randy" and "Windmills Not Oil Spills" T-shirts ($15 each). This is not a new approach within the environmental movement. Greenpeace's online store, for example, features a myriad of wildlife-themed buttons, stickers, postcards, and greeting cards available for purchase. It feeds an appetite for member participation and accrued cultural capital through the merchandising of commercial products. Such merchandising of green activism, then, not only raises important operational funds for organizations. It also provides a means for audiences to weave the appeals of the organization into their personal lives and life narratives. However, such consumption activity can render activism more vulnerable to outsider charges of commodification or commercialization.

Merchandising wasn't the only visible byproduct of commercial activity at Harvest the Hope. On March 15, 2015, a curious headline appeared in the pages of the *Omaha World Herald*: "Bold Nebraska sues for beer revenues from Willie Nelson–Neil Young concert." After the Harvest the Hope festival, Bold Nebraska had litigated against "the husband and wife owners of a small-town restaurant that contracted with the organization to operate the beer garden at the September show"—for $25,000 damages based on sales of 12,000 cans of beer (Omaha.com 2015, para. 2). Here is a reminder that Bold Nebraska, even as a not-for-profit entity, engaged in commercial activity to sustain its operations and amplify its message. The 8,500 tickets available for entry to the event were hardly given away; they were sold for $50 each (though many of the tickets were donated to community members and partners). While this is not a shocking cost when one considers the exorbitant ticket prices for high-profile rock artists such as the Rolling Stones and U2, or even Neil Young and Willie Nelson themselves, it represents a major cost for working families and economically marginalized citizens. Even as a fundraiser, the necessary commercialization of Harvest the Hope, including ticket and beer sales, highlights the possibility of a hierarchy of participation in movement events—a stratification between movement member haves and have-nots. Bold Nebraska's foray into concert organization necessitated at least some degree of commercial savvy and promotion. And of course, to not engage in commercialization of any sort would mean that there could be no Harvest the Hope. Here, too, Bold Nebraska had to find its comfort-zone on the purity-pragmatism spectrum.

The funds raised from Harvest the Hope were distributed to Bold Nebraska, its associated Cowboy and Indian Alliance, and the Indigenous Environmental Network. The positive net impact for recipients is obvious, as the funds generated from fundraising events such as this (Harvest the Hope cleared $125,000, according to Kleeb) sustain operations for not-for-profit entities and inject necessary capital into current and new projects. At the same time, commercialization of this order makes issue advocates vulnerable to accusations (even when they are not justified) of co-optation by business interests or the selling out of the grassroots base. Harvest the Hope provided a pipeline metanarrative for Nebraskans to rally around steeped in powerful symbolism; yet it also posted a market price for this high-profile and historic rock concert.

Being a protest movement did not stop the group from suing a small business vendor in arrears over beer sales (as was Bold Nebraska's right), nor did it mitigate commercialization of the movement through the Bold Store. There is a business cost to staging activism. An example from Australia shows how merchandising adds to an organization's appeal even while its followers are dismissed as "armchair activists." Recognise, a movement addressing Aboriginal and Torres Strait Islander peoples' rights in that country, offers an array of T-shirts, hoodies, buttons, and

Fig. 10. A poster promoting the Harvest the Hope concert. Event proceeds from the sold-out concert went to Bold Nebraska, the Cowboy and Indian Alliance, and the pipeline opposition effort. Concert poster artwork by Justin Kemerling (justinkemerling.com). Image courtesy of Bold Nebraska.

badges for sale that is similar to the Bold Store. In 2014, an Australian journalist used the merchandising to undermine Recognise's credibility and authenticity: "The Recognise brand offers a great deal to the consumer-activist . . . a sense of participating in something morally good, without the requirements to make sacrifices, forego pleasures or endure discomforts that usually accompany a moral cause" (Pholi 2014, para. 1). Such a critique is overwrought, but its basic premise—that the commodification of activism can have unintended consequences, including being taken less seriously by outsiders—is not completely without merit.

Even so, the merchandising of Harvest the Hope served to reinforce Bold Nebraska's engagement with its audience, not undermine it. Consumption of this brand—yes, a brand—played an important role in fostering an identification between its audience and the anti-pipeline movement. In addition to wearing them at the concert, participants wore these hats, T-shirts, and other items during community gatherings, demonstrations, and other public events—which in turn were mediated through photographs and video published on Bold Nebraska's website and social media platforms. In this sense, these commercial items, incorporating phrases such as "Pipeline Fighter," "Windmills Not Oil Spills," and "I Stand with Randy," provided key visual, contextual, and metaphorical rallying cries. Importantly, these bumper-sticker slogans were worn not just by Bold Nebraska's leadership but by the disenfranchised community members, including farmers and ranchers, it ultimately sought to influence and mobilize.

Yet for Bold Nebraska, the intersection of a harmless (and arguably necessary) commercialization with the ever-present risk of potential appropriation (whether real or perceived) of Indigenous symbolism does make its message more susceptible to charges of exploitation. The use of sacred Native American artifacts in fleeting editorial appeals and special events is safeguarded as activism and free speech. However, it is harder to qualify the commodification of an Indigenous headdress in a retail store with the same distinction. Without adequate context, a T-shirt design featuring the tribal prophecy of a black snake destroying land

and water can either represent support for Indigenous environmental justice or more ominously be construed by critics as profiteering from Indigenous culture. To Bold Nebraska's credit, one particular T-shirt matching that description was modeled by a tribal member. However, the Bold Nebraska store reminds communicators tasked with forging identities in the name of pluralist causes that they hold a special responsibility to dignify cultural heritages and identities. Bold Nebraska's usage of cultural symbolism was ultimately legitimized by the engagement and support of Indigenous tribal leaders and community members at Harvest the Hope. As Kleeb pointed out, it was also rooted in trust. Members of Bold Nebraska spent years building a relationship with local tribes and understanding their unique plight in the pipeline struggle.

Coalition politics are impossibly complex yet infinitely rewarding for participants when they succeed. The Cowboy and Indian Alliance highlights the fact that anti-pipeline activism, including the variety deployed by Bold Nebraska, operates within a larger framework of coalition responsibility and communication ethics. The merchandising of Harvest the Hope served to reinforce Bold Nebraska's engagement with its audience, not undermine it. Consumption of the organization's brand played an important role in fostering an identification between organization, group members, and the larger anti-pipeline movement.

At the individual- and group-levels, these brand appeals further fostered a style of speech and writing within Bold Nebraska's established discourse community (Suddaby and Greenwood 2005; Berkenkotter and Huckin 1995) while solidifying Bold Nebraska's ecological metanarrative. The sloganeering provided small but powerful image events (DeLuca 2005) that helped to shape public consciousness and provide a ready-made "vocabulary of ideographs" (McGee 1980, 15) to induce member belonging in the moment and amplify these appeals beyond the event.

Toward an American Environmental Metanarrative

Harvest the Hope demonstrated the power of rhetorical appeals embedded in environmental activism. Bold Nebraska's metanarrative railed against TransCanada's Keystone XL pipeline and simultaneously advocated for the rural citizenry of Nebraska. Such advocacy integrated multiple narratives—centered on populism, celebrity culture, rural America, and Indigenous communities—to diverse audience members with interests not traditionally aligned. Here, Bold Nebraska's arrival at a narrative-driven grassroots communication style was built upon powerful persuasive devices and the activation of the innate core values of its audience. But it also relied on the construction of a metanarrative in order to both unify its audience and underlie multiple stories about the threat of Keystone XL. It did so by constructing cohesive narrative appeals: stories that toggled between facts and values, reason and emotion, intellect and imagination.

This communication strategy hearkens back to the legacy of one of the foremost historical figures in environmental public relations: John Muir. An early advocate of wilderness preservation in the United States, he is considered "one of the patron saints of twentieth-century American environmental activity" for his prolific, poetic writings about wild landscapes, which helped ordinary Americans rethink their relationship with nature (Holmes 1999). Such preservation efforts led to the establishment of Yosemite National Park, among other nationally protected geographies. Muir also cofounded in 1892 an environmental group known today for its wide-ranging green advocacy and activism across the United States: the Sierra Club, one of Bold Nebraska's key allies in the fight against Keystone XL. Bold Nebraska's foray into rhetorically charged environmental appeals merely revived a century-old American tradition.

Material conditions were fundamental to this process. Bold Nebraska's Harvest the Hope conveyed a unique sense of ecology in the state: bountiful cornfields, agricultural equipment, and an overriding call to protect land and water. At the same time, it drew from the symbolism of the prairie to inspire a much larger public constituency—a key communication strategy that is echoed repeatedly in American environmental history. That larger narratives were molded by Bold Nebraska's images and symbols echoes Dunaway's (2008) assertion that American environmental reformers have turned to such strategic devices because they infuse aesthetics and emotion into political debates. Such tactics are effective because they can "elicit an emotional response in spectators, awakening them to the beauty of nature and arousing their concern for its protection" (Dunaway 2008, xviii). Bold Nebraska was building on a long-standing tradition within environmentalism of leveraging historic and cultural symbols to construct powerful rhetorical appeals. At the same time, these striking, seminal visual moments stand in as the image events described by DeLuca (2005)—defining not only the event but the larger ecological issue. Harvest the Hope, with its incorporation of multiple ecological appeals and tropes as part of a larger rhetorical performance, helped attendees and audiences make sense of both the organization and the movement. By bringing rural and Indigenous communities together, it also justified Bold Nebraska's broader pipeline activism and helped audiences see the pipeline through the lens of a broader coalition, and ultimately a metanarrative that was recognizable to the country.

Rhetorical appeals propped up key messengers and spokespersons to elevate a broader narrative about the organization's mission and work, and it did so with the intention of creating new interest in the pipeline's construction and environmental impacts among rural Nebraskans. In this sense, it produced what Fisher (1987) describes as social knowledge—an account of reality that is shared among citizens—as well as civic action, by encouraging broader public participation through engagement in synchronous and mediated venues. Furthermore, the appeals' constitutive nature provided the basis for political identification among the ranchers, farmers, environmentalists, and Indigenous communities represented. As Stokes (2013) notes, tapping into the story of America serves a constitutive function, at once celebrating differences of culture, geography, and faith and elevating common social and environmental goals.

Harvest the Hope reminds us that activist appeals are effective when steeped in storytelling and performance. While strategic communication is driven by information and relationships, its potential for influencing human cognition is activated through the power of story. Such a perspective is sometimes overlooked, in part because some rhetorical approaches can move parties away from conditions of mutuality or agreement—a key component of normative approaches to public engagement. This event has shown that these narrative appeals and tropes not only can be used for constructing larger meaning within activist and advocacy messaging but also play an important role in how the collective sees itself. Furthermore, the building of a powerful rural metanarrative provides the foundation for coalition-building and outreach to multiple stakeholders.

Environmental activists in particular are wise to consider how rhetorically influenced communication tactics, including powerful persuasive symbols, can align an organizational metanarrative with strategic objectives such as movement support, recruitment, media coverage, and public policy change. The focal points of contemporary environmental debates—wildlife, natural resources, and ecological relationships, along with the living and working conditions of individuals and communities—also necessitate an environmental persuasion that articulates the materiality of the spaces being contested. A rhetorical approach weaves timely universal narratives into its persuasion, but it also draws from more than a century of American environmentalism to build broader public support and engagement in an effort to stave off threats of ecological degradation to precious waterways, productive agricultural lands, and the communities of rural and Native Americans.

The legacy of Harvest the Hope was carried out not only within the pipeline-fighter metanarrative but also in the corn fields where it was hosted. In 2018, with Keystone XL continuing to loom large over the prairie, Art and Helen Tanderup once again hosted Bold Nebraska's coalition of farming, ranching, and Indigenous communities. On this occasion, the couple signed over part of their farmland—a plot of 1.6 acres that lies both on the Trail of Tears and the route of the pipeline— back to the Ponca Tribe. The gathering brought the legacy of Harvest the Hope full circle, yet it also marked the beginning of a new era for the rural activists. As with their original music festival, Bold Nebraska had deployed symbolic appeals steeped in history and culture to sustain a powerful, strategic metanarrative—one that embraced the dualism of the Great Plain's material conditions and a collective ecological idealism. An emergent land ethic was bolstering democratic engagement and a sense of public duty to the larger community.

4 Framing a Movement

In the earliest days of the Keystone XL pipeline proposal, Art Tanderup was planting soybeans in his fields when a representative from TransCanada came knocking on his door. Tanderup and his wife, Helen, the farmers from Neligh who retired to their family acreage after careers in teaching and education service, had suspected this day would come. Two weeks before, Art had seen a headline in the *Omaha World Herald* that instantly caught his attention—announcing TransCanada's proposed new routing for the Keystone XL Pipeline. A map featured in the story showed the pipeline's routing as being extremely close to his property. "We were looking at that tiny map in the newspaper and we were like, 'well, it's close to us,'" Tanderup recalled when interviewed by the author at his Neligh home in 2018. On the day that the TransCanada employee came calling, it was Helen who answered the door. As Art recalled, Helen "said there's a lady here from TransCanada and she needs to talk to us. So I came in and we talked and talked and, I swear, these people, they train them to sell. And everything is so positive." TransCanada, in Tanderup's opinion, had situated the pipeline's construction as a sort of Nebraska civic duty—requiring the Tanderups' blessings but also part of their land. "When they get done talking to you, you feel that if you don't sign this dotted-line you're unpatriotic," he said, invoking the rhetorical appeals that occur during a wartime effort. "They do such a sales job on you. It's like we got bombed, and you've got to join the army, and so you do."

Despite the arm-twisting, however, the Tanderups weren't interested in making a deal to help give right-of-way for the oil and gas pipeline.

Soon after, they heard about a meeting in town being organized by Jane Kleeb. Even though it was still planting season, Helen made time for the first meeting, and Art attended a second. Soon, they were part of a growing local group who lived and worked along the path of the pipeline who wanted no part of the project's construction. "You start researching this crap, and you don't find anything that you like," said Tanderup. "There is nothing good on this: The tailings ponds, the wildlife being totally killed off, the [other] potential impacts. And it's not just the fact it's running over our farm—it's running over the Ogallala Aquifer. And it's in the sand. And if there's a leak, it's going to be in that water." It wasn't just the high-profile oil spills that scared the Tanderups. It was the ones that didn't make the news—until it might be too late. Tanderup referred to a defective weld hole on a pipeline in South Dakota that had been leaking for weeks without detection. "If that happened here, we'd wake up dead. It's the little spills that really worry me, because those are the ones that don't get shut off, their system doesn't detect it." In the case of the South Dakota leak, residents living nearby dodged a potentially devastating scenario. "They didn't ruin their water supply, because they have to go very deep to get a well—they have rural water that is piped to the farms so they were saved by that," he said.

The meetings in Neligh, and other locations along the pipeline route in Nebraska, continued as the TransCanada push gained momentum. The Tanderups were part of a growing environmental movement to stop the project. Before long, Kleeb asked them to travel to a protest against Keystone XL in Washington DC and to do related media interviews in New York City. As meetings turned into protests, Art in particular was becoming a voice for the collective of ecologically minded ranchers, farmers, and Native Americans. He was hardly a textbook environmentalist, however. "I believe in the environment, I believe in conservation, I believe in protecting water, a lot of things that [environmentalists] believe in, but I wouldn't put that label on me," he said. He admits to having done some conservation farming previously, and he had become a proponent of no-till farming. But, said Tanderup, "if somebody would have asked me if I was an environmentalist I would have said no."

Fig. 11. Art Tanderup indicates the trajectory of the Keystone XL Pipeline that would run under his farm in Neligh. Photo by Derek Moscato.

His involvement with Keystone changed his worldview and his life. "Today they can call me a tree hugger and it wouldn't bother me," he said. The Tanderups, then, might be understood as accidental environmentalists. They didn't gravitate toward the pipeline proposal initially; instead, it literally came to their front door. The bright orange flags placed by TransCanada employees at the boundary of their property and marking the path of the pipeline through their cropland provided them with an unwelcome and ongoing reminder of this fact. Yet their involvement in the pipeline fight seems more inevitable than accidental. "We wanted to be retirees and living on the farm and traveling and growing old," said Helen Tanderup during that same 2018 interview in Neligh. Instead, the couple found themselves locked into a decade-long fight not only over their family farm but over the future of agriculture, ecology, and energy in their home state. They would also become a crucial part of a larger, emergent prairie movement that drew from the cultural and ecological heritage of Nebraska, one that was mediated strategically to audiences across the Great Plains and the country through strategic organizing, messaging, and rhetorical appeals. This was the reawakening of heartland environmentalism.

The Green Persuaders

Environmental activism is defined broadly as action and discourses on behalf of environmentally focused organizations and collectives (Seguin et al. 1998). Fundamental to such activism is the materiality of the spaces being contested: wildlife, natural geologies, and human-inhabited environments along with their living and working conditions. Environmental activists are more actively committed to changing environmental conditions or policy, and this is reflected in their attempts to influence people's attitudes and behaviors toward the environment through acts of persuasion, protest, advocacy, fundraising, and related forms of political communication (Seguin et al. 1998).

One way to understand environmental activism, then, is to situate it within the conceptual sphere of strategic communication, which explains how organizations purposefully use discourses to engage audiences and create favorable conditions for reaching policy objectives and organizational goals. Theoretical paradigms such as framing, persuasion, and public relations allow the outside observer to fully analyze the complex dynamics between activists, stakeholders, local citizens, journalists, politicians, and the larger public. Activists thus play multiple roles in their communication efforts as message creators and framers for a variety of audiences. As an organization advocating for the environmental protection of natural landscapes, farmland, Indigenous territories, and specific geological features such as the Ogallala Aquifer, Bold Nebraska therefore provides an appropriate case study for exploring these questions regarding environmental activism.

"We Don't Care Too Much for Politics"

Three years into their pipeline fight against Keystone XL, Bold Nebraska embarked on an ambitious construction project to build a clean energy barn on the path of the petroleum pipeline in order to change the way Nebraskans understood the future of energy. The Build Our Energy project drew support from national and state environmental partners, more than 1,300 donors, and hundreds of volunteers within the state who traveled to farmland near Bradshaw, Nebraska, to help build the solar-powered structure. "Mess with the bull, you'll get the horns," warned Meghan Hammond in a 2013 Bold Nebraska press release. The sixth-generation farmer, who along with her family donated part of their land to the cause, made her position clear. "We don't care too much for politics, but this is our land, and our water. It's who we are, and that's way more valuable than any hush money they can offer." In one swoop, Bold Nebraska had cast TransCanada as a corporate villain, but it also pivoted the pipeline issue away from the inevitability of oil as an energy source toward the possibility of powering the state's agricultural economy with clean, locally produced energy. At the same time, the community barn initiative had engaged hundreds of Nebraskans in real time, and tens of thousands more through fundraising and social media engagements. Bold Nebraska was framing the pipeline proposal, and the pipeline fight, in a way that best served its mission—and this was before the news media arrived to echo and amplify this emerging narrative to millions more across the state and the country.

Journalists' framing of events and issues in the media has been shown to be a critical dimension to successful activism and other forms of political communication. Framing does not emanate exclusively from the media, however. Activists enjoy significant agency and can frame issues, events, and even entire movements for journalists as well as for organization members, political elites, and the general public. Activists' use of framing, in terms of both motivations and outcomes as well as the composition and construction of such activist frames, is a critical part of understanding the communication embedded in environmental advocacy. Studies of activist and social movement organizations, including environmental groups, have incorporated a range of theories and disciplinary perspectives reflecting the widespread interest in the topic. Social movements have been analyzed from domains such as sociology and political science, while grassroots environmental protests and campaigns have received special attention in fields such as environmental history. Social movement literature often focuses on the group-level, psychological, and political circumstances and contexts behind the mobilizing forces trying to create change. At the same time, approaches from within media and communication studies have also been used to study these movements. Public interest communication scholarship has increasingly explored the relationship-building and communication strategies on the part of activists, while studies from rhetoric and persuasion have explored the conception and construction of movement messages themselves. These different positions allow for a more careful and well-rounded understanding of environmental organizations like Bold Nebraska, as they are understood through their social-psychological dimensions but also through their overarching rhetorical appeals and advanced public relations strategies. This evolution points to a shift in the playing field of environmental communication, an altered terrain that TransCanada was forced to adjust to.

Social Movements and Collective Action Framing

Studies of social movement organizations have historically incorporated numerous theories to account for the rise and fall of groups committed to social and environmental change, including resource mobilization (Jenkins and Perrow 1977; Walsh 1981), political process (McAdam 1982), and transnationalism and globalization (Brysk 1996; Seidman 2000; Widener 2007). More contemporarily, these organizations are analyzed through frameworks of digital mediation and social media algorithms (Etter and Albu 2020); international development (Martinez and Cooper 2017); and the formation and longevity of coalitions (Van Dyke and Amos 2017). Examinations featuring representation and identity also loom large. Gender mainstreaming has been a recent focus of theoretical development (Rademacher 2020) alongside insideroutsider strategies (Gulliver et al. 2020) and relational fields approaches involving the deliberate construction of movement identity (Clark et al. 2021). This amalgamation of strategy, identity, social engagement, and global dialogue has led some scholars to establish a theoretical resonance between social movement activism and civil society volunteerism (Della Porta 2020). It has also moved more research about social movement organizations into the scholarly disciplines of media and mass communication.

A long-standing interest in individual participation and engagement in social movement organizations, as well as meaning-making by movement actors, has led to significant scholarly inquiries through the study of framing (Snow et al. 2018; Wiktorowicz 2004, 15). In turn, some significant milestones in recent decades have connected framing theory to social movements literature and have helped to define this research area. To date, these have included the application of frame analysis to media portrayals of social movements (Gitlin 1979, 1980; Tuchman 1978) and the introduction of the "injustice" frame as a key catalyst for protest macromobilization (Gamson et al. 1982; Gusfield 1994). Social movement organizations have long been understood to both articulate and disseminate frames of understanding that are meant to resonate with their constituents and the general public. Snow and Benford (1988) position movements as carriers of beliefs and ideologies through a range of activities including recruitment and messaging, in turn constructing meaning for supporters and opponents. They focus on the idea of collective action frames while acknowledging that social movement organizations are typically embedded in a field in which multiple actors are vying for framing dominance or salience (Wiktorowicz 2004). Multiple groups vie for membership, funding, political support, and favorable public opinion. Consequently, movement organizations strategically develop specific frames—conveyed verbally, visually, interpersonally—around which their constituents are able to mobilize. In the U.S. debate regarding abortion, for example, different groups specifically use terms "pro-life" versus "pro-choice" to frame different perspectives of the same issue (Gusfield 1994, 69).

Thus, collective action frames provide groups with a means to understanding and articulating an issue and placing it in a larger context. Such frames are understood as representing a shared understanding of a condition or situation in need of change, an attribution of blame, an articulation of a different course of action, or a call to action for interested parties (Snow and Benford 2000). This also corresponds with frame alignment processes, which explain the alignment of different frames within a movement, and the amplification of frames to larger audiences through public events and media outreach (Snow et al. 1986). These micromobilization processes are used to align the social movement organization's goals and ideology with the values and beliefs of targeted individuals. Far from guaranteeing success, however, these processes are prone to failure and can even be counterproductive. Key to these different outcomes is "the content or substance of preferred framings and their degree of resonance" with existing and potential supporters: "Does the framing build on and elaborate existing dilemmas and grievances in ways that are believable and compelling? The higher the degree of frame resonance, the greater the probability that the framing effort will be relatively successful. Many framings may be plausible, but we suspect that relatively few strike a responsive chord" (Snow et al. 1986, 477).

Because framing processes can be conceived as rhetorical strategies to align personal and collective identities (Gusfield 1994) and build broader support with publics, an understanding of framing composition and content becomes key for organizers, activists, and issue advocates. This also highlights the need for better understanding of how activists strategically conceive and craft frames for resonance with different constituents, including supporters, the general public, and various members of the media. Public discourse is central to this framing process, hinging upon persuasive communication during mobilization campaigns along with consciousness raising through collective action (Klandermans 1992). Despite recent studies that adjoin social movement organizations to communication focal points such as digital strategy (Etter and Albu 2020) and civic engagement (Della Porta 2020), there exists a chasm between knowing social movement framing practices and their communication or media outputs. For example, scholars have identified a relative lack of understanding of how communicator frames and audience frames can coexist with frames that emerge from media content (Matthes 2009). In the case of environmental activism, a critical question thus emerges: Are frames from the relatively messy sphere of collective action successful in producing meaning and engagement around ecological issues, and do they persuade stakeholders and publics?

The Strategic Advocacy Framing Taxonomy

Frames are largely understood as inherently rhetorical and their deployment is connected to collective identity (Gusfield 1994), human cognition (Snow and Benford 2000), and awareness-building (Klandermans 1992). A taxonomy for an organization's strategic framing of public issues offers a key approach for activists, advocates, and not-for-profit organizations to position public discourse on specific issues in order to achieve desired policy outcomes. This is known as the strategic advocacy framing taxonomy, and it calls special attention to the key role played by the news media in constructing public perceptions of issues along with how organizations might identify and communicate alternative frames (Gilliam and Bales 2001). This quest for an altered media narrative is also known as "reframing" because of the communicator's ability to shift predominant discourses and the potential for encouraging publics to reconsider previously held conceptions (Lakoff 2014). Newly developed frames by organizations can help counter dominant or outdated narratives when news reporting is steeped in old conventions or stereotypes (Gilliam and Bales 2002). Thus, instead of responding to the language of a dominant paradigm, organizations should strive for message development that is closely aligned with campaign goals. This requires the translation of a group or organization's policy positions into language that considers a target audience's knowledge and beliefs about the issue (Bales et al. 2004). The pipeline politics of rural America make this process particularly challenging, since understandings of environmental topics, including climate change, are often tangled up with closely held political values and socially constructed knowledge.

Elements of Strategic Framing

On a fall afternoon in the state capital of Lincoln in 2015, Bold Nebraska and the Nebraska Sierra Club organized a game of kick-the-can outside the governor's mansion. These opponents of Keystone XL were not merely passing time while waiting for an in-person meeting with Governor Pete Ricketts. Rather, they staged the game to metaphorically send a message—to politicians, the public, and the media—that Nebraska needed to quit procrastinating and meet its goal of reducing carbon emissions by 40 percent. What they wanted was a state energy plan, a sentiment they did not see as being shared by Nebraska's political leadership. "Don't Let Ricketts Kick the Can," implored a media advisory distributed a week before the event by communication director Mark Hefflinger. "The opportunity to transition from dirty fuels [will] usher in more clean wind and solar energy in Nebraska." The advisory included an invitation for the public to join the fun, a petition for the public to sign, *and* the unflattering image of a tin can with the governor's face, featuring a similar refrain: "Tell Ricketts it's time to submit a Nebraska plan to reduce carbon pollution." Within one communication tactic, multiple rhetorical elements were being used—and synchronized—to elevate the issues of renewable energy and climate change and ultimately provide a new narrative about carbon emissions policy within the state. This was a perfect demonstration of strategic advocacy framing in action. Governor Ricketts's inaction had been effectively reframed from the official message of cautious delay to an activist narrative of ecological neglect.

In environmental and social advocacy, frames form around a variety of persuasive devices geared toward influencing how the public understands an issue (Gilliam 2006). In conjunction with one other, these elements organize situational interpretations in new and different ways or provide mental shortcuts. The strategic framing taxonomy is particularly instructive here, identifying six influential elements: numbers, messengers, visuals, tone, metaphors and simplifying models, and context (Bales and Gilliam 2010). Fully developed frames often draw from more than one element (such as visual cues in conjunction with numbers or messengers)—otherwise known as a "a proper orchestration" of variables—in order to generate new thinking about an issue (Bales and Gilliam 2010). The selective usage of these cues triggers "shared and durable cultural models that people use to make sense of their world" (Gilliam and Bales 2002). These elements are defined below, and are subsequently discussed in the context of other framing studies of activism that have featured these elements.

Numbers. While the use of numbers by themselves (in terms of statistics and other data) fail to produce the kind of frames that can emerge as dominant, they can and do orchestrate with other framing elements to provide a persuasive interplay between facts and narrative (Gilliam and Bales 2001). The framing of statistics for charitable organizations, for example, can influence the way issues are interpreted or perceived to be made salient. A social issue framed with large numbers in occurrence rates or annual aggregates, such as child poverty, is more likely to garner attention and consideration (Chang and Lee 2009). In this sense, numbers are leveraged for their informational but also rhetorical value. What becomes important it not just which numbers are presented but how they are presented.

Messengers. As the people who bring issues to the public, messengers play a pivotal role in the strategic framing process. They provide comments to the media, write op-eds, appear in photographs, publish messages on social media, and are often seen as the physical symbol of the issue—thus rendering their role as important as the message itself (Gilliam and Bales 2002). In climate change activism, for example, variations in messengers allows the issue to be seen through scientific, social justice, economic, or even ethical lenses. A climate change message delivered from a church leader casts the issue as a religious or moral crusade—giving it greater traction with members of the church (Wilkinson 2012).

The role of messengers within social movement organizations enjoys growing prominence thanks to the changing communication environment. Within emerging media forms such as online social networks, activist spokespersons can have follower networks that rival the readerships of large newspapers, in turn enhancing their ability to be represented in the mainstream media as well (Tufekci 2013). Furthermore, because environmental sources are sought out by the media for issues like global warming and sustainability, Reber and Berger (2005) call for the training of spokespersons to enhance the framing of public opinion and take advantage of media opportunities at the local, regional, and national levels.

Visuals. Photographs and images serve as visual shorthands in advocacy, producing the same mental models and frames that words do (Gilliam and Bales 2002). Images can also undermine frames constructed with words and have the power to narrow audience focus on a particular detail or emotion. Environmental reformers in the United States have long felt an attraction to photographic images because they infuse aesthetics and emotions into ecological politics, they record the reality of nature, and they bring Americans closer to the natural world (Dunaway 2008). So-called image events—where visual communication emerges as a potent and particular means for social activists to communicate on a level playing field against companies and governments—help explain why organizations like Greenpeace rely upon seminal visual moments in their communication (DeLuca 2005). Drawing from this understanding of visual media, the success of Martin Luther King's 1963 campaign and the Children's Crusade in Birmingham, Alabama, is explained as "an exercise in cross-racial vision" and a triumph for Charles Moore's widely shared, emotional photographs of civil rights protests (Johnson 2007).

In the realm of economic and environmental justice, a much lighter form of visual rhetoric involves the subversion of popular and consumer cultural artifacts (Harold 2004). Three contemporary cases highlight the success of this approach, which pairs conflict with humor: the Barbie Liberation Organization, the Biotic Baking Brigade, and the American Legacy Foundation's Truth Initiative. All three examples integrate a subversion of existing corporate or cultural entities with comedic posture and the creation of colorful imagery for the media. The Biotic Baking Brigade, which throws pies in the faces of captains of industry to express opposition to neoliberal economics, environmental degradation, and corporate monopolies, hijacks already-orchestrated media and publicity events. In this sense, these activists provide "entertainment and consumption" to visually deliver a very real environmental or social message (Harold 2004).

Tone. The tonality of activism can range from polarizing and confrontational to reasonable and neutral. Some confrontational forms of communication emanating from marginalized publics have been shown to ultimately resonate with the media and the general public in the short term (Harold 2004; Weaver 2010; DeLuca 2005). An examination of the successes and failures of working-class and poor people's movements argued that activists are most effective when they are at their most radical and disorganized, and less vulnerable to co-optation by political elites: "We may begin to consider alternative forms of organizations through which working class people can act together in defiance of their rulers in ways that are more congruent with the structures of working-class life and with the process of working-class struggle, and less susceptible to penetration by dominant elites" (Piven and Cloward 1978, xvi).

A study of student activism at Columbia University demonstrated how one polarizing image depicting heavy-handed police response to student protesters helped sway public opinion in favor of radical student protesters (Klumpp 1973). The image, showing the kind of violence that university leaders decried, delegitimized the administration and undermined its moral authority. This analysis points to a sense of conflict fueled by student activists that ultimately set the stage for converting opposition to the administration's position into support for their own: "The traditional theory of identification through compromise has fit well with the goals of representative democracy. Yet today situations in which purity of ideology and polarized opposition are the goals have gained new importance" (155).

It is worth looking to the environmentalists opposing whaling ships in the Pacific to garner a better understand of how activists emphasize or deemphasize these modes. Well-publicized skirmishes between groups like Sea Shepherd Conservation Society and whaling boats that appear on the news and in entertainment programs may turn off some audiences at home, but they also energize others. Where activist organizations like Sea Shepherd position themselves on a spectrum that ranges from outright conflict to cooperating with policymakers becomes important in terms of the psychologies of their would-be members, volunteers, and donors (Conner and Epstein 2007). Thus, the diverging activisms of Sea Shepherd and Greenpeace hint at a complex ecosystem of movement organizations within any particular issue. If Greenpeace's role in recent years was to influence global publics or lobby lawmakers on the topic through traditional institutional channels, Sea Shepherd's radical and sometimes illegal actions are what have allowed the issue to garner the public's attention in the first place, criticism of their tactics notwithstanding (Conner and Epstein 2007). An emphasis on radical action and disorganization can be useful for short-term impact but is less successful in building a broader base of supporters and allies.

Another revealing study of Sea Shepherd's activism looks at the first season of Animal Planet's reality program *Whale Wars*, which focuses on Sea Shepherd's campaign to stop Japanese whalers in the Antarctic Ocean (Russill 2009). An entire season's worth of footage both raw and televised revealed that, beyond image events depicting boat rammings, vandalized whaling equipment, and stink bombs launched at Japanese vessels, there was another side to this activism story seen only in the raw footage and previously left untold:

> For all the tough talk and black flags, it is obvious that Sea Shepherd is not really at war, or simply about whaling. When they launch an action, the activists refuse to imperil the lives of whalers, even as they risk their own. When Sea Shepherd loses some crewmembers at sea, they radio the Japanese ship for help, and the whalers offer assistance. Nor does Sea Shepherd oppose all whaling. In the brief moments when Sea Shepherd volunteers share their beliefs on the public screen, they suggest vague connections between whales, ocean life, and the future of humans.... These examples and explanations evoke moments of a broadened sense of shared finitude, which is the experience motivating a wide variety of eco-centric thought. (Russill 2009, para. 12)

This finding suggests that even polarizing forms of activism can be rooted in a strategic orientation, with Sea Shepherd's members toggling between oppositional and reasonable based on whether or not the television cameras are rolling. Perhaps counterintuitively, Sea Shepherd constructed a more polarizing image for mass audiences in order to capture their interest but displayed a more reasonable tact during private moments with their Japanese adversaries.

Metaphors and simplifying models. Metaphors enjoy an outsized presence in environmental activism and communication, with terms like *population bomb* and *carbon footprint* regularly injected into debates (Cox 2012). Analogies and simplifying models about the environment are useful because they help audiences make extensive inferences through streamlined patterns of reasoning (Gilliam and Bales 2002). They have also been shown to be popular with the media. A study of carbon reduction activism and subsequent news coverage argues for an interplay of issues frames, which help articulate a language of climate change activism, and media frames, which deployed conceptual metaphors for the environment like religion (climate activism as a moral imperative), dieting (equating the carbon footprint to human health), and finance (climate activism as financial management) to make such activism understood by a wider audience (Nerlich and Koteyko 2009). Climate activism was also framed as a battle or war, or as a journey in which the final destination is the reduction of carbon emissions: "A first step toward such a change is always to make people think differently about a topic, to change old cognitive habits, and entrench new cognitive habits to see things in a new light, in fact to create new ontologies. However, new thinking has to be rooted in something already well-known and familiar to make the jump from old to new possible" (Nerlich and Koteyko 2009, 219). Such metaphorical language not only democratizes debates about climate change by simplifying the language and making it more widely available to audiences; it also brings about behavior change.

Context. By focusing on issues that are common to groups and go beyond individual-level problems, context helps broaden frames to family, community, regional, or even national levels (Gilliam and Bales

2001). Long-term or national trends are considered, positioning the issue as part of a wider public discourse. Situating events within a time or place elevates the roles of geography, history, and culture. In the bid to maximize support across the political spectrum, Chong (2012) argues for activist appeals that integrate dominant cultural norms such as individual liberty, limited government, patriotism, and respect for private property. To this end, the framing strategies of bipartisanship, patriotism, and narrative are recommended to adjoin to the more traditional movement frames of legality and radical social justice. The bipartisanship frame in particular recognizes the importance of the political center in the United States and argues that key economic values and principles are shared by conservatives and liberals, Republicans and Democrats, workers and executives (Chong 2012). Along with patriotism and narrative framing strategies, it reflects an alignment with the values and beliefs of mainstream audiences: "The cultural resonance of a frame is therefore even more important than its veracity, as is demonstrated by the ongoing effectiveness of political messages that are refuted by fact-checking organizations. In the cultural context of the United States, then, economic and social rights must be promoted in a manner that appeals to the dominant cultural norms . . . even as activists seek to co-opt or modify these cultural norms" (Chong 2012, 125). Social problems, as Guttman (2000, 74) notes, are "time-, place-, and context-bound. . . . The particular view of the ideal state is what determines what is considered problematic." With their ability to draw from dominant cultural norms such as patriotism and private property rights, framing strategies highlight a political style that is potentially driven by the hyperlocal and the historical.

Gilliam and Bales's (2002) strategic framing taxonomy, with its six elements of numbers, messengers, visuals, tone, context, and metaphors, responds to the confluence of activism with strategy and framing to understand how specific compositional elements inform frames. As a form of strategic communication, this framing taxonomy closely parallels scholarly inquiry within persuasion and public interest communication about how it advances the objectives of activist organizations.

Table 2. Strategic advocacy framing taxonomy

STRATEGIC FRAMING ELEMENT	DESCRIPTION
Numbers	The provision of data or statistics to highlight a problem or opportunity
Messengers	Individuals who bring personal experiences, perspectives, and actions to an issue
Visuals	The usage of photos, illustrations, maps, cartoons, charts, and other graphical representations
Tone	The degree to which advocacy is strident or oppositional in tone
Metaphors	Simplifying models or figures of speech representative of more complex issues
Context	Recognition of the problem or opportunity within the boundaries of time, space, and community

Source: (Gilliam and Bales 2001)

Ideology versus Strategy: Lessons from Nigeria's Ogoni Movement

An ongoing dialectic exists within social movements between frames that serve collective action and member beliefs and those that serve the strategic or long-term interests of the organization, including a movement's ability to affect policy change, attract new supporters, and gain preferred standing with media and audiences. A recognition of this tension between ideology and strategy comes from a study of the long-running Ogoni movement in Nigeria (Bob 2001). The insurgency of the Indigenous Ogoni people of Central Niger Delta was critical of not only the Nigerian state over human rights issues such as poverty and medicine, but also the impacts of the petroleum industry. The latter, environmental stance helped the movement garner a greater standing with NGOs, including an alliance with Greenpeace, and a subsequent global media spotlight both domestically and internationally. Its broader human rights focus did not attract the same attention internationally, in great part because it was competing for attention with other political groups. This led the Ogoni activists to increasingly frame themselves as an environmental movement.

The case highlights a reality for social movement organizations: While global media has afforded all oppressed groups new avenues for disseminating their cause or issue, only those organizations with preexisting linkages with political actors and expertise in international public relations will reap greater opportunities and resources. Garnering favor from media, politicians, or international NGOs (non-governmental organizations) sometimes requires the shifting or even contortion of an issue. The Ogoni case study echoes the assertion that local movements, in a bid to secure new allies, are often tempted to tailor their goals and tactics to appeal to both local and nonlocal audiences, even while running the risk of having their concerns diluted or subverted by outsiders (Jasper 1997). In other words, this ability of movement members or advocates to strategically navigate a complex network of global political, economic, and media institutions becomes prerequisite for the successful "insurgent marketing campaign": "Something as simple as a leader's fluency in English or another world language enables NGO staff or journalists to appreciate insurgent claims. An understanding of public relations techniques, permitting a movement to project a coherent and pleasing image, can subtly influence hardened NGO professionals" (Bob 2001, 45).

This public relations "pitch" ultimately paid dividends for the Ogoni people in terms of securing much-needed resources and attention for their cause. It also underscored not only the importance of media coverage for global activists but also the tensions inherent in projecting certain frames to secure publicity or financial support from global NGOs. While securing media coverage helps a movement, activists simultaneously run the risk of emulating, to some degree at least, the approaches used by the institutions they seek to oppose: "Using sophisticated approaches, they seek to influence the media, NGOs, and broader publics. In this, of course, insurgents do nothing more than their opponents—governments, multinational corporations, and international financial institutions with huge resources and privileged access to the international press. But where the powerful buy the world's best public relations machines, challengers must bootstrap themselves to the fore" (Bob 2001, 7).

In short, activists have the ability to exist on a level playing field with their better-funded opponents if they emulate their communication practices. Such an approach is vulnerable to critique on the grounds that the Ogoni movement shifted its activism to adjust to the global media environment. It also suggests that many social movements, like their adversaries, are results-driven entities dependent on media coverage and broad public support. While this view is "more skeptical of movements and NGOs than is most existing scholarship, this is a tribute to their highly strategic choices" (Bob 2001, xi). We must ask: Does activism exist as a tangent of public relations, a communication practice better known for serving the organizational missions of companies, governments, and other established institutions?

In grappling with the interplay of activism and public relations, scholars from the genre have emphasized the primacy of the organization and its relationship with audiences or stakeholders. The heightened role of public relations in potentially resolving confrontations with green activists for companies and navigating contentious communication terrain is one example (L. Grunig 1989). Referring to it as a more constraining force for companies than the government itself, activism is defined here as "the organization of diffused publics into a powerful body attempting to control the organization from the outside" (L. Grunig 1987, 55). To achieve an optimal operating environment, organizations should aspire to good relations through symmetric engagement: the usage of communication to negotiate, resolve conflict, and foster mutual understanding with publics (Grunig and Hunt 1984). Organizations should maintain good relations with strategic publics—including customers, shareholders, community members, and activists—in order to achieve the goals of both the organization and its publics, and to reduce negative publicity (Grunig and Grunig 2008). This is understood as symmetric communication, and it emphasizes the primacy of active publics. When members of the public are invested in organizations like the Sierra Club across a range of environmental issues, they are more likely to participate actively with that group than are those who engage with these organizations for other purposes.

Public communication scholars have also explored these issues from the perspective of organizations such as corporations and government agencies, which regularly square off with green activists. From the company perspective, to reach agreement through mutual communication would be preferable to engaging in conflict. A normative, two-way symmetrical approach to communication maintains that "individuals, organizations, and publics should use communication to adjust their ideas and behaviour to those of others rather than try to control how others think and behave" (J. Grunig 2006, 156). This call for harmonious, interactive engagement was asserted in situations where companies were confronting adversaries such as environmental activists. This was in part because activists were seen as often garnering stronger support from publics than their corporate adversaries being called out in the media and via public demonstrations (L. Grunig 1986). Similar environmental activism case studies from other countries provide further granularity in this regard (Anderson 1992; Guiniven 2002).

Building on this notion of symmetric dialogue between institutions and activists is the conceptualization of strategic communication or public relations as the facilitation of interpersonal dialectic (Pearson 1989). A focus on the structure of organization-public interactions is argued to remove the problem of ethical relativism in public relations practice by focusing on communication rules. This in turn brings public relations practice to a goal of symmetric, dialogic, and ethical communication relationships. Reaching mutually desirable outcomes are not the sole objective of such dialogue. The opportunities for such dialogue between organizations and publics became more apparent with the rise of Internet communication (Kent and Taylor 1998). Drawing from Pearson's original conceptualization, a dialogic theory between parties proposed the transmission of ideas and ideology through two-way interaction but also for the sake of the communication itself (Kent and Taylor 2002).

Many of these ideas borrow heavily from a larger philosophical tradition established by the German philosopher Jürgen Habermas. A key underpinning of dialogic theory is ethics discourse, a form of dialogic ethics conceived by Habermas as the "procedure through which persons can live up to the imperative of the moral principle" (Heller 1985, 5). Habermas argued in favor of a public moral discourse that is free of power imbalances and one in which the superior argument for society as a whole ultimately prevails. It explicitly includes as participants of argumentation all those affected by a norm (Hoenisch 2005). This freedom of access positions public discourse differently from arrangements such as government hearings, university seminars, parliamentary debates, or corporate meetings: "Anyone who seriously engages in argumentation must presuppose that the context of discussion guarantees in principle freedom of access, equal rights to participate, truthfulness on the part of participants, absence of coercion in adopting positions, and so on. . . . This must be distinguished from the institutional arrangements that obligate specific groups of people to engage in argumentation" (Habermas 1993, 31). The degree of a society's liberality hinges upon institutional expressions that are non-coercive and non-authoritarian, giving way to an autonomous morality that takes on a life of its own (Habermas 1993, 171). A key tenet of this discourse ethics is the ideal speech situation, which necessitates equal opportunity for all to participate, for participants to be true to themselves, and for participants to have the equal ability to influence others. This suggests an ideal condition that real discourse must measure up to or roughly satisfy.

The central importance of optimized communication procedures is further explicated by public relations' relationship management theory. Drawing from interpersonal communication and management theory, this theoretical tradition recognizes organization-public relationships as distinct from the perceptions held by parties in the relationships and underscoring their unique properties (Broom et al. 1997). In other words, the organization-to-organization relationship takes on a life of its own—distinct from the individuals embedded in those organizations.

A fundamental goal of public relations practice, then, is the cultivation of strategic relationships between parties (Hon and Grunig 1999). This emphasis on relationship-cultivation pays dividends at the organizational level as well as the societal level. Increasingly, scholars have called for the application of strategic communication on the part of organizations as a means to uniting diverse audiences: "Establishing relationships built on common interest and helping to coordinate activities in civil society is a clear path for public relations in democracy. Public relations also has a more practical role in facilitating organizational participation in public dialogue" (Sommerfeldt 2013, 286). Public interest communication as an applied communication discipline and a means to coalition-building can therefore play a key role in supporting democratic institutions and more civil societies (Sommerfeldt 2013). This is because it provides a means to voicing collective opinion and shared meaning while building relationships among groups. Here the intersection of activisms and public relations activities gains new complexity, as carefully constructed messages travel from organization to first- and second-level audiences (such as local publics, politicians, or the media), and then on to wider audiences. A study of how LGBT advocates used ground-up public communication strategies in the United States provides a case in point. During campaigns for the Equality Agenda across multiple states, advocacy messaging spiraled from grassroots activists and supporters at the state level to national-level audiences and decision-makers, providing the underpinnings necessary for critical mass support and a demonstration of how public relations can serve as an instrument for democratic change (Mundy 2013). Crucial in this process was the conveyance of authentic, personal, and locally specific stories that emphasized LGBT issues as community issues, establishing a foundation for ground-level support, and allowing the movement to progress at subsequent state and federal levels. Initial public discourse resulted in local positive action from town councils or school boards before advancing to state-based advocacy for LGBT protections at higher levels. A key facet of this public discourse was the makeup of the local audience for such advocacy—"neighbors, friends, families, coworkers"—who began to hear LGBT stories in locally relevant terms and helped build a critical mass of ground-level support (Mundy 2013, 388). This spiral of advocacy also embraced the crafting of positive messages that emphasized the linkage between LGBT individuals and the communities they lived in. This example provides strong evidence that the interplay of strategic activism with increasingly empowered grassroots supporters can power a bottom-up approach to movement activism (Mundy 2013). The identification of audiences as "neighbors, friends, families, coworkers" hints at an activism that emphasizes locality and community as the catalysts for inclusivity.

At the same time, activists must deal with a reality in which the outcome of a single public policy issue can be even more important than the long-term viability of their movement organization. This is a marked difference from the corporate or government bodies more commonly studied in public relations. This was certainly the case in Nebraska, where the pipeline project was a driving force for a decade of Bold Nebraska's activism, and in turn overshadowed other environmental narratives in the state. The construction of meaning within the disseminated communication about a specific issue or situation, and how this communication helps cultivate the organization-audience relationship, becomes a pivotal process. The relationship between public relations strategies and framing becomes potentially symbiotic and mutually reinforcing. Building on the premise that human behavior is predicated on how people interact and use symbols to create meaning (Blumer 1971), framing theory is invoked as a useful vehicle for examining what occurs within public interest communication (Hallahan 1999). Here, seven models of framing have potential application: situations, attributes, choices, actions, issues, responsibility, and news. Underpinning these framing approaches is the argument that framing is connected to the psychological processes people use to digest information, make choices, and make sense of the world around them. This recognizes both the construction of messages intended to influence publics and the importance of the publics themselves in deciphering content.

Yet public relations scholarship in particular had historically been remiss in its dismissal of the material conditions within environmental campaigns and movements, and the result was a stifling of research within the discipline pertaining to social responsibility (Karlberg 1996). In attempting to understand environmentalism as a public communication process, framing becomes a valuable vehicle for negotiating meaning of humankind's relationship with natural matter. Yet framing processes have too often overlooked the dialectic of materialism and idealism in environmental discourses. When framing is understood strictly in terms of generic or reductive explanations of mediated phenomena, it becomes oblivious to the heightened role it plays with environmental communicators.

To position framing as something that happens *to* ecological controversies by third parties unwisely relegates social movement organizations to passive status in the communication process. In other words, what if environmental stories are subject exclusively to the whims of journalists, media institutions, audiences, and other media production factors? The agency of environmentalists is removed. And indeed, many communicators have historically been content with abiding by traditional media and public relations protocols that turn over narrative agency and what story gets told to public appetite or journalist interpretation. However, looking at frames as rhetorical, persuasive phenomena changes this reality and puts power back into the hands of the communicator whose organizational story is being told. In particular, thematic frames by their very nature position an issue in subjective terms. They connect audiences to a particular issue and imbue it with meaning, thus shifting the paradigm in which ecological issues are consumed.

Scholars in environmental studies have previously carved out so-called issue history as a methodological approach (Szasz 1994). For example, "hazardous waste" exists as a topical representation in the mass media but also as an object of the public's imagination, even as it is also addressed by federal and state laws. For the social scientist, the challenge is to make use of a variety of data materials in tracking the issue as it is deliberated by the organization, the press, and the public. To this end, framing is especially well suited to contending with material themes. That's because understanding media coverage of a topic in isolation doesn't go far enough in analyzing environmental movements. Of greater import is understanding the conditions allowing for attitudes to underpin the formation of a new social movement (Szasz 1994).

Previous studies have adjoined persuasive issue frames to successful collective action. A previous analysis of the Sierra Club's newsletters and national/regional newspapers bears out this organization-audience dialectic. Activist organizations constructed and used issues frames, among their repertoire of public relations strategies, to influence the attitudes, perceptions, and behaviors of internal and external audiences (Reber and Berger 2005). The use of a diversity of issue frames (such as urban sustainability or wilderness protection) can attract and mobilize supporters or expand awareness of a topic but can also dilute the potential power of any single frame to impact media coverage or galvanize public opinion. These are collective action frames that can help recruit and mobilize members, reach out to other groups, and influence public debate (Reber and Berger 2005). The Sierra Club's media successes reflected the potential usefulness of framing theory at the intrapersonal, interpersonal, group, organizational, and societal levels in which activist groups and NGOs operate.

This premise can be extended in arguing for an understanding of audiences though an issue-specific context (Hallahan 2001). Four key types of publics are understood based on their knowledge and involvement of an issue: active (high knowledge, high involvement), aroused (high involvement, low knowledge), aware (high knowledge, low involvement), and inactive (low knowledge, low involvement). In turn, responses on the part of organizations are designated for each public grouping: negotiation (for active publics), intervention (for aroused publics), education (for aware publics), and prevention (for inactive publics) (Hallahan 2001). This suggests more generally that audience cognition is subject to change on an issue-by-issue basis and requires carefully calibrated messaging and response on the part of activists.

Underscoring the strategies behind movement framing, and activists' use of public relations, is the importance of rhetorical device. Rhetorical approaches infuse persuasive messages with their actual meaning (Hallahan 1999). And specific elements such as visuals, metaphors, and messengers help drive meaning-making within strategic framing. Returning to the case of Bold Nebraska, this begs important questions about the organization's communications and activism strategy within this bigger picture of movement framing: What specific issue frames helped to drive Bold Nebraska's years-long advocacy, and how did these topical frames interact with the rhetorical and persuasive framing variables featured in the strategic framing taxonomy? Furthermore, what strategic framing elements did the organization put into play during its anti-pipeline crusade, and to what extent? Finally, how did these issue frames, grounded as they are in history and materiality, interface with these strategic framing approaches?

To answer these questions, the author conducted a quantitative framing analysis to understand Bold Nebraska's own framing of the pipeline issue through its strategic website communication, including media releases and feature stories. By focusing on one organization, Bold Nebraska, and its campaign against the construction of TransCanada's Keystone XL pipeline, it drew from the case study methodology. Case studies are well known in the domain of business schools, and most notably at Harvard Business School, where MBA students use the case method to test their knowledge in real world business scenarios. Yet case studies offer much to the scholar of communication or environmentalism. The term *case study* identifies a specific form of inquiry that is different from two other predominant forms of social research, the experiment and the survey (Gomm et al. 2000). The method has been found to be a direct means to building upon experience and improving understanding (Stake 1978).

Data collection in case study research is extensive and can draw on varying sources of information such as documents, interviews, observations, and audiovisual materials (Creswell and Clark 2007). Notably, the researcher needs to make a case for their sampling strategy and information-gathering approach. Additionally, the researcher should also be able to set boundaries around the case to give it clean beginning and end points (Creswell and Clark 2007). Content analysis, meanwhile, holds up the text as a medium of appeal, positioning it as one that is trying to reach out to or convert an existing audience.

To understand how Bold Nebraska strategically framed its environmental activism, the author collected materials for content analysis from the extensive news section of Bold Nebraska's website. This section included Bold Nebraska's press releases, media advisories, editorials, statements, updates, information about petitions and other forms of political action, organization-generated stories, and recaps of mainstream media stories devoted to Bold Nebraska or Keystone XL pipeline developments. Content analysis can help the researcher identify inaccuracies when prevailing "wisdom" attributes certain characteristics or attributes to a text or artifact (Bauer 2000).

To measure the extent to which Bold Nebraska incorporated strategic framing elements in its website communication, texts were coded on the basis of whether they recognized or engaged with their audiences by incorporating the six elements put forth by Gilliam and Bales (2001): numbers, messengers, visuals, context, metaphors and simplifying models, and tone. The author also inspected each article in Bold Nebraska's news section, which represents one webpage, to identify what issues were present. Key issues promoted by an activist organization provide means to study master frames in activist websites as well as media coverage (Reber and Berger 2005). From an organizational perspective, these frames are collective action frames—intended to help recruit and mobilize members and other concerned citizens and groups—that can become potentially integrated into media or news coverage as issues frames (Reber and Berger 2005). In the case of Bold Nebraska's website communication, these issues deemed most prioritized after a review of tags (or index system) from Bold Nebraska's website articles from 2011 to 2015 were farming/ranching, Indigenous rights, climate change, land rights, alternative energy, environmental threats, and globalization. Metaphorical ecological conceptualizations from Nerlich and Koteyko (2009) were also coded: environmentalism as religion, dieting/nutrition, finance, battle/war, and journey (a sixth category of "other" accounted for metaphors that did not fit the description of the first five categories).

To establish a sample, articles were collected from the Bold Nebraska website between January 1, 2011, and December 31, 2015. The years indicated covered a significant timeframe of Bold Nebraska's activism against TransCanada and the Keystone xl pipeline. In these articles, written communication was the predominant mode of transmission, informing audiences through verbal text. Most content analysis articles involve text because it is the primary vehicle for preserving mass-produced content (Riffe, Lacy, and Fico 2014). However, it is important to note that the author also recorded the presence of visuals in the stories. As a condition for content analysis to be valid, intercoder reliability was tested and reported in order to gauge the reliability of the coding protocol.

From the Bold Nebraska website, more than a thousand articles were identified in the organization's news section during the five-year timeframe. The news section includes all blog posts, media releases, information updates, opinion articles, and other public-facing strategic communication and editorial materials. Once their meta-data was gathered, these articles (1,032 in total) were documented in a Microsoft Excel spreadsheet. From this list, a total of 236 articles were randomly sampled using Microsoft Excel's randomizer function. With a second coder independently coding website articles, intercoder reliability of the content analysis was established.

Attributes of Bold Nebraska's Communication

Before the meaning-making within the communication could be assessed, the values for the physical characteristics of the articles (including length and format) were first coded. Articles were also coded as 1 (yes) or 0 (no) for whether or not they contained an action item, such as imploring readers to sign a petition to sign, make a donation or purchase, attend an event, or phone or write to politicians. This area is addressed later in the chapter. Suffice it to say, these "action items" played an outsized role. Finally, the article's origin or authorship was coded: 1 (Bold Nebraska staff member), 2 (Bold Nebraska member or guest contributor), 3 (partner or third-party organization), and 4 (media outlet contribution or reprint). An overwhelming majority of articles (78 percent) were six paragraphs or more in length, indicating both a substantiveness in terms of quantity but also ideas. Only 10 percent of the articles were between three and five paragraphs, and less than 10 percent were one or two paragraphs. Of the 236 articles measured, 14 percent were formal media releases originally created for distribution to media. The remaining 86 percent included a variety of stories, updates, republication of media coverage, calls to action, and event information.

Issue Frames

The values of each issue framing variable were coded as 1 (frame present) or 0 (frame not present). As noted, these issue frames were farming/ranching, Indigenous/tribal issues, climate change, land rights/eminent domain, alternative/clean energy, environmental threats, and globalization. Figure 12 details the use of each issue frame as a percentage of all articles. Three issue frames were found in a majority of news articles: environmental threats (67 percent), globalization (65 percent), and land rights/eminent domain (50 percent). Farming and agricultural issue frames were present in 44.5 percent of articles, followed by climate change (31 percent), alternative/clean energy (22 percent), and Indigenous/tribal issues (8.9 percent). A majority of articles contained multiple issue frames; for example, farming/agriculture was often situated alongside land rights and globalization, Indigenous and tribal concerns often existed in conjunction with land rights and also environmental threats, and discussions of alternative/clean/solar energy coexisted with the issue of climate change. More than 20 percent of all articles contained three or more issue frames, while a further 40 percent contained four or more frames.

Each of the seven issue frames in Bold Nebraska's communication were analyzed to determine association with inclusion of an action

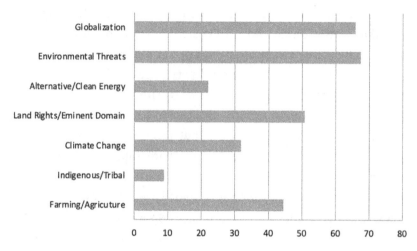

Fig. 12. Issue frames (percentage of all website articles). Created by author.

item (as discussed previously) in the article, including calls for readers to sign a petition, donate money, participate in an event, or write a letter to a politician or government agency. Pearson chi-square tests showed a significant association between the use of an action item and only one issue frame, that of farming/ranching (χ^2=9.29, df=1, p<0.05). Significance was not found in the associations between action items and the other six issue frames. The next chapter features a comprehensive analysis and discussion of the integration of issue frames in Bold Nebraska's pipeline discourse.

Strategic Framing Elements

To determine which of the strategic framing elements were used and to what extent, the six variables—numbers, messengers, visuals, metaphors, tone, and context—were coded as 1 (present) or 0 (not present). Figure 13 shows that each element was used in more than half of all Bold Nebraska articles analyzed. Context (89 percent) and messengers (86 percent) were the most popular elements, followed by oppositional tone (71.6 percent), metaphors (69.5 percent), numbers (59.7 percent), and visuals (55.5 percent). Chi-square tests were also conducted to assess the relationship between the strategic framing elements employed by

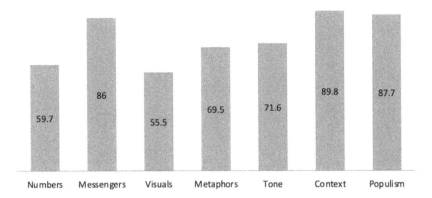

Fig. 13. Strategic framing elements (percentage of all website articles). Created by author.

Bold Nebraska. The element of context enjoyed significant relationships with other elements: tone, metaphors, and numbers. The element of visuals did not enjoy significant associations with any other element. The element of messengers enjoyed significant associations with tone and metaphors.

Conceptual Metaphor Frames

Articles that contained the strategic element of metaphor usage were further analyzed for their containing of conceptual metaphors for environmental and climate activism as suggested by Nerlich and Koteyko (2009): financial/money (1), religion (2), health/diet (3), battle (4), journey (5), and other (6). This latter category included metaphors that did not fit into the existing framework, including representations of environmental struggle and crisis as a sporting or popular culture event, or as an agricultural or wildlife scene. Figure 14 shows that of the articles coded for metaphors, 40 percent contained metaphors that did not fit the existing framework. The most pervasive individual conceptual metaphor was battle/war, represented in 34 percent of the stories containing metaphors. This was followed by journey (11 percent) and finance (9 percent). The conceptual metaphors of diet/health and religion were represented in only 5 percent and 1 percent, respectively. Figure 15 shows the break-

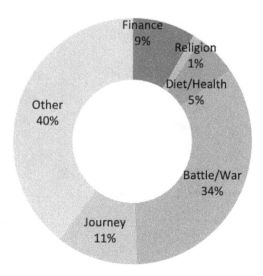

Fig. 14. Metaphorical frames (percentage of all website articles). Created by author.

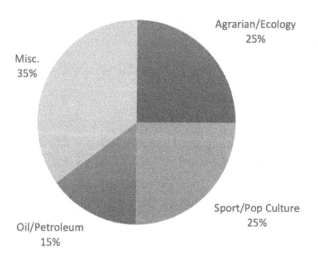

Fig. 15. Other metaphorical frames (percentage of all website articles). Created by author.

down of all Bold Nebraska articles containing metaphors. Metaphors within the "other" category were recorded and further analyzed. Three new categories of metaphors emerged: agrarian/ecological themes, sport and popular culture, and oil industry/pipeline themes. Examples of the first category, which comprised 25 percent of the "other" metaphors, included "bold boots kicking in the doors," "chickens hiring the fox to look after their interests," and "fixing the fence." The second category, sport and popular culture, which also garnered 25 percent of the "other" category, included references to Dr. Seuss's Grinch character, horror movies, and the college football Hail Mary pass. A further 15 percent of the "other" metaphors fell into the third category of oil/pipeline themes, and these included references to "pipe dreams," an "oil sands academy," and "towering mountains of petcoke."

Thus, while some metaphorical frames that are regularly used in climate change communication were integrated into anti-pipeline discourses, they didn't tell the whole story about environmental framing strategies in a rural context. The metaphorical frames of battle/war and journey were apparent, but most other metaphorical strategies from climate fights outside of Nebraska were invisible. Notably, the metaphorical frame of religion was almost entirely absent. This points to prairie activists distancing themselves from appeals that conflated climate mitigation with human sacrifice and redemption. Instead, Bold Nebraska's metaphorical frames once again drew from Nebraska's material conditions: people, place, history, and ecology.

5 Níbtháska

During their crusade against Keystone XL, Nebraska's pipeline opponents showed an uncanny ability to mobilize support through regionally
relevant and contextually dependent appeals that relied on a recurrent
theme of hyperlocalization. How did they do this? By channeling the
ecological heritage of their home state. Among the leading issue frames
discussed in the previous chapter, at least three (environmental threats,
land rights/eminent domain, and farming/ranching) were steeped in
discourses that spoke to how the pipeline's construction would impact
specific rural geographies and properties, including public lands and
privately held farms. Both the Ogallala Aquifer, the shallow water table
sitting under most of Nebraska, and the national landmark–designated
Nebraska Sandhills warranted special mention in numerous stories and
media releases. The Ogallala Aquifer plays an outsized role in Nebraska's quality of life and rural economy, supplying more than 80 percent
of the state's drinking water (U.S. Geological Survey 2009). In north
central Nebraska, sitting above the aquifer, lies the state's Sandhills. The
region's geographic mix of sand dunes and grass prairie have garnered
the status of National Natural Landmark (National Park Service 2021).

These ecological assets do not exist in a natural resources vacuum;
rather they are linked to the state's broader ecosystem, including wildlife, wetlands, lakes, rivers, forests, cropland agriculture, and cattle
ranching. The quantitative content analysis results provided in chapter
4 demonstrate a particular kind of environmental framing in pipeline
politics. Throughout its campaign against Keystone XL, Bold Nebraska
highlighted environmental threats to land and water brought on by the

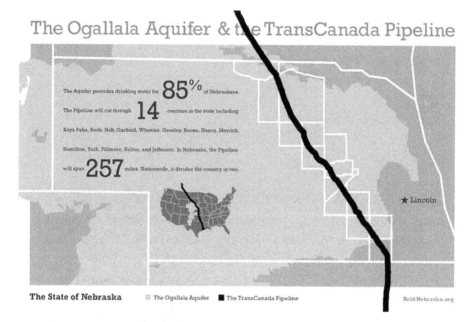

The Ogallala Aquifer & the TransCanada Pipeline

The Aquifer provides drinking water for **85**% of Nebraskans.

The Pipeline will cut through **14** counties in the state including

Keya Paha, Rock, Holt, Garfield, Wheeler, Greeley, Boone, Nance, Merrick,

Hamilton, York, Fillmore, Saline, and Jefferson. In Nebraska, the Pipeline

will span **257** miles. Nationwide, it divides the country in two.

★ Lincoln

The State of Nebraska   ▒ The Ogallala Aquifer   ■ The TransCanada Pipeline   BoldNebraska.org

Fig. 16. A Bold Nebraska website infographic details how the Keystone XL Pipeline would travel through the Ogallala Aquifer. Graphic design by Justin Kemerling (justinkemerling.com). Image courtesy of Bold Nebraska.

possibilities of pipeline leakages, spills, or even explosions. "Protecting land and water" became a key message in Bold Nebraska's controlled communication such as website articles and press releases. The inclusion of Nebraska's valuable ecological assets also provided a platform for Bold Nebraska to authentically develop its identity and appeal to its local and national audiences, including journalists, policymakers, and the general public.

A plains-style land ethic emerges here. Within the popular genre of Westerns, including films, television shows, and literature, a sensitivity for the land and environment is a core value, one that brings communities together. Thus, the presence of a western frontier mythology inclusive of specific ecologies provided ready-made narratives for anti-pipeline activism: "Attunement to natural environments and material interests mark western heroes" (Nelson 2018, 115). Even those opposed to Bold Nebraska's environmental appeals would be hard-pressed to argue against the outsized role of the Sandhills or aquifer to the identity and well-being of Nebraskans.

Jane Kleeb pointed to ready-made narratives from literature and poetry about Nebraska's ecology that resonated with the state's citizens. She held up the celebrated Nebraska author Willa Cather as a prime example. Cather's critically acclaimed novels from a century ago were praised for their plainspoken language about the people and landscapes of Nebraska's frontier, which in turn helped form a cherished part of the state's identity. "People know the Sandhills, because that is where all of our ranchers are; this is cattle-ranching country," said Kleeb. "These are tough communities that have been through difficult times that still continue to rise. So when you think of the Sandhills you think of wildlife and beauty, but also the tremendous amount of grit of the families who lived there." The same idea held true for the inclusion of the Ogallala Aquifer, the state's critical water resource for farmers and residents. Its existence as a public resource ultimately entrusted to the citizens of Nebraska has made it an eternal point of pride and ownership for Nebraskans.

Meanings of Land and Water

The issue frame of land rights and warning of the government's usage of eminent domain rules to expropriate private farmland for the pipeline was also a crucial issue frame for Bold Nebraska's advocacy. The frame of land rights provided Bold Nebraska with the opportunity to maximize support across Nebraska's political spectrum and integrate dominant cultural norms in American life, notably individual liberty, limited government, patriotism, and respect for private property. This bipartisan emphasis on land rights created an additional layer of meaning within Bold Nebraska's activism. The repeated mantra of "protecting land and water" became a rallying cry for conservation and environmentalism, but also for individual property rights. This double-entendre messaging provided Bold Nebraska with a powerful tool for recruitment and mobilization by offering a new lens through which to understand the environment, especially for those individuals and families who didn't fit the traditional activist mold. Keystone XL was no longer just a threat to the collective via threats to waterways, wildlife, and public lands; it was also a danger to the independently held agricultural land holdings of individual farmers and ranchers. Such a symbiosis fostered ease of entry to the environmental cause and a politically welcoming tent. When Bold Nebraska's self-styled Pipeline Fighters were protesting, marching, or writing with the hopes of staving off the TransCanada project, they were doing so on their own political terms, whether it was progressivism from the political left or the championing of individual liberties and land ownership from the right. This approach was critical given the state's historic leanings toward conservative politics and the previous understanding of environmentalism as a long-standing issue exclusive to one political paradigm. Such bipartisanship was thus contingent upon the deployment of different issue frames that activated individual beliefs, attitudes, and values from across the political spectrum. Instead of marginalizing individuals from one side of the political divide, Bold Nebraska rhetorically communicated social-psychological variables that would be compelling to farmers and ranchers who identified as Democrats or Republicans.

The Climate Change Conundrum

This bipartisan strategy helped inform the organization's cautious approach to what is arguably the planet's most pressing environmental issue of climate change. While the climate change crisis was featured with some regularity in Bold Nebraska's website communication, it did not emerge as the most prolific issue frame, nor was it even among the top three. This is surprising given the salience of climate change in national environmental debates over the past decade. The issue frames of environmental threats, globalization, land rights, and farming/ranching all garnered substantially more attention from the organization. While Bold Nebraska recognized the relationship between the pipeline's construction and the exacerbation of climate volatility, and allied itself with organizations such as 350.org that are devoted to solving the global climate challenge, this did not drive the dialogue conceived by pipeline activists. Other frames emerged more often because they represented a more immediate concern to Nebraskans. The issues of farming and ranching, as well as land rights, framed the pipeline as immediately antagonistic to Nebraskans' way of life in a way that the climate change topic could not. The issue of environmental threats similarly showed how the pipeline's construction and potential spills were a danger not just to land and water in general but to specific land and water entities, most notably the aquifer and Sandhills. This points to an ongoing conundrum for climate change as an issue: short of an epic storm or devastating drought linked to fluctuating global temperatures that affect a locality, it does not always fit the profile of a hyperlocal issue frame as effectively as land rights or threats to regional ecology. Short-lived weather events notwithstanding, climate change as a phenomenon that operates over a timeframe of decades and across global geographies is much more difficult to see. Despite the scientific community overwhelmingly uniting on climate science, and international weather volatilities increasingly linked to the outcomes of a warming planet, the impacts of global emissions are more easily abstracted than a local oil spill, even if the results are equally devastating.

Climate change as an issue in the national public sphere has also collected political and cultural baggage over the years. A subset of the population is inclined to stubbornly dismiss it not because of the science but because of its place in America's polarized ideological battles and well-publicized "culture wars," which points to a failing of both political parties. Furthermore, conversations about climate change tend to be led by cultural and political elites, including government bureaucrats, academics, journalists, think tanks, and NGOs. And because of their top-down nature, they exist in tension with the lateral, interpersonal communication and social relations that define rural life. Weighing into these discussions can be intimidating for those citizens on the ground who are immediately affected, especially when the rules of dialogue are already established. At the same time, national discourses about climate change are often laden with predictable tropes that emphasize no-win outcomes. For example, Arnold's (2018) examination of climate change impacts on Alaska's Native American communities notes that national media stories have fallen into a repeated narrative pattern emphasizing doom, tragedy, and hopelessness, which situates community members as victims and leaves the public feeling powerless. This dynamic produced by national and international journalists "has not resulted in a groundswell of support for mitigation or adaption. Nor has it resulted in public policy at the state or federal level" (Arnold 2018, para. 3). Fostering individual and community agency in climate discourses from national policymakers and media therefore deserves greater emphasis.

In his 1979 book *Dust Bowl*, historian Donald Worster (2004) closely examined the role of local culture and discourse during the Great Plains' devastating drought of the 1930s, particularly in western Kansas and Oklahoma. In searching for an answer to how this disaster was exacerbated and prolonged, he located an important but overlooked dynamic on the dust bowl: the role of interpersonal communication and social bonds between local community members, including farmers and ranchers, at social clubs, diners, and churches. This was a powerful form of discourse that deepened local engagement even as it raised suspicion of federal intervention, including messaging and aid. Ultimately this insider/outsider dynamic may have exacerbated the ecological damage inflicted on family farms. The dust bowl era's social world provides a stark reminder that authoritative sources do not have a monopoly on transmitting ideologies; in rural life they often emerge from the bottom up. Through this material/discursive lens, it would be easy to understand why impacts to a nearby waterway or grazing field would generate more discussion at the local lunch counter than a global climate report. Bold Nebraska certainly tried to incorporate the climate change issue explicitly as a driver of activism dialogue (it was present in roughly one-third of all stories), but the issue's communication production was neither prolific nor authentic. A number of stories published by Bold Nebraska involving climate change had their origins with third parties, such as other activist groups like 350.org and the Sierra Club, academic researchers, or national and international media outlets. The organization sometimes resorted to rehashing press releases from other groups on this topic.

There were occasional indicators of a livelier climate change issue frame driven by Bold Nebraska and its state-based agenda. An example comes from the summer of 2014, when Kleeb appeared on MSN-BC's *The Ed Show* to discuss severe weather events across the United States connected to global warming, including flooding in Kearney, Nebraska. This was the exception, however. A more common scenario was Bold Nebraska's outsourcing of the climate change topic to state and national experts. For example, a major report on how the pipeline would worsen climate change and fail the climate test set by President Obama was republished on Bold Nebraska's website but was originally produced by the National Resource Defense Council. This example also demonstrates how national-level appeals to the issue of climate change, while rich in statistical data and scientific expertise, did not always make the local connection. The NRDC missive dated July 23, 2013, despite its depth and alarming warning, did not once mention the locale where the pipeline's construction was being contested: the state of Nebraska.

The Bold Nebraska experience highlights an ongoing challenge for climate change as an environmental issue: in spite of increasingly volatile weather events, it is still vulnerable to abstraction as it is explained by scientists and politicians. Kleeb, who has had conversations with hundreds of farmers and ranchers across the state, puts the challenge in starker terms. "The climate change community has not figured a way to explain what climate change means," she said. As an issue frame, it did not align as effectively with the rhetorical, emotional, and cultural appeals of the strategic framing taxonomy, in part because it was viewed as a more diffuse and internationalized issue. While some national media stories championed climate change concerns as a leading catalyst for anti-pipeline activism, the analysis from Bold Nebraska's own activism reveals a different story. Climate change still held an important and aspirational place in the group's campaign, and it was implied in a majority of Bold Nebraska's communication, but it did not energize its grassroots base to the same degree that agriculture, land rights, or threats to the Ogallala Aquifer and Sandhills did.

"An Act of War against Our People"

Of the issue frames examined in Bold Nebraska's website discourse, the frame of Indigenous/tribal rights and concerns garnered less coverage than other issue frames. This comes as something of a surprise because Bold Nebraska's activism had regularly integrated Indigenous concerns and narratives in its campaigns, events, and public protests. For example, one of the most impactful elements of both the Harvest the Hope festival and Bold Nebraska's Reject and Protect rally in Washington DC was the powerful symbolism of an American cowboy reaching out and shaking hands with a Native American, a representation of the Cowboy and Indian Alliance. In part, this lack of prolific representation within topical frames might be attributed to the distribution of Nebraska's population, as Native Americans make up only 1.5 percent of the state's total population, though that number approaches 9 percent in neighboring South Dakota (U.S. Census Bureau 2019). It stands to reason that there were fewer individual messengers, activists, and newsmakers from the tribal nations to feed Bold Nebraska's prolific communication output, which amounted to more than one thousand articles published over a five-year period. However, tribal members *were* disproportionately affected by the Keystone XL proposal because of where they lived. The pipeline was slated to run through the heart of the Oceti Sakowin Treaty area. Tribes along the pipeline's route included the Oceti Sakowin, Lakota, Dakota, and the Nakota nations (Boos 2015, para. 13). Rosebud Sioux Nation president Cyril Scott referred to the authorization of Keystone XL as "an act of war against our people."

Yet as the movement framing analysis shows, Indigenous and tribal-specific issues, while still present, were overwhelmed by issue framing related to more general environmental threats, the role of globalization, land rights, and challenges facing farmers and ranchers. This points to Bold Nebraska's ability to foster a symbolic alliance of hope for broader appeals and high-profile protest events but also some shortcomings in bringing Indigenous topics (and by extension Indigenous peoples) into a more prolific, granular, and daily activism. This finding corresponds with a previous study that analyzed a video production about a Washington DC anti-pipeline protest (Wilson 2017). During the video, environmental organizations like Tar Sands Action and 350.org projected a diversity of participants, including Indigenous peoples, but such diversity tended to be more aspirational than realized. As a political vehicle with sweeping implications for citizens from across the demographic spectrum, climate activism in particular has remained "stubbornly white" (136). In this regard, Bold Nebraska was well ahead of its environmental peers in fostering larger representation, especially in light of Nebraska's unique politics and the Great Plains' demographics.

There is one other dimension to Bold Nebraska's integration of Indigenous issues that should be mentioned. The group didn't start actively discussing a Cowboy and Indian Alliance publicly until 2013, at which point Indigenous messengers and narratives become woven more regularly into the pipeline campaign. Bold Nebraska's communication was subsequently energized from the integration of another aggrieved group into its campaign (evidenced by national media stories, support from Indigenous organizations and media, and arguably a more compelling narrative for the national media). This speaks to the assertion that those movement organizations willing to adjust their activism in order to access superior resources (political, economic, media) will ultimately be more successful than their counterparts unwilling to evolve (Bob 2001). As Bold Nebraska embraced tribal-specific pipeline concerns, it also enjoyed its most highly visible moments as an organization, including the Harvest the Hope festival and its Earth Day Reject and Protect rally in Washington DC—stories that enjoyed significant attention from the *New York Times*, the *Wall Street Journal*, the *Washington Post*, and other influential national media outlets.

An interesting account of the Cowboy and Indian Alliance logo comes from tribal artist Richard Vollaire of the Tongva Nation, who designed the artwork initially for a Bold Nebraska water bottle as part of a fundraising effort. The logo quickly moved from low-key art design to the iconic image used on signs and flags at marches and protests, as Vollaire explained on his website. The #NoKXL crop art installation on the Tanderups' farm, meticulously led by John Quigley and featuring Vollaire's logo, attracted public attention across the country and the world. And it ultimately became the centerpiece of the 2014 Harvest the Hope concert. Media coverage of these events, which featured the contrarian imagery of ranchers and Native Americans protesting in unison and the cultural heritage and artifacts of both groups, showed that tribal engagement wasn't peripheral to existing activism but rather essential to Bold Nebraska's emergent identity and its credibility as a regional leader in resisting Keystone XL.

Mitigating Abstraction in Pipeline Politics

A key goal in reviewing Bold Nebraska's public-facing materials, including media releases, event advisories, and website stories, was to determine what strategic framing elements—numbers, messengers, visuals, tone, context, and metaphors—were woven into the movement's strategic communication, and of these what elements were most pervasive. The original strategic framing taxonomy encourages public issues advocates, such as activist and not-for-profit organizations, to strive for message development that is aligned closely with campaign goals, and to translate policy positions into language that considers the target audience's existing knowledge and beliefs. Fully developed frames, comprised of these "shared and durable cultural models that people use to make sense of their world," are argued to develop new thinking about an issue (Gilliam and Bales 2002). They are also argued to help integrate universally resonant norms such as patriotism, property rights, and individual liberty. In Bold Nebraska's case, the author found multiple strategic framing elements in an overwhelming majority of website articles. The most common element found was context, featured in nearly 90 percent of all articles. Context helps broaden advocacy to family, community, regional, and national levels by positioning an issue within a time and place (Gilliam and Bales 2001). In the case of Bold Nebraska's activist communication, this included a multitude of references to specific geographic entities such as the Ogallala Aquifer, various rural communities in the state of Nebraska, and even specific family farms. Such contextualization not only provided a means to localizing content; it mitigated abstractive or conceptual styles of communication.

The pipeline was real, and it was headed for watersheds, valleys, ranchlands, and rural fields. The #NoKXL crop art provides an excellent example of how the pipeline's material characteristics were articulated. The art installation (led by the artist and activist Quigley, who specializes in mixed and experimental art forms, including aerial perspectives and earth/land patterns) wasn't merely distributed to publics as a stand-alone photograph (or media photo opportunity) without contextual information. Rather, organizers implored citizens to head to Antelope County, where the massive Cowboy and Indian crop art was carved into a cornfield, to volunteer and "help pull weeds in the rows of hand-planted sacred Ponca corn and organic soybeans" (Hefflinger 2014, para. 1). The crop art itself was therefore embedded in a time and place. And grassroots volunteers would help put the finishing touches on what would emerge as a symbol for the world.

The predominance of contextual elements in Bold Nebraska's framing shouldn't come as a great surprise. By virtue of its name, Bold Nebraska, the movement had declared that civic policy within the state was an organizational priority. The adjective *bold*, which the *Oxford English Dictionary* defines as "showing an ability to take risks" and to be "confident and courageous," highlights a willingness by the organization to shake up the state's political status quo and perhaps even the status quo of the environmental movement. The state's name, Nebraska, is also contextually rich, rooted in Indigenous conceptions of local ecology. It comes from the Omaha-Ponca word Níbtháska, meaning "flatwater," used to describe the state's Platte River (Koontz 2003). Thus, the organization's historic, geographic, and cultural appeals were even embedded in the Bold Nebraska name. Such a contextualization is especially poignant when it invokes sacred Native ground (the Ponca Trail of Tears), sensitive ecological geography (the Nebraska Sand Hills), and utopian-ecological gathering spots (the #NoKXL Clean Energy Barn).

Fig. 17. Pipeline opponent Art Tanderup inspects the planting of the sacred Ponca corn on his farm in Neligh, Nebraska. Photo by Derek Moscato.

Messengers as Activism Narrators

Within political communication forms such as activism, messengers can be as important to the issue as the message itself. They not only provide compelling quotes as part of speeches or media interviews; they also appear in photographs, reach out to audiences on social media, and even write op-eds for influential newspapers. In some cases, they can become the embodiment or physical symbol of a cause. Bold Nebraska proved itself to be particularly adept at bringing messengers as a framing element into its communications; only the element of context was used more. These messengers included the obvious spokespersons (such as founder Jane Kleeb) but also ordinary citizens (such as the Tanderups and Randy Thompson) and even celebrities (one website story invoked celebrity activists Daryl Hannah, Mark Ruffalo, Neil Young, *and* Willie Nelson alongside climate change thought leader Bill McKibben). Other messengers took the form of government officials (members of the Natural Resources Committee, for example) or specific politicians (such as Nebraska State Senator Ernie Chambers, who fought to repeal TransCanada's eminent domain land acquisition powers). The inclusion of messengers is a reflection of civic exchange within strategic communication. Messengers provide necessary narration, opinion, expertise, and leadership. They also foster an emotive and human-scale quality to political or ecological events.

Their prolific involvement showed that advocacy does not exist within a communication vacuum but rather incorporates the voices of activists, citizens, and other community members. These people had stories to tell—stories that resonate with audiences and a constituency of invested citizens. In constructing rhetorical appeals, messengers make important contributions to the three elements of persuasion: ethos, pathos, and logos. They establish the credibility of the organization and community, they help conjure up emotions connected to the issue, and they provide arguments and expertise based on logic. In conjunction with the previously discussed contextual elements, messengers were especially important in building ethos and pathos on behalf of Bold Nebraska, helping audiences to make sense of the organization's connection to the pipeline and fusing this authenticity with human sentiment.

Metaphors: Plainspoken Politics

The usage of metaphors and simplifying models, also included in a majority of Bold Nebraska's communication, allowed the organization to take what was a nuanced process involving a multinational company's energy proposal and make it readily digestible for public consumption. While conceptual metaphors are often used to describe more abstract concepts in concrete or simplified terms, Bold Nebraska proved especially adept at connecting the nuances of ecological and resource extraction debates to rural experience and terminology. Officials with various conflicts of interest were labeled as "foxes watching the hen house." Pro-pipeline officials deserved "coal for Christmas" and were implored to "work a day in our boots." Members were encouraged to watch TransCanada "like a hawk," while the pipeline itself was "shovel ready for the grave." Other metaphorical expressions used equally blunt force or humor. State officials were described as "keystone cops" and "puppets of rich foreigners." Others were accused of procrastinating on key decisions (the aforementioned "kicking the can") or receiving perks from TransCanada, including trips to Alberta to play golf with oil lobbyists ("when is tee time?"). An oil and gas industry project was described as a "horror movie," another as a "pig on the loose." Some of these metaphors leveraged conceptualized themes such as the environmental "battle" or "journey." However, Bold Nebraska was also successful in developing metaphors rich in contextual and populist sentiment. Metaphors containing agrarian/ecological themes were a natural fit for the organization's activism, as were metaphors containing sporting or popular cultural references, such as Hollywood movies or the Nebraska Cornhuskers football team. The petroleum industry also provided Bold Nebraska with ready-made metaphors depicting environmental hazards or corporate ambivalence toward Nebraskans.

Seen through the Aristotelian model of persuasion, the usage of metaphors also played an outsized role in establishing pathos or emotional appeals. These metaphors interfaced effectively with other framing elements in developing a style of communication for Bold Nebraska that was equal parts provocative, colorful, and grassroots. For example, a

Christmas campaign promoted to media involved the fictional character created by Dr. Seuss, the Grinch, visiting Nebraska governor Dave Heineman and asking him to "not be a mean one" by denying any pipeline route that crossed the Ogallala Aquifer. The accessible theme provided a strong hook for the media ("great visuals to kick-off holiday," Kleeb pitched earnestly in a media advisory) and also provided a lighter, simpler approach to engaging the public on the pipeline's routing. Similarly, a Pumpkins against the Pipeline event allowed Nebraskans to engage with the issue through Halloween. The group's members carved ninety-one pumpkins to represent the troubling ninety-one oil spills projected to occur over the lifetime of the Keystone XL pipeline by University of Nebraska professor and environmental resources expert John Stansbury. Here again, a metaphorical model for pipeline resistance provided member engagement, a compelling photo opportunity for both Bold Nebraska's internal communication as well as the media, and a ready-made public message about what was otherwise a complex, lengthy academic report. As a vehicle for persuasion, the metaphor also helped develop logos by disseminating an argument about pipeline accidents based on scientific evidence.

Visuals: A Currency of American Environmental History

Bold Nebraska's unwavering focus on the hyperlocal was perhaps best articulated through visual imagery. Within its thousands of website messages, Bold Nebraska embedded hundreds of images, conveying a pivotal sense of time and place in Nebraska. The organization also posted many more images to photo sharing sites and social media channels such as Facebook, Instagram, and Flickr. These photographs and graphics conveyed a unique sense of ecology in the state: farm work, bountiful cornfields, agricultural equipment, and the well-publicized clean energy barn. At the same time, they drew from the visual symbolism of the prairie to inspire a much larger constituency.

This is not a new tactic in American environmental history. A century ago, the Sierra Club (one of Bold Nebraska's chief allies in the pipeline fight) used a combination of powerful images and words to

Fig. 18. Scene from Bold Nebraska's pumpkin carving party on October 30, 2015. Members gathered at Harmony Nursery in Bradshaw, Nebraska, to carve "#NoKXL" messages for U.S. president Barack Obama and Canadian prime minister Justin Trudeau. Photo by Michael Roach. Photo courtesy of Bold Nebraska.

resist the Hetch Hetchy dam development in the northwestern corner of Yosemite National Park. In this fight, the Sierra Club benefited from forerunners in activist public relations, the environmentalist John Muir and the photographer Herbert Gleason: "Gleason's photographs became a centerpiece of the campaign, not only in his popular lectures but also in a pamphlet distributed nationally . . . The photographs authenticated Hetch Hetchy's aesthetic value and testified to the sacredness of the site" (Dunaway 2008, 22). Bold Nebraska's #NoKXL crop art installation emulated these objectives of conveying a natural spirituality. Though crop art as a communication tactic might be dismissed as a publicity stunt, in this case it leveraged an ideal medium to tell a story about the convergence of Native American and rural interests against a common environmental threat to land understood as sacred and agriculturally productive. Seen from an aerial vantage point, the inscription of the

Fig. 19. Aerial image of the #NoKXL crop art installation in Neligh, Nebraska, near the Ponca Trail of Tears. The artwork was led by artist-activist John Quigley and based on the original logo by tribal artist Richard Vollaire. Aerial photograph by Lou Dematteis/Spectral Q. Photo courtesy of Bold Nebraska.

outline of the cowboy and Indian standing side by side in a cornfield above the words "Heartland" and "#NoKXL" signified the sacredness of Nebraska's heritage and environment. It had come to represent not just one Nebraska farm but many.

While visuals were featured in roughly half of all of Bold Nebraska's website communication, many of these visuals were qualitatively more important than the numbers would suggest. The crop art installation, for example, was used multiple times in Bold Nebraska's own communication and was also featured in mainstream news stories, including national and international media coverage. Another visual used frequently was that of the black snake. For Lakota tribal members, it represents a second coming as a result of a destruction to the earth's natural resources. It was used in several anti-pipeline media messages, including the cover of the July/August 2015 issue of *Omaha Magazine*, where it was seen emerging from a pool of oil and crawling along Kleeb's arm. Finally, the organization regularly featured the political cartoons of

Nebraska cartoonist Neal Obermeyer. The prolific usage and publication of political cartoons helped fulfill a satirical yet confrontational strategy with government and "big oil" officials. In doing so, it was emblematic of Saul Alinsky's "Rules for Radicals," which called for the usage of ridicule, humor, and an understanding of local values to mobilize publics and marginalize those in power (Alinsky 1989). That environmental narratives were embedded in Bold Nebraska's photographs and other images echoes the assertion that American environmental reformers have turned to images because they infuse aesthetics and emotion into political debates. Such images are effective because they can "elicit an emotional response in spectators, awakening them to the beauty of nature and arousing their concern for its protection" (Dunaway 2008, xviii). Bold Nebraska was building on a long-standing tradition within environmentalism of leveraging photographs and visuals to construct powerful rhetorical appeals.

Drinking the Kool-Aid

There is one other visual dimension of Bold Nebraska's strategic activism that needs to be considered alongside powerful photographs and symbols, and that is brand identity. To understand this aspect of strategic communication, one might start with a visit to Jane Kleeb's hometown of Hastings, Nebraska. With a population of 25,000 people, Hastings is an attractive town located 15 miles south of the Platte River and about 160 miles southwest of Omaha. It sits at the south end of the Tom Osborne Expressway, named for the legendary University of Nebraska football coach. In addition to being Osborne's birthplace, Hastings is known for its impressive mix of historical architecture and a buoyant, diversified economy. This is also a rail town, one that was established in 1872 at what was then the meeting of the Burlington and Missouri River Railroad and the St. Joseph and Denver City Railroad. That legacy of rail continues with a downtown Amtrak station listed on the National Register of Historic Places. But its downtown core also features yoga studios, coffee shops, and even a craft brewery. One could do worse than Hastings as a place to visit or raise a family. But what is also striking about Hastings is its legacy in the story of American consumer brands, and in particular the tribute it pays to another son revered as much as Coach Osborne.

Here in Hastings, almost a century ago, an entrepreneur named Edwin Perkins turned a fruit-flavored liquid concentrate startup into the beverage empire known today as Kool-Aid. A plaque commemorating Hastings's role in the birthplace of Kool-Aid is located directly across from the historic rail station downtown. Every August locals and visitors alike celebrate the legacy of the popular children's drink at the Kool-Aid Days festival. The beverage was even designated as Nebraska's official refreshment by the state in 1998, in a bid to boost tourism to the city. The brand also introduced the world to Kool-Aid Man, a mascot of sorts in the shape of a glass pitcher who bursts through walls to entice children with the sweet beverage. Today, the brand's reputation doesn't resonate with the public the way it did in the 1970s or 1980s, as consumers gravitate to less sugar-laden beverages. But the advertising and promotional legacy of Kool-Aid lives on. Branding was and is central to the success of consumer products, and Kool-Aid was one of the great examples from the last century, highlighting how the interplay of product marketing and mass promotion situated a business idea in the national public consciousness. The power of brands isn't just limited to consumer goods or for-profit enterprises, however. It can help publics to quickly understand the attributes or benefits of other entities, including advocacy organizations and political issues.

It is worth pausing here to consider the degree to which Bold Nebraska cultivated what would be best described in the corporate world as a brand. Of course, the idea of an environmental advocacy group constructing an image for audiences in the same style as a consumer brand is anathema to traditional green thinkers and social activists. This is not to say that Bold Nebraska deployed an approach that looked anything like that of a multinational beverage company. But it is fair to assess some of their approach as akin to what happens in branding. Its persuasion layered a consistency of textual and verbal messaging with nonverbal cues: symbols, graphics, color schemes, photographs, cartoons, logos, and other visual artifacts. Furthermore, it built a brand consistency across its media ecosystem: the organization's "look" included the Bold Nebraska logo, with the word "Bold" situated in a blue-cube adjacent to a red "Nebraska"—an ode to the colors that represent the state and the nation, and an allusion to bipartisan advocacy. Its website and social media channels shared the logo and colors, with a continual mix of hard-hitting headlines and compelling visuals. It would be hard for outsiders to confuse Bold Nebraska with TransCanada. And it would also be difficult for outsiders to confuse Bold Nebraska with any other organizations opposing TransCanada. The organization's unique mix of appeals and strategies stood alone not only on account of the meaning embedded within the communication, but also because of attention paid to their considerations of brand. This dimension is often ignored on account of being shallow or superfluous. This hearkens back to the paradox of purity-pragmatism in environmental activism: to brand successfully, in the eyes of some critics, is to ostensibly sell out to the system even if it means shifting public opinion.

But for Bold Nebraska, effective image-making always mattered, so a proper brand was cultivated by a team of communication experts, spokespersons, and artists. Kleeb admits as much, noting that while she herself was not a visual communication expert, an aspired consistency in look and feel was a deliberate choice from the very beginning. Early on, she went looking for a graphic designer whose work aligned with her personality as well as the impactful visual look she wanted. She would join forces with an Omaha-based graphic designer named Justin Kemerling to give the organization a visual aura that blended a rural grittiness with a contemporary, user-friendly flavor. Kemerling's design philosophy "focused on making it [the Great Plains] beautiful, moving people to action, and getting things done" (Kemerling 2019, para. 1). The look he helped develop also found its way into protest sloganeering found on signs, posters, and T-shirts. "I always gravitate towards the communication and design," said Kleeb, who neither studied visual communication nor journalism while in university. "I think it's a strength of our organization," she said. "I am always very aware of the visual look of events." An example Kleeb likes to give is that of the planting of the Ponca corn, an event held annually. She noted that not everybody could drive several hours to a remote farm to participate in an event that simultaneously raised awareness and civic goodwill. Yet the photographs from the event became especially powerful when they were transmitted through the press and social media to audiences of thousands, if not millions, making the planting an environmental story that could be told to potentially all Nebraskans. A picture may tell a thousand words, but its potential for mediation and transmission is equally exponential. As any Instagram user will attest, photography travels well.

The degree to which Bold Nebraska was deliberate and strategy focused with its communication and activism ultimately afforded the organization a critical voice for pipeline opponents at the local, state, and national levels. The organization's ability to cultivate a message that ultimately resonated with both its followers and a larger constituency emphasized the critical role of strategic communication within environmental politics. While some studies from the domains of sociology and political science have pointed to the critical role of media and communication in assisting movements (Bob 2001; McAdam 1982; Wickham 2002), others have overlooked the construction of the messages and appeals themselves, thus assuming a uniformity in their composition. Other studies yet from these realms have simply ignored, or have taken for granted, the role of strategic communication in rallying publics and fostering public policy change. Yet political history is littered with well-intentioned organizations and activists who ultimately failed to gain traction with the public because they couldn't figure out how to publicize their efforts or calibrate their story. In some cases, this is because some self-conscious protest movements intentionally downplayed the "strategic" part of their communication for fear of being seen as co-opted, favoring instead more radical or disorganized approaches (Conner and Epstein 2007).

Bold Nebraska showed no such nervousness concerning its affiliation with tried-and-true public relations practices, including institutional outreach, and media relations. The organization's online news site offered the same kind of press relations materials offered by traditional organizations: press releases, media advisories, statements, fact sheets, photo opportunities, and interviewee contact information. In short, its communication output was not only prolific but emulated a public relations approach developed historically for corporate and government entities.

This media savvy can be contributed in part to Kleeb's background as a political organizer as well as MTV journalist. That Kleeb, as the founder and director, was also the de facto communicator in chief says much about the organization's reliance on a continual outflow of communication and media messaging. Other key Bold Nebraska communicators leveraged professional backgrounds and interests. These included Mark Hefflinger, the former journalist from California who served as Bold Nebraska's communication director, and Ben Gotschall, the writer and agriculture expert who worked on behalf of farmers and ranchers with the Nebraska Farmers Union. The involvement of these experienced communicators and policy experts underscored the organization's commitment to effective strategic communication, on top of the emergence of an organizational brand or at least the semblance of one.

Not all environmental activist organizations embrace such a high level of professional competence, one that emulates best practices from industry and government. Some intentionally steer clear of it. Paul Watson, founder of the Sea Shepherd Conservation Society as well as Greenpeace, disparaged his former colleagues at the latter organization as "the Avon ladies of the environmental movement" and "a bunch of wimps" for having moved toward user-friendly approaches to environmentalism, including collaborating with corporate sponsors at the 2000 Sydney Summer Olympic Games (Conner and Epstein 2007, 2). Watson's case serves as a reminder that pragmatic professionalism potentially risks alienating core members and diluting the organization's identity over time. Yet Bold Nebraska's strategic communication was careful to foster grassroots action and protest—movement "purity"— alongside its sophisticated, people-friendly public engagement strategies and tactics. In short, Bold Nebraska found its ideal location on the

Fig. 20. Cover of *Omaha Magazine*'s July/August 2015 issue, "Nebraska's Most Controversial Woman." Photo by Bill Sitzmann and creative direction by John Gawley and the *Omaha Magazine* team. Courtesy of *Omaha Magazine*.

purity-pragmatism spectrum, one that answered Conner and Epstein's (2007, 2) call to "understand the price of being practical, as well as the cost of being pure."

Bold Nebraska's committed strategic communication agenda was evidenced in different ways. Over half a decade, the organization was featured prominently by media in local and national publications. Kleeb herself earned the title of "Nebraska's Most Controversial Woman" on the cover of *Omaha Magazine* (the publication of which inspired a subsequent magazine launch party for Bold Nebraska members) and significant personal and organizational coverage in a *New York Times Magazine* article entitled "Jane Kleeb vs. the Keystone Pipeline." But the success of this communication agenda was also made possible by the publication of thousands of website articles and a multitude of public policy meetings, fundraisers, rallies, parties, and concerts. So too was Bold Nebraska's ability to infuse its "action item" micromobilizations into its messaging, thus engaging Nebraskans through hundreds of community engagements. Perhaps no outreach activity was more important, however, than its engagement with a critical entity in American public life: the national media.

6 A Fight on Your Hands

"What do you do with 10,000 dead cows?"

For loyal readers of the *New York Times Sunday Magazine*, this was the worst-case scenario, posed by an aggrieved Nebraska cattle rancher and pipeline opponent named Terry Van Housen. The rhetorical question was also part of a national newspaper story that underscored Bold Nebraska's media strategy for over a decade. The complex interplay of grassroots environmentalism and media advocacy fosters compelling questions about the growing role of green activists in national public life. For many years, activism has been examined by scholars from the disciplines of sociology and political science, where activities such as organizing, direct action, and group mobilization have been emphasized, sometimes at the expense of the role of media which is relegated to a supporting or passive role. This oversight has been addressed by some scholars who have elevated the prominence of media relations within those domains (Bob 2001). Within the strategic communication and public relations literature, much analysis of activism has considered its role from the perspective of the institutions they are opposing. Missing in much analysis, however, is a granular understanding of how green activists strategize and persuade publics through intentional media coverage and in turn how journalists mediate this careful outreach to audiences and policymakers. Such outreach is the focus of this chapter.

The relationship between environmental activists and journalists is complex but necessary. Environmentalists serve as key sources for media, providing expertise, opinion, and commentary. They also serve as newsmakers, providing both new story ideas and newsworthy events for reporters. Along the way, they must contend with other political actors in the media—including institutional elites and, yes, their direct opponents—while getting their message amplified or providing alternative perspectives. Finally, they are cognizant of the audiences for whom media serve and must craft their communication accordingly.

As a case in point, one returns to the *New York Times Sunday Magazine* and the question of the ten thousand deceased cattle. It was May 17, 2014, and, four years into Bold Nebraska's back-and-forth jousting with TransCanada over the latter's proposal to build the Keystone XL Pipeline across the state, reporters beyond Nebraska's borders were becoming well-versed in the state's pipeline politics, as evidenced by a wave of major news stories. This was highlighted by media treatment devoted to not only company and government officials engaged in the years-long battle but also the work of on-the-ground activists and environmentalists. National reporters were looking to tell the Nebraska story to those outside flyover country in a way that adequately conveyed the urgency of the fight, the sweeping frontier backdrop, and the political stakes of a seemingly endless ecological battle. One cattle rancher's dystopic vision of a catastrophic oil spill and a landscape of perished livestock was therefore the perfect opening act for a much larger story.

As the heartland narrative gained national attention, Bold Nebraska wasn't just asked to provide background or quotes for stories about the latest government legislation, court action, or pipeline routing. Rather, Bold Nebraska *became* the story. And the best example comes from the *Sunday Magazine* feature, which provided more than 4,600 words from freelance journalist Saul Elbein and a series of dramatic, gallery-worthy prairie photographs from Los Angeles–based photographer Michael Friberg. The print version's headline, "This Land Is Our Land," promised a Great Plains narrative of agrarian back-to-the-landers fending off a foreign interloper while protecting people, livestock, and soil (a promise, it's safe to say, that the talented Elbein delivered on). That set the stage for an extensive journalistic treatment featuring names and themes well known to anyone familiar with the Keystone pipeline controversy. The story of Sandhills rancher Randy Thompson was put forth as central to the national pipeline fight. Thompson, of course, was the Republican who had joined Bold Nebraska's coalition of green populists. Here, he offered up one of his irresistible, media-friendly quotes that boiled down a politically complex topic to a resonant metaphor that captured the essence of the issue—and TransCanada's alleged aggression—in two sentences: "They came out here with this great sense of entitlement and we were just supposed to get out of the road," Thompson told the *Times*'s Elbein. "These guys just treat you like bugs they can squash."

Thompson's role in the feature was to help explain the story of the pipeline. However, what Elbein was doing with the rest of his narrative was constructing a profile of Bold Nebraska's founder. Indeed, the different headline in the online version of the story—"Jane Kleeb vs. the Keystone Pipeline"—was probably the more accurate summary of his journalistic output. Bold Nebraska was emerging in national stories not just as a political influencer, but rather as an entity that could move the entire pipeline paradigm in flyover America into the domains of rural discontent and green advocacy. As a result, its leadership was being increasingly subjected to media coverage that was both sympathetic and critical. This is the price organizations pay for wooing reporters and gaining media traction. Kleeb and her team had recognized early in this process that journalists would factor extensively into their success, and that awareness of the power of news helped cultivate their public profile and actions. But their success wasn't earned overnight. Rather, it happened incrementally, through hundreds of media engagements, interviews, photo opportunities, and a communication philosophy that emphasized the agency of environmental advocates in stories that appeared almost daily in television newscasts, social media feeds, and newspaper headlines.

The materiality embedded in stories such as the *Times*'s homage to the hypothetical ten thousand dead cows conjures up the legacy of Canadian political economist Harold Innis and his decidedly grounded interpretation of media systems and mass communication. Innis's research about the development of the Canadian railway system, and later the role of hinterland commodities such as timber and minerals, would form the basis for his staples theory, which came to be known as "dirt research." Commodified staples, such as fur, fish, wheat, and lumber, dictated the underpinnings of economic as well as political and cultural life in North America's frontier settlements, according to Innis. His original interest in resource commodities such as timber and subsequently pulp and paper eventually led him to analyzing both newsprint and the newspaper industry. That scholarly turn brought the geographer and historian straight into the study of media and technology, particularly as North American corporations and government institutions leveraged journalistic processes to secure "monopolies of knowledge" in shoring up economic growth and political power. In particular, Innis was interested in the impact of media technologies such as the printing press and electronic broadcasting on institutions and social structures. His focus remained on the form and structure of media and technologies rather than their content (Patterson 1990). Marshall McLuhan, Innis's colleague at the University of Toronto during the 1950s, was significantly influenced by this decidedly material, structural view of media and its political economy. McLuhan's famous adage that the "medium is the message" spoke to forms of media delivery such as newsprint and television sets and their relationship to human cognition, but it was drawn directly from the commodities analysis that underpinned staples theory. Inherent in Innis's research was a recognition that disruptive media technologies and the mediated societal discourses they created were predicated on natural resources. Dirt research, then, was a means to understanding the linkage between the natural world, the mediated world, and transformative upheavals in the global economy. When extended to strategic environmentalism, Innis's understanding of media through staples is simultaneously imbued with rhetorically charged appeals and literal ecological matter.

Eco-activists and the Media Sphere

This dialectic of materialism and idealism is the media terrain in which communicators fight for hearts and minds while audiences attempt to make sense of their political, cultural, and environmental worlds. For

Americans living in the path of existing and proposed oil and gas pipe-lines, engaging in debates about their country's energy future means navigating local, state, national, and even global politics, as well as mes-sages emanating from corporate enterprises and the media. This new reality has fostered necessary linkages between environmentalists, citi-zen groups, and tribal communities in the United States. TransCanada's Keystone xl pipeline proposal became a prominent example, emerging in the media as a symbol of the global energy economy but also of humankind's relationship with the environment. Given their collective role as a conduit between publics, politics, and policy, environmental activists have emerged as a leading voice in a national issue with geo-political, economic, and environmental consequences. Yet their reach and influence are inevitably tangled up with national media coverage, which necessitates intentional, strategic outreach.

Media Framing: Journalist Interactions Matter

When *New York Times* journalist Gail Collins dedicated her op-ed col-umn on November 8, 2014, to the politics surrounding the Keystone xl proposal, she initially highlighted the issue of jobs creation from the pipeline's construction. TransCanada's public relations team would have been pleased with the article's lead. Yet a quotation from Kleeb situated later in the story—"When you start to mess with Nebraska water, you definitely have a fight on your hands"—pivoted the focus of Collins's column. Bold Nebraska's founder had successfully reframed Collins's story from one of jobs and the economy to conflict, human health, and Nebraska water.

Media framing, therefore, shows the power of the media to shape public debate, but it also shows how social movement organizations can influence their coverage. Framing in the media underscores the social construction of news and involves the highlighting or selection of information to provide a distinct or different perspective of reality. Describing the power of a communicating text, Entman (1993) empha-sizes the role of media framing in articulating social problems, diagnos-ing their causes, and projecting both moral judgments and remedies.

This largely mirrors understandings of framing from the sociological tradition. Snow and Benford (2000) describe collective action frames as representing a shared understanding of a condition or situation in need of change, an attribution of blame, or a call to action for interested parties. While social movement organizations must tend to membership recruitment and retention along with issue articulation, the media's role in framing is one of selection and salience, directing attention to how a communicated text exerts its power by directing the audience's attention toward a particular focus (Entman 1993). Drawn from a range of theoretical positions, including cognitive, constructivist, and critical, media framing analysis examines images, stereotypes, metaphors, actors, and messages (Matthes 2009). It has been used to study a range of communication within media discourse, including political, economic, and social topics.

Given this range of disciplinary perspectives, how researchers understand and measure frames is the subject of significant debate. For example, a conceptual divide has been located between issue-specific frames, such as the economy or environment, and generic frames, such as conflict or personalization (Matthes 2009). Other media framing literature has identified regularly occurring frames in news across multiple issues. These include frames featuring conflict, human interest, economic consequences, morality, and responsibility (Semetko and Valkenburg 2000). In nondemocratic environments, two main patterns of framing—overt propaganda and hidden manipulation (Baysha and Hallahan 2004)—exploit cultural values and past political events. They can also be used in the struggle over meaning as audiences adopt either pro-government or pro-opposition perspectives.

The presence of specific groups and individuals in media coverage of polarized media topics can be explained as episodic in nature (Iyengar 1990). These frames revolve around isolated events and breaking news without broader societal context. However, frames can evolve to become more thematic, attributing responsibility of a problem or issue to societal or political forces as opposed to specific groups or individuals. Over time, episodic frames can give way to thematic ones, suggesting that coverage in the media is dynamic and subject to evolution and continual influence because of larger contextual factors (Dimitrova et al. 2005). Thus, while media frames can be misunderstood as unnecessarily rigid or dualistic, their construction is subject to a tapestry of journalistic practices and contextual variables.

Media Framing of Environmental Activism

The eco-philosophical adage featured in Mann and Twiss's book *Physics* (1910) raises a poignant environmental question: "If a tree falls in the forest, does anybody hear?" The query has been posed more recently in popular culture artifacts, including the 1989 song "If a Tree Falls" by Canadian musician and environmentalist Bruce Cockburn, which concerned the decimation of rainforests. The invocation highlights an enduring question for both ecologists and media scholars: Does an environmental debate exist without an audience? In the early 1970s, Terry Simmons, a founding member of Greenpeace in Vancouver, British Columbia, grappled with this fundamental issue. Then a graduate student at Simon Fraser University in nearby Burnaby, British Columbia, he argued in his graduate thesis that one such example, the decades-long High Ross Dam controversy on the border of British Columbia and Washington State, would not have existed without active interest from members of the media: "A public controversy is in large part a media campaign" (Simmons 1974). He and his media-savvy Greenpeace colleagues, many of whom were journalists and considered themselves hardwired to the media theories of Marshall McLuhan (Dale 1996), were onto something early on that countless others from the environmental community would eventually emulate. Frames emanating from green activists need to be deliberated in the mass media in order to be successful. For environmentalists, a key challenge emerges in bringing an issue to the public's attention. Helping to shape the right kind of media frames plays a role in this process. A further challenge comes with retaining control and influence over the media narrative when other political actors deploy competing or disruptive frames of their own. To this end, the role of strategic communication in media framing has historically been overlooked, and whether frames in media content align with either source communicators or audiences ought to be considered (Matthes 2009).

Given the prominent role media play in environmental and social debates, media framing therefore emerges as a key lens through which to study activism. The ways in which language is used go beyond logic and reason and can activate existing ideologies on the part of publics, thus situating framing as a process that connects media discourses to a range of human emotions (Lakoff 2010). Here again, the strategic framing taxonomy allows activists to reposition public discourse in order to achieve desired media (and policy) outcomes (Gilliam and Bales 2001). The framework identifies those influential rhetorical elements: numbers, messengers, visuals, tone, metaphors and simplifying models, and context. And it calls special attention to the key role the news media play in constructing public perceptions of social or ecological issues and how organizations might identify and communicate alternative frames. Such "reframes" have potential for encouraging publics to reconsider previously held conceptions (Lakoff 2014). Because news reporting can be steeped in old conventions or stereotypes, newly developed frames by organizations can help counter a dominant narrative (Gilliam and Bales 2002). Furthermore, organizations should strive for message development that aligns with campaign goals and translates policy positions into language that considers a target audience's knowledge and beliefs (Bales et al. 2004).

In creating frames for media, movement organizations have three overarching goals: standing, which refers to the press taking such movements seriously; preferred framing, which occurs when the news media provide coverage of the specific movement and its views; and sympathy, which is the tone with which the movement is covered (Gamson and Wolsfeld 1993). That said, scholars also have emphasized how social movement organizations should use a variety of means to navigate media frames that either distort or ignore them. For example, Salvadoran newspaper coverage of a movement's struggle against health-care privatization revealed how the third-party endorsement of government policymakers lent credibility and legitimacy to public health-care advocates, paving the way for better media coverage (Kowalchuk 2009). Activists leveraged credibility through government engagement to be taken more seriously as a provider of information to the media. This goes against other accounts of media coverage of activism, which are often informed by the assumption of journalistic norms and decision-making or by structural forces such as the political economy of media. Like their institutional counterparts who practice media relations, activists enjoy a certain degree of agency in the news coverage process while serving as occasional or even prolific sources for journalists.

Activists as News Sources

Contested issues playing out in the media, such as environmental debates, highlight the influence of mass media in the context of whether movements are successful. In turn, social movement organizations have become a source for the news media, as they convince journalists that their frame is the most useful in organizing a story (Reese 2001, 20). A framing study of the Tea Party movement, for example, addressed some movement organizations' lamenting of what they perceived as just or unjust portrayals on television news (Boykoff and Laschever 2011). In that case, the television network Fox News used frames to legitimize the Tea Party, in stark contrast to MSNBC. The latter in fact described the group as a construction of news media (Boykoff and Laschever 2011), suggesting the perceived ability of media outlets to not only frame a movement's issue but also to legitimize or delegitimize an entire movement. This tension over representations of a movement is manifest in framing battles including everyday American versus non-mainstream, and grassroots versus establishment. Media frames, then, depend on journalistic affinity and are shaped by a changing mainstream media culture favoring partisanship and polarization.

This environment creates obstacles for some activists but an opportunity for those with a greater degree of media sophistication. A study of the interaction between frames advanced by community groups and the frames employed by journalists found that marginalized voices are able to enter news discourses when they are afforded economic and cultural resources (Ryan et al. 2001). However, their viewpoints are often limited because of trends like sensationalism, diminished story length, and attention paid to soft news. Despite these setbacks, framing is still upheld as a useful tool in expanding civic dialogue and improving communication between the news media and communities whose stories are underreported (Ryan et al. 2001). However, this requires community advocates to be prepared for their interactions with media and improve their ability to articulate frames.

The production of environmental communication in the media specifically hinges on activist sources who make environmental or scientific claims while trying to influence what is communicated to the public (Hansen 2011). In turn, the media supplement coverage of environmental issues with these contributing perspectives. Eco-activists who interface with the media provide commentary on existing stories and direct media to further expertise within their organizations. Like their communicator counterparts from government and the private sector, they also prepare story ideas that are both compelling for and easily digestible in the mainstream news cycle.

Activists as Newsworthy

The establishment of newsworthiness has direct bearing on whether an organization or issue succeeds or fails in making the news (Lester 1980). Regardless of their profile, organizations need to generate new stories to garner public interest and journalistic coverage. Evidence suggests that the presence of activist viewpoints in media stories is hardly an organic process where reporters somehow stumble across what environmental groups are doing or saying. Rather, this transmission of information and arguments from movement to media involves research, strategizing, and the deployment of tactics on behalf of the activists. It also requires a nose not only for what makes news but also for who is reading or watching the news and who else might be trying to influence the news. This is evidenced in a study of the U.S. news media's coverage of global production practices by athletic footwear manufacturer Nike (Greenberg and Knight 2004). The greater presence of activists versus company representatives in analyzed coverage was attributed to a larger repertoire of tactics and strategies such as demonstrations, fashion shows, and student protests that fit a criterion of newsworthiness.

These findings contradict the notion of government and company sources as being the only actors to help determine news and policy agendas in the media (Greenberg and Knight 2004). In a global environmental context, advocates and communication organizations not only help shift the framing of specific news topics. They are also argued to have altered broader media discourses. Media coverage of pollution in South Africa, for example, points to an increase in environmental stories arising from NGOs' and community activists' ability to provide journalists with newsworthy information such as chemicals dumping, industrial leaks, and health impacts (Barnett 2003).

This ability to provide journalists with important scientific and social data and information is not a sole driver for prolific or sympathetic media coverage. In health news, for example, the mere presence of activists in a story helps to amend existing media frames about disabled individuals. An analysis of advocacy in support of the American with Disabilities Act showed traditional media representations of disability to be more malleable and favorable in the face of disability activism. Newer media representations didn't entirely do away with old stereotypes, but they did include more progressive representations (Haller 1998).

Tropes and Metaphors

An environmental organization can't always count on sympathetic media coverage by virtue of its mere presence, however, especially when its advocacy is situated against an opposing viewpoint. Given that ecological or scientific information by itself doesn't translate into newsworthiness for media practitioners, communication techniques such as emotional appeals, tropes, narratives, and argumentation can play an outsized role in environmental news controversies (Cox 2012). Environmentalists have long recognized that some media coverage minimizes nuance or issue expertise in favor of richer narratives. This is a long-established strategy and is underscored by scholarly analysis of the Mohawk-white conflict in upstate New York during the 1970s. At the time, national media outlets provided sympathetic coverage to Mohawk activists even as they used outdated stereotypes or romanticized depictions of Native Americans. Mohawk organizers embraced this irony because the stories resonated with non-Indigenous readers, even if these selective representations did not match contemporary Native American lifestyles or priorities (Landsman 1987). This is an example of a public media event existing as an interpretive construction fostered by activist input, audience feedback, and journalistic conceptions. Newsworthiness, then, can be socially constructed and is contingent upon features, meanings, and consequences of a story or topic (Lester 1980). An embrace of these features is not a precursor for guaranteed success, however. Activists by their nature contest policies and actions deployed by other institutions, which means they are not the sole political actors within a given media frame and as a result face constant competition. This can even take the form of competing metaphors to describe an environmental controversy.

The use of metaphors is considered to be an effective approach to gaining coverage and an upper hand within environmental and scientific media discourses. Metaphors transmit information or meaning through audience interpretation, but their impact goes beyond individual cognition. They also communicate ideas between disciplines, institutions, and discourses (Väliverronen 1998). For scientists, the benefit of such an approach is readily apparent, but it also presents a potential moral dilemma when negotiating the tension between scientific detachment and advocacy within the production of ethical scientific communication (Larson 2009). And, as discussed, metaphors are often used by groups opposed to scientific discourses to undermine environmental advocacy. The so-called climate-gate scandal of 2009, which saw emails by climate scientists leaked to Internet sites and media outlets, saw use of religious metaphors to associate climate science with cult worship (Nerlich 2010). Such metaphorical framing is powerful because it invokes affectual and emotional responses in readers and establishes optimal conditions for political mobilization. Across the political spectrum and in different nation-state contexts, metaphors help drive populist rhetoric in the media (Lundgren and Ljuslinder 2011; Steinert 2003; Semino and Masci 1996).

Within environmental and scientific media the usage of metaphors is prominent and impactful in discourses about climate change (Flusberg et al. 2017; Shaw and Nerlich 2015; Nerlich 2012; Cozen 2013) and nuclear energy and accidents (Ausmus 1998; Gamson and Modigliani 1989; Demeritt 1994). A case in point comes from the extensive media coverage of Japan's Fukushima nuclear disaster in 2011, where specific metaphorical frames devoted to themes of rebirth, devastation, and sickness shaped both discourse and specific public engagements with energy policy (Renzi et al. 2017). The powerful metaphorical frames arising from disasters both natural and manmade are common with environmental media. During Louisiana's Hurricane Katrina disaster, media metaphors that emphasized civil unrest and urban warfare served to reflect and reinforce an ideology of militarism (Tierney et al. 2006). The effectiveness of metaphors, therefore, can be measured in different contexts and at different levels, but even when they seek to find common ground they are often subject to contradictory meanings that can turn a contended issue into a battle ground instead (Väliverronen 1998). Yet as a reductive strategy, the metaphor can't help but further promote populist discourses that juxtapose grassroots movements with loftier institutional or establishment discourses.

Activists versus Elites in the Media

As the previous discussion suggests, the depicting of environmentalism in the media is not a black and white affair. Overwhelming evidence suggests that the balance of power in media coverage shifts back and forth between activists and elite sources such as government and companies, even within a single event. Protesters who made national and international news at the 2009 G20 Summit in Pittsburgh demonstrated how this phenomenon works. While media commentators and city officials generated media frames such as violence and anarchy to describe their action, the anti-globalization protesters were successful in deploying their own frames through the media, such as First Amendment/right to protest and nonviolence (Kutz-Flamenbaum et al. 2012). This also means that protesters, when dealing with reporters looking for ready-made storylines, can punch above their weight in terms of how much coverage they receive vis-à-vis their establishment opponents. Predictably volatile political events like global nation-state summits provide protesters with the opportunity to be positioned as central figures when journalists are motivated to cover protest stories, as they often are.

This ability to be politically opportunistic and exploit normative journalistic practice leaves activists with a potential conundrum. In positioning themselves as oppositional to garner attention, do activists or protesters reinforce existing negative media frames, such as violence and anarchy? Analysis from another global summit offers important insight here. The 2001 G8 Summit in Italy, and specifically the Battle of Genoa clash between police and protesters, evoked "images of tear gas, burning cars, and black clad protesters hurling stones and Molotov cocktails at advancing lines of heavily militarized riot police" (Juris 2005, 413). While these violent protests as reported by the media helped generate significant visibility for anti-globalization activists and energized their larger movement, they also helped justify repressive government strategies, including efforts to criminalize dissent (Juris 2005). Evolving media frames contingent upon the presence of elites, then, can help or hurt activists. This underscores the point that while the media in a free press context is malleable and subject to outside influence, it is still an uncontrolled media entity. Other studies of media framing paint a challenging picture for marginalized groups when they are presented as "rhetorical enemies" (Bowe and Makki 2015), engaged in disturbance or radical action (Kruse 2001), or even as fleeting or apathetic (Entman and Rojecki 1993).

Coverage of climate science in the media shows how this diminishment can even occur when activists have access to more conclusive or fuller scientific evidence to justify their views. Other scholars have shown activists being outdueled by opponents who are willing to simplify or obfuscate environmental debates. An analysis of U.S. and UK media coverage of anthropogenic climate change has highlighted the role of climate change contrarians, those dissenters who argue that such a warming trend is a falsehood (Boykoff 2007). That climate change deniers can undermine scientists in the news suggests a divergence between scientific agreement on anthropogenic or human-created climate change and the role of the media in affirming or undermining such consensus (Boykoff 2007). A public debate over the logging of old-growth forests similarly reveals the media's potential for mitigating scientific facts (Liebler and Bendix 1996). Campaigners intent on saving the forest and protecting the native spotted owl tried to frame the debate as a choice between preserving an ancient geological resource for the public or propping up an industry in decline. They were outflanked by the pro-logging side because the latter defined the debate more narrowly as a simple conflict between an obscure bird and people losing their jobs.

This demonstrates the importance of beliefs and narrative in environmental media coverage relative to scientific information. The framing of an environmental controversy in concise or more simplistic terms allowed sources and journalists to move past scientific data, asking audiences to make decisions based on storylines laden with personal values and experiences. Activists are thus vulnerable to opponents who weave more compelling or easily digested narratives. To get to positive media framing, then, activists must navigate a complex ecosystem of supporters, opponents, journalists, and mass audiences. The sympathetic media framing of a deaf rights movement demonstrates how attending to these different groups can prove successful (Kensicki 2001). Positive frames were attributed to several factors: a lack of expedience on the part of elite sources, the availability of protesters as sources and their peaceful nature, support from corporations and liaisons with journalists, and sympathetic assumptions from the public about disability.

Activists and Media Audiences
Breaking through to the audiences served by media outlets with the right kind of news coverage, known as message pull through, becomes

paramount for activists who risk public disinterest or, worse, alienation with the wrong kind of media treatment. Studies of feminist activism reveal the power of the media to frame movements in negative terms and disrupt activist efforts in the media. An analysis of third-wave feminism identifies frames such as demonization, personalization, trivialization, and victimization, which prevented a fuller account of modern feminism for readers (Bronstein 2005). Terkildsen and Schnell's (1997) study of U.S. coverage of the United Nations Conference on Women and NGO forum suggests the value of media frames that emphasize a common denominator between marginalized groups and the broader public. Noting that adversarial media frames exerted a negative impact on gender-related issues and support for women's rights, they call for messaging that integrates universal values. A focus on long-term or national trends can position an issue as part of a wider public discourse. This consideration of media audiences within a larger societal context underscores Iyengar's (1990) explanation of thematic framing and the importance of contextualization.

More comprehensive appeals have enjoyed success in the environmental policy arena. The universality of food and its inclusion in contentious debates about biotechnology provides a case in point. Ten Eyck and Williment (2003) examined how the U.S. elite press develops discourses around genetics and genetic technology, producing seven frames: progress, economic prospects, nature/nurture, public accountability, ethical concerns, runaway technology, and Pandora's box. Concurrent with the assertion that genetics debates are fiercer when the topic of food or crops is present (Thompson 1997), the study found more critical discourses of biotechnology when food or crops were the central issue, as opposed to when considering the integration of genetics in medical innovations. In other words, topicality can influence the kind of science frame invoked in news coverage. That food trumps medical and scientific innovation in critical environmental reporting shows that news media are embedded in larger cultural contexts, with environmentalists having made a more deliberate and successful push to reveal the negative impacts of genetically modified foods (Ten Eyck and Williment 2003). Media framing, therefore, can elevate the prominence of some environmental problems while overlooking or even disguising others.

These resonant, totalizing messages can also activate larger audiences through real-time and digital social networks. During the 2010–11 Tunisian uprising, for example, such an approach helped connect online human rights activists with working-class populations and labor movements (Lim 2013). An image of a fruit vendor lighting himself on fire after his stand was confiscated by the government served as an archetypal image that had iconic value for many groups. This suggests the effectiveness of overarching narratives that culturally and politically resonate with large populations as one approach to successful framing by a movement. Combined with the activation of a large, dense network of bloggers and other social media users, it helped to transform local actions and contentions into a successful movement at the national level (Lim 2013). Similar to this is the tactic of deploying emotionally or rhetorically charged images in the environmental sphere as a means to leveraging the power of technological media and influencing existing discourses (DeLuca 2005).

Media framing ultimately emerges as a key site for influencing public policy and affecting policy change for activists. Their interest goes beyond observing the results of media discourse, however. Activists have become important sources and newsmakers for the media in the development of news stories. To this end, and like their media relations counterparts from government and the private sector, they interact with journalists and prepare stories that are digestible in the mainstream media. Additionally, their actions—when they fit a criterion of newsworthiness, such as demonstrations and events—can shift existing media discourses about an issue. This goes against some assertions of media framing being controlled exclusively by elites from government and business. A number of studies, however, show media framing to be a complex process that delivers mixed results for activists. Media coverage may include more progressive representations of a movement while simultaneously communicating outdated stereotypes. Other times, a media frame deployed by activists fails to compete with other frames based on cognitive or cultural factors. Activists must contend with opposing forces within media discourse, including those from government and corporate elites. They must also be cognizant of the audiences for whom media serve.

Within environmental communication in particular, the tension between scientific data and metaphorical or storytelling approaches becomes especially significant. Defining conflicts in simple terms or storylines that match up with existing personal or cultural beliefs allows sources and journalists to define issues beyond scientific evidence. It also allows activists to develop larger narratives resonant with broader publics and networks. In a contemporary news context notable for sensationalism and diminished journalism resources, activists need to be prepared for their interactions with media and improve their ability to articulate their frames, especially to overcome media environments in which movement voices are obscured or marginalized. In spite of challenging media environments, scholarship to date suggests a variability of media framing outcomes that present opportunities for activists to gain traction for their causes in terms of salience, cognition, and support. To this end, three overarching questions arise with regards to Bold Nebraska's engagement with the media. First, were strategic advocacy framing elements observed in national media stories (and if so, which ones were most pervasive)? Second, were conceptual metaphors and simplifying models about environmental communication used within national media coverage? And finally, what science or environmental frames were used within national media coverage?

To answer these questions requires an understanding of how national media in the United States and Canada used news stories to frame stories involving Bold Nebraska and its activism directed at the Keystone XL pipeline. News discourse is presented as a socio-cognitive process involving all three players in the process of mediation: sources, journalists, and audience members (Pan and Kosicki 1993). Entman (2007) links frames and sources, arguing that content analyses should be informed by explicit theory linking patterns of framing in the media to priming and agenda-setting effects on audiences. Framing analysis examines news discourse by conceptualizing news texts into empirically opera-tionalizable dimensions—syntactical, script, thematic, and rhetorical structures—to ultimately show evidence of the media's framing of issues in news texts (Pan and Kosicki 1993).

The framing paradigm as method ensures the collection of data that represents media messages being picked up by most audience members. Analyzing media texts highlights information that is more or less salient by placement, repetition, or association (Entman 1993). Because the debate over the Keystone XL pipeline entailed a North American audi-ence and a strongly political dimension, the author analyzed four pub-lications through quantitative framing analysis. These four newspapers were the *New York Times* and the *Washington Post* in the United States and the *Globe and Mail* and *National Post* in Canada. Leading national newspapers are optimal for framing studies because news stories are far more likely to have a cascading effect on other media outlets, elite views, and ultimately mass opinion (Entman 2008). The newspapers were selected because of their national presence within their respective countries. The *New York Times* is generally considered the most influen-tial newspaper in the United States. The *Washington Post* is notable for its coverage of national political issues and events. The *Globe and Mail* newspaper is Canada's highest-circulated national newspaper and has been dubbed the country's "newspaper of record." The *National Post*—originally built around the *Financial Post* newspaper and currently the flagship newspaper of Canada's Post Media Network—draws from its business journalism tradition to offer a more conservative perspective of national and international affairs.

Using the LexisNexis database, stories published between January 1, 2011 and December 31, 2015 about Keystone XL that included the term "Bold Nebraska" were obtained. In the case of all four publications, the author removed articles where the term "Bold Nebraska" was mentioned only in passing. The author also removed letters to the editor about Bold Nebraska, as were duplicates that were published in more than one edi-tion of a certain publication. However, editorials, op-ed contributions, and blogged articles remained for analysis.

In total, the author collected 68 articles from the *New York Times* (17 stories), the *Washington Post* (18 stories), the *Globe and Mail* (14 stories), and the *National Post* (19 stories). As opposed to a subset or sampling of media articles that is seen in some content analyses, this set of articles represented full coverage from these national media publications. Riffe, Lacy, and Fico (2014) note that when the focus is on a particular critical event such as a major environmental disaster, probability sampling can miss important parts of the coverage. Additionally, research is more successful in examining the entire population of stories devoted to certain topics when such topics receive comparatively scarcer coverage. The author developed a written protocol that could be shared with other researchers and instructs coders on how to assign values to content units. The unit of measure for the study was the article. Stories related to coverage of Bold Nebraska's activism against the Keystone XL pipeline were subsequently coded for whether they deployed media frames marked by conceptual metaphors, making them more digestible for larger audiences. Drawing from Nerlich and Koteyko's research on climate activism in the media, these metaphors were environmentalism as religion (stopping the pipeline as a moral imperative), dieting (equating the health of the threatened environment to human health), finance (environmental activism is good financial management), battle or war (environmental activism as a battle) and a journey (with the final destination being the elimination of the pipeline). Stories were also coded according to media frames based on Ten Eyck and Williment's (2003) examination of media treatments of an environmental issue: progress, economic prospects, public accountability, ethical concerns, Pandora's box, and runaway resources extraction (what Ten Eyck and Williment had originally labeled "runaway technology"). The author added a seventh frame, globalization, in order to reflect the binational nature of the Bold Nebraska versus TransCanada dispute and the activists' appeals to patriotism and regional culture. Finally, the author coded for the presence of strategic advocacy framing taxonomy elements (Gilliam and Bales 2001) in order to understand how source organizations construct media stories. These five elements were context, numbers, messengers, metaphors and simplifying models, and tone. (The author removed the element of visuals, which is part of the original taxonomy, due to the limitations of the archived newspaper articles). To establish reliability and replicability, two well-trained coders analyzed the articles independently. In addition to frames and framing variables, the author coded articles for additional elements related to the content. These included physical attributes such as the length of the story (assessed by number of words) and whether the story appeared on the front page of the newspaper or not. Of the stories, only a small percentage (10 percent) were located on the front page of a newspaper section. A majority of articles were between 500 and 1,000 words, while a further 21 percent of all stories were longer than 1,000 words. Those coded as less than 500 words accounted for 19 percent of the stories. A majority of articles were general news stories (63 percent), while a smaller number were either feature or magazine stories, or commentaries or editorials (29 percent and 6 percent, respectively).

Strategic Framing Elements in Media Stories
Media frames were analyzed for the existence of one or all of the elements of strategic framing. Of the measured elements, all were featured for at least 50 percent of the articles. Context was the most commonly used framing element in the media coverage, featured in more than 89 percent of articles. The numbers frame, which includes statistics about the pipeline, environmental impacts, and climate change, appeared at least once in 85 percent of the newspaper stories, while messengers were also identified in 85 percent of the stories. Metaphors were identified in 53 percent of the articles, along with the framing element of tone.

Metaphorical Frames
Among conceptual metaphorical frames, the metaphor of battle/war was most prevalent, appearing in 51 percent of stories measured. The environmental metaphor of the journey followed, present in 31 percent of news articles, along with the conceptual metaphor of finance (also 31 percent). Two other metaphors, diet/health and religion, were used

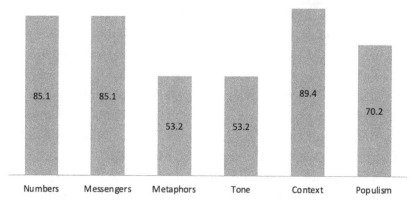

Fig. 21. Strategic elements of framing in media articles (percentage). Created by author.

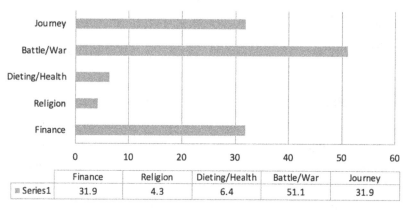

	Finance	Religion	Dieting/Health	Battle/War	Journey
▪ Series1	31.9	4.3	6.4	51.1	31.9

Fig. 22. Metaphor frames in news articles about Bold Nebraska. Created by author.

with less frequency, as they appeared in only 6 and 4 percent of all stories, respectively.

Science and Environmental Frames

News articles were also examined for the presence of Ten Eyck and Williment's (2003) frames of scientific and environmental discourse: progress, economy, public accountability, ethical concerns, runaway technology/resources extraction, and Pandora's box. The frame of globalization was also measured. The top four environmental frames in media coverage featuring Bold Nebraska were ethical concerns (67 percent), globalization (61 percent), economy (46 percent), and public accountability (46 percent). The frames of progress and runaway resources extraction were used in 38 percent and 36 percent of the articles, respectively. The frame of Pandora's box saw much sparser usage at 15 percent.

Movement Framing versus Media Framing

Figure 24 shows the degree to which strategic framing elements were used in both the contexts of Bold Nebraska's controlled media (website articles) and uncontrolled media (mainstream newspaper coverage of Bold Nebraska). Context, which was the most pervasive element in Bold Nebraska's communication (89 percent), was also the most popular element in news coverage by the major newspapers (89 percent). Similarly, the element of messengers, another leading element deployed within the group's communication (86 percent), was also a top element within newspaper coverage (85 percent). While the element of populism was featured in a majority of Bold Nebraska and newspaper articles, it enjoyed greater popularity within the movement's communication (87 percent of articles) compared to newspaper coverage (70 percent). Conversely, the element of numbers was more pervasive in newspaper coverage (85 percent) than in Bold Nebraska's website communication (59 percent). Figure 24 also shows a drop-off in the usage of oppositional tone and metaphor in newspaper coverage of Bold Nebraska compared to the group's own discourse.

Overall, national media coverage of Bold Nebraska's activism featured significant usage of strategic framing elements. Conceptual metaphor frames were found in a majority of website articles, although they did not always line up with Nerlich and Koteyko's (2009) proposed frames for environmental and climate activism. The most popular environmental metaphor within media coverage was that of battle/war, followed by the metaphors of journey and finance. Within Ten Eyck and Williment's (2003) science and environment frames, the frame of ethical concerns was most frequently located within stories. Globalization, as an added

■ Bold Nebraska Articles ■ News Articles

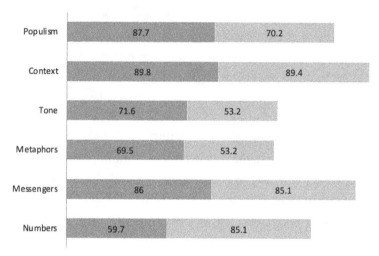

Fig. 23. Science/environment frames in news articles about Bold Nebraska (percentage). Created by author.

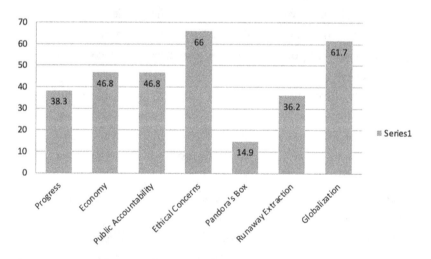

Fig. 24. Strategic framing elements: Bold Nebraska and news articles (percentage). Created by author.

frame to the science and environment framework, was also present in a majority of media articles. Roughly half of the articles featured themes of economy and public accountability.

Molding the Media Narrative

Newspaper articles from the *New York Times* and *Washington Post* in the United States and the *Globe and Mail* and *National Post* in Canada used strategic framing elements extensively in reporting about Bold Nebraska's rural environmentalism. This provides a reminder to advocates and other strategic communicators that modes of issue engagement are transferable to journalistic coverage. Bold Nebraska's emphasis on contextual factors, notably its Nebraska location, geography, and state culture became embedded in the broader media narrative. Context was the most used element among all framing variables, as journalists situated the pipeline fight squarely in Nebraska's farms and ranches as well as tribal communities. Such contextualization was realized through the emphasis of specific family farms, townships, geological features, and regional histories. Even the organization's name, Bold Nebraska, projects a contextualizing messaging. Furthermore, such variables moved the pipeline saga away from abstraction by repeatedly emphasizing the state's unique rural character but also its distinct ecological features. Neither the Nebraska Sandhills nor the Ogallala Aquifer are particularly well known geological landmarks outside of the Great Plains. Thus, their mediation was especially important in situating Nebraska as a valuable ecological geography.

On-the-ground human communicators, as official messengers, were also integral to Bold Nebraska's pipeline narrative. Messengers, according to Gilliam and Bales (2002), can be as important to the issue as the message itself. They not only provide compelling quotes within media stories but also appear in photographs, reach out to audiences on social media, and even write op-eds for influential newspapers. In some cases, they can become the embodiment or physical symbol of a cause. These messengers included the obvious organizational spokespersons (such as founder Jane Kleeb) as well as ordinary citizens and even celebrities who supported the organization, such as actress Daryl Hannah and musicians Neil Young and Willie Nelson. Another distinct advantage imparted by messengers is their ability to frame or reframe stories featuring different narratives, as journalists look to set off a perspective from one organization with another point of view or lived experience. The mainstream media treated the Keystone XL proposal as a political story, an economic story, and an environmental story. As a result, a wide range of reporters wrote stories about Keystone XL and situated the pipeline within larger debates over energy policy, climate change, jobs creation, and national politics. Consequently, such stories also featured voices from government (such as the State Department, tasked with overseeing the permitting process), TransCanada executives, other oil and gas companies, and think tanks (such as the Center for International Policy). Amid this ecosystem of media sources, which can simultaneously confuse and dilute preferred frames for activists, the rhetorical implications of a well-placed quote become heightened, particularly if they create or support existing metaphors or environmental issue frames.

A January 23, 2013, story in the *Washington Post*, describing the backing of the pipeline by Nebraska's governor, highlighted the ability of Jane Kleeb as a messenger to rhetorically reroute a story's narrative back to Bold Nebraska's favored frames and away from the state government's perspective. "The fight continues, even though Governor Heineman sided with a foreign corporation and turned his back on our water and property rights," said Kleeb to the newspaper. Other Bold Nebraska messengers, such as rancher Randy Thompson, provided even blunter assessments of the pipeline project while cementing the saliency of a resonant issue across the state—eminent domain and farmers' and ranchers' land rights. "They just keep you in a pressure cooker all of the time," he said of pipeline builder TransCanada's demand to run the pipeline across his family's property in a 2011 *National Post* story. "To me, it's obscene. I thought, screw you, bring your attorneys." The writer echoed Thompson's sentiments within the same story, referring to TransCanada's correspondence with Thompson as "a blunt missive . . . [with] all of the charm of a high school bully threatening to punch a third-grader's lights out." Here, the school bullying metaphor not only amplified Bold Nebraska's appeals; it ultimately synchronized the journalist's voice and thus the broader narrative with the rancher's unique point of view.

In some cases, the messengers themselves became the story. A September 10, 2013, *Globe and Mail* article reported on Neil Young's description of Fort McMurray, a key site for oil sands production in Alberta, as a "wasteland" and more: "The fact is, Fort McMurray looks like Hiroshima," he said, describing his visit there. "The Indians up there and the native peoples are dying. . . . The fuel's all over—the fumes everywhere—you can smell it when you get to town." In the same story, Canada's Natural Resources Minister Joe Oliver responded that while he was a fan of Young's music, he disagreed with the singer's assertions. Kleeb showed no hesitation in responding to both Young *and* Oliver in the same story while rerouting the story to a preferred metaphorical frame of prairie activists dueling corporate lobbyists: "Neil Young is speaking for all of us to stop the Keystone XL," she said. "Joe Oliver can say anything but the reality is people are dying and the alliance between cowboys and Indians is stronger than any K Street lobbyists Canada hires." This time, drawing from sympathetic and oppositional voices, Kleeb was able to reshape a related story about Fort McMurray and the Canadian oil sands into yet another narrative warning against Keystone XL's intrusion into Nebraska.

From Activist Frames to Media Storytelling

In addition to seeking a greater understanding of communication emanating from contemporary environmental activism, this study also sought to identify the elements from this strategic communication that carry forward into mainstream media coverage. This study's analysis of newspaper articles from the *New York Times* and *Washington Post* in the United States and the *Globe and Mail* and *National Post* in Canada found that the strategic framing elements embedded in movement communication can also be found in subsequent national media coverage. Bold Nebraska's continued emphasis on contextual factors, notably its Nebraska location and geography, became embedded in the broader media narrative. Context was the most used element in both movement framing *and* media framing, as journalists situated the pipeline fight squarely in Nebraska's farming and ranching communities. This was especially important because dozens of reporters from a myriad of beats were assigned to report about Keystone XL and Bold Nebraska. At the *New York Times* alone, articles were authored by Michael Shear, a White House correspondent; Coral Davenport, an energy and environmental policy reporter; Mitch Smith, a reporter with the *Times's* Chicago bureau; Dan Frosch, a Denver correspondent; Saul Elbein, a Texas-based freelance journalist; and Ian Austen, the *Times's* Canada correspondent. The provision of contextual information in Bold Nebraska's messaging was important in relaying to a wide swath of reporters from a range of media outlets the circumstances, setting, and history of Bold Nebraska's fight against Keystone XL especially when almost all of the national reporters were based outside of the state.

Nebraska's agrarian storytellers were instrumental in attaching this context to the pipeline proposal. Nebraskans such as Art and Helen Tanderup, the corn and soybean farmers from Custer Township, and cattle rancher Randy Thompson from Merrick County were put forth as the protagonists in Bold Nebraska's years-long eco-drama. In explaining the I Stand with Randy campaign, one of several engineered to energize Nebraskans in their fight against TransCanada, the *New York Times* described Thompson as "a lifelong Republican who had never done anything more political than vote" (Elbein 2014). The Tanderups, whose farm hosted the Harvest the Hope festival, garnered similar attention, including attention from *Rolling Stone* magazine, which detailed Art Tanderup's meeting with Neil Young at a Keystone XL protest in DC and their subsequent plan for a benefit concert on Tanderup's property (Kreps 2014). In a statement delivered to media, Kleeb even situated the group's salt-of-earth messengers as celebrities in their own right: "Farmers, ranchers and tribes that have been standing up to TransCanada are rock stars in my eyes," she said (Saldana 2014, para. 5).

Not all elements were as well represented in both movement and media framing, however. Bold Nebraska's feisty oppositional tone, which was featured in nearly three-quarters of the organization's website communication, was more or less muted in the media. At least, it garnered much less inclusion in the media coverage, in great part because journalists control the tone and also determine which quotes to incorporate in news stories. Similarly, Bold Nebraska's use of metaphors saw a similar drop-off in media articles, again demonstrating how journalists construct their stories based on different professional practices that may or may not incorporate specific communication styles. This also helps explain why numbers and data were featured in media stories to a greater degree than Bold Nebraska's own articles. Reporters, unsurprisingly, were living up to their professional obligations by including quantifiable economic, environmental, and financial information. Still, a telling result is that Bold Nebraska's rhetorically infused strategic framing elements were found in a majority of both Bold Nebraska missives *and* national media articles. This can be explained in part to Bold Nebraska's ability to provide not only a prepared narrative to the media (complete with compelling protagonists and colorful commentary) but also specific components helpful in reconstructing it as part of the reporting process. The organization's press releases, statements, advisories, and interviews given to the media closely mirrored what was communicated in primary missives to Bold Nebraska's primary audience. For example, the organization's mantra of protecting Nebraska's "land and water" from a foreign corporation in website communication was repeated near-verbatim by metropolitan and national daily publications, including the *Washington Post, Chicago Tribune,* and *Omaha World Herald.* So while media coverage didn't mirror the exact usage of Bold Nebraska's framing elements, it did convey the same master frame emanating from Bold Nebraska's advocacy.

As public interest communicators, activists do not control media coverage or media frames, but they can wield influence in how media discourse about organizations and issues is shaped through their actions and words, as well as their engagement with journalists by providing interviews, background information, quotes, and contextualizing details. Such attention admittedly requires time, resources, and an ability to weather media coverage that can toggle between positive and negative portrayals or sympathetic and critical perspectives. Yet by engaging deeply as sources, activists are well positioned not only to make news but to push back against prevailing narratives supporting institutional elites with counternarratives of their own.

While national publications play an important role in influencing political and economic debates, the Keystone saga also highlighted the role of regional media, including metropolitan and community newspapers. Newspapers from Omaha, Lincoln, and other Nebraska cities and towns provided their own critical coverage of Bold Nebraska and the Keystone proposal. The key role of regional and local media supports a growing call for journalists to pay heed to civic issues and concerns outside of the major media and political centers of the United States and contributes to a greater understanding of the media's role in potentially propping up civic engagement in rural communities. Furthermore, Bold Nebraska's coverage in social media, on television broadcasts, and in lifestyle and entertainment magazines such as *Rolling Stone* and *Omaha Magazine* were also important in widening the debate over pipelines to specific demographics. A recurring theme in much of this coverage was conflict between the ordinary citizens of Nebraska's hinterland and wealthy corporations from outside the state and country. The disgruntled cowboys and environmentalists who represented a major part of the anti-pipeline fight were taking aim at political and financial elites in Nebraska, in Washington DC, and well beyond U.S. borders. Bold Nebraska was dancing with a powerful force in prairie politics, one that revived agrarian traditions but also grievances on the Great Plains.

7   From the Grass Roots

The town of Neligh enjoys a significant place in Nebraska's collective consciousness, and not just because recent years have brought national and even international media attention to Art and Helen Tanderups' farm, the sight of Bold Nebraska's Harvest the Hope concert and a series of crop art protest installations by artist-activist John Quigley. The picturesque farming community of 1,500 residents, located on the north bank of the meandering Elkhorn River, is also home to a well-known marker that precedes the Keystone fight by over a century: the grave site of White Buffalo Girl. In 1877 U.S. government agents removed the Ponca people from their traditional territory about forty-five miles north of Neligh, near the Niobrara River, a tributary of the Missouri River. Agents marched tribal members six hundred miles south to a reservation in Oklahoma. The journey ended badly for the Poncas. Nine members died along the way due to brutal weather conditions; many more died after arriving in Oklahoma.

The north–south journey across the state is now remembered as the Ponca Trail of Tears, and it runs directly across the acreage where the Tanderup farm now sits. About eight miles further south, closer to Neligh's town center and the Elkhorn River Valley, is where White Buffalo Girl succumbed to the journey. She was still a baby—only one year and six months old at the time of her passing. Her parents, mother Moon Hawk and father Black Elk, were forced to continue marching on, and they asked the white settlers of Neligh to care for their daughter's grave. In turn, the Neligh locals honored their pledge to White Buffalo Girl's parents to honor their daughter's memory. A century and a half later, a stone monument remembering her is well tended by volunteers at Neligh's cemetery, and the story continues to captivate Nebraskans who visit the historical marker to reflect on the site's complex history. Visitors regularly leave flowers, coins, and other offerings. As Helen Tanderup pointed out, it is the most decorated gravesite in the community. This is a point of pride in Neligh. It is also a site of hope amid an otherwise challenging historical legacy for Native Americans on the Great Plains, highlighting the power of civic engagement and communication to at least provide a platform for both healing and nurturing a collective memory. And in its own way, the Cowboy and Indian Alliance—founded in an effort to stave off encroaching pipeline infrastructure and conserve land and water for Indigenous and white settler communities—fostered its own civic engagement, a useful antidote to the heightened political partisanship that has ravaged public life in Nebraska and across the United States over the past decade. Even as rallying in favor of the state's ecology necessitated conflict with government and industry, it also bridged divides between previously disenfranchised communities.

Strategic grassroots events like Harvest the Hope remind us that national media were not the sole entities responsible for broadly defining anti-pipeline activism. With or without mainstream media coverage, Bold Nebraska actively defined its environmentalism on its own terms at the iconic music festival. The media, in turn, mostly parroted an established narrative too compelling to ignore. Bold Nebraska therefore forged the terms of its story to the media, and not the other way around. As a cultural venue for protest and public activism, Harvest the Hope represented the aggregation of Bold Nebraska's rhetorical appeals. This in turn fostered a metanarrative of united rural Americans, both Native and non-Native, resisting the environmental threat wrought by a foreign corporation. Judged by different measures, including attendance, star power, local interest, and media coverage, the event was a considerable success. The concert was sold out, attracted two of the highest-profile musicians in the world, and garnered extensive attention in publications as diverse as the *Lincoln Journal Star*, *Indian Country Today*, and *Rolling Stone*. At a regional level, the event paralleled the trajectory of equally iconic and much larger music festivals. Harvest the Hope stood in for an idealized prairie grassroots activism in the way that the Woodstock Music and Art Fair symbolized American counterculture in the 1960s or Live Aid represented the global effort to address the 1980s famine in Ethiopia. Woodstock is remembered as participatory, communitarian, and noncommercial, and an opportunity for counterculturalists to seek "refuge in the social relations of an idealized past," while Live Aid's loftier activism opened new spaces for cultural politics (Garofalo 1993, 189). The immortalization of these events through mass media has given them a mythology of their own (Cunha 1988). Similar in some ways to the labor strikes of the 1940s and student protests in the 1960s in terms of how they mediated a civic counternarrative, such festivals represented a collective rethinking of fundamental social issues and conflicts (Peterson 1973). While the involvement of celebrity musicians and other entertainers is shown to be a long-standing tactic in social and environmental activism, its effectiveness has been debated. One study found that most people aren't persuaded by celebrity appeals, but they believe that other people are (De Waal 2016). In this operating environment, the legitimacy of Neil Young and Willie Nelson, through their long-standing connection to American farming and Indigenous issues (in other words, their own narrative fidelity) became paramount. It is difficult to dismiss either musician as a social issue grandstander when both performers have historically engaged deeply with rural, environmental, and Indigenous issues over the courses of their respective careers going back roughly a half-century.

It was Bold Nebraska's construction of a "Cowboy and Indian" coalition involving farmers, ranchers, and Native American tribal members that stood out from other rock festivals. The image of the cowboy maintains symbolic power steeped in American ruggedness, frontier adventure, and expansionism, but it also carries baggage that to this day divides many Americans. Among its many legacies, the conquering of the American West by white settlers is remembered for tragic conflicts with Indigenous communities, some of which included mass human atrocities, as well as devastating ecological impacts to land, water, and wildlife.

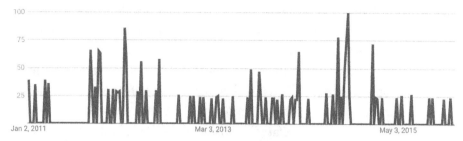

Fig. 25. Usage of the search term "Bold Nebraska" between January 1, 2011, and December 31, 2015, from GoogleTrends. Numbers represent search engine interest relative to the highest point on the chart for the given time-frame. The value of 100, reached on August 18, 2014—the day the Harvest the Hope concert was announced—indicates peak popularity for "Bold Nebraska" on the Google search engine. Created by author on trends.google.com.

By itself, then, the cowboy is a contended symbol representing the histories of both pioneering and violence. A cowboys-alone crusade could not do justice to the simultaneously patriotic and environmental overtures of the Bold Nebraska cause. Yet the master frame evoked by the Cowboy and Indian Alliance at Harvest the Hope ultimately helped mitigate mistrust of the American cowboy from other quarters. It recognized that the American West was founded not by one particular group, ethnicity, or nationality, but rather multiple entities. As first peoples, the role of Native American tribes is not merely complementary to North American Great Plains history; it is both central and absolute. To this end, the alliance implicitly recognized the rights, responsibilities, and contributions of both groups to the land, even while skirting over the contended history between the two groups, both in Nebraska and nationwide. Here, the farmer and rancher achieved ecological goals in harmony with their Indigenous neighbors. Bold Nebraska's cowboy, then, stood in for the American patriot fending off the Canadian interloper—gaining a greater moral authority by standing as an equal with a former adversary.

At the same time, the Cowboy and Indian Alliance raised key environmental, political, and economic challenges and opportunities facing

Indigenous communities. As a partner in the Cowboy and Indian Alliance and a cohost of Harvest the Hope, tribal members shared many of the same objectives as non-Native farmers and ranchers. Like their partners, they maintained an interest in ecological protection but also protection from hostile corporate or government acquisitions. Symbolically, the alliance with farmers and ranchers allowed these Native American environmental advocates to be seen less as adversaries or victims of the state but rather as a part of the American fabric fighting against outsider institutions. Standing with cowboys, they too were situated as patriots, protecting their nation's soil in the most literal sense from the imposition of global "big oil."

This bridging of cultures and histories creates a distinct American pluralism, one that situates the master frame as a rhetorically developed narrative to help the collective make sense of itself, to set the boundaries for discourse, and to create a new audience for subsequent appeals (Bridger 1996). In its own way, the Cowboy and Indian Alliance metanarrative redefined American environmentalism, rendering it an act of patriotism and imbuing it with rural, civic values. It also moved it away from its association with traditional environmental messengers, notably coastal urbanites and "radical" protesters and nudged it closer to the political center. Last, it served as a vehicle for what has been described as the punctuating and coding of reality, and the assignment of attribution (Snow and Benford 1992). Here, the master frame of the Cowboy and Indian Alliance presented to its audience a novel yet innovative way to reconfigure the essence of rural America, including its history and its ecology.

There remain some disquieting tensions within this alliance, however. Given the historical marginalization of Indigenous peoples in the United States, questions linger under the surface about the usage of powerful Native American symbols in propping up a movement that served a largely non-Indigenous constituency. The potential issue of cultural appropriation provides a reminder that movements are capable of invoking cultural heritage and symbols to further specific agendas, even when the ownership of such symbols remains contended. The power of self-representation and autonomy, then, remains critical within these movement coalitions. This is part of the reason why Bold Nebraska spent years working with tribal nations to establish mutual trust and rapport before embarking on projects as fraught with potential misunderstandings as the Cowboy and Indian Alliance and Harvest the Hope. Such endeavors necessitate goodwill and moral leadership.

A necessary underpinning of ethics lies at the heart of much environmental discourse in the sense of moral ecological action and environmental behavior that serves the well-being of communities, nation-states, larger geographies, and indeed the planet. Mainstream media coverage of Bold Nebraska's fight against TransCanada's pipeline incorporated ethical concerns in a majority of articles. It is worth noting that while Bold Nebraska raised ethical problems in terms of its opponents in government and the oil sector, it was also on the receiving end of ethical questions and moral criticism. Some discourses from pipeline proponents painted Bold Nebraska's activism and communication as less than genuine. A spokesperson for TransCanada labeled group leader Kleeb as "a very effective misinformer" and someone who staged a rural uprising for the benefit of East Coast environmentalists: "She uses hyperbole and fear to make reasonable people think that something awful is about to happen. She's embellishing to susceptible people" (Elbein 2014, para. 39). A pipeline-friendly politician on Twitter, referring to her photograph with the black snake on the cover of *Omaha Magazine*, accused her of cultural appropriation.

Here I invoke the conception of manipulative rhetoric developed by Walter Fisher (1969, 117), a term used for when an audience is being "played, worked, or otherwise used." Evidence of this manipulation include communication expertise used in a self-serving way, the fostering of dialogue that distracts from or dilutes the truth, and communication that serves personal ambition over social knowledge or public action (Fisher 1987). While Bold Nebraska's communication did prop up key messengers and spokespersons to elevate a broader narrative about the organization's mission and work, it did so with the intention of creating a new interest in the pipeline's construction and environmental impacts among rural Nebraskans. In this sense, it produced what is described as social knowledge—an account of reality that is shared among citizens (Fisher 1987)—as well as civic action, by encouraging broader public participation through engagement in real-time and mediated venues. It is true that Jane Kleeb elevated her personal profile during Bold Nebraska's decade of opposition to TransCanada. This included the feature profile in the *New York Times Sunday Magazine* entitled "Jane Kleeb vs. the Keystone Pipeline" and the controversial cover story of *Omaha Magazine* featuring the black snake. However, such profile-building always occurred in the name of bolstering pipeline opposition. Spokespersons like Kleeb, and especially farmers and ranchers like Randy Thompson and the Tanderups, were providing a voice for those who chose to remain silent for reasons of their own. As Art Tanderup explained, farmers don't gravitate to the spotlight, and most avoid the media as a matter of habit. As a result, he and others were compelled to give voice to the issue. This is persuasion informing public life, not the self-serving manipulative rhetoric cautioned against by Fisher (1987).

How has this kind of advocacy impacted the way we think about areas of research such as environmental public relations and public interest communication? Contentious battles over the logging of old-growth forests in the U.S. Pacific Northwest during the 1980s spurred much discussion about the changing nature of company versus activist public relations, including the heightened role of the practice in potentially resolving confrontations with environmentalists (L. Grunig 1989). A two-way symmetrical approach was considered necessary not only to mitigate the fallout from public demonstrations and negative media coverage but also because the reaching of mutual understanding was preferable to engaging in conflict (L. Grunig 1986; Grunig and Grunig 2008). The assertion that activism represents "the organization of diffused publics into a powerful body attempting to control the organization from the outside" (L. Grunig 1986, 55) was proven true through the case of Bold Nebraska's years-long fight against TransCanada. Yet such an argument positioned public relations as institutional activity, the domain of corporations and governments. Such a normative model for public communication places such entities at the center of an ecosystem surrounded by their stakeholders: customers, employees, shareholders, community members, and finally activists. But Bold Nebraska never saw itself as a stakeholder at the periphery of a public debate, as its relationship to TransCanada existed only in relation to the pipeline. This dynamic is closer to the view that marginalized publics are best understood, and most effective, when they are situated at the center of civic dialogues; in other words, it is about putting the public back into public relations (Karlberg 1996). And this reality left TransCanada continually at a disadvantage. For the most part, the company simply couldn't engage with Bold Nebraska directly, but rather was forced to play constant catch-up with its green adversary, one that enjoyed an environmental momentum fueled by coalition politics and a distinct homefield advantage.

Grassroots or Astroturfing?

While Bold Nebraska was forging new pathways for engaging publics and reframing a dialogue about environmentalism in rural America its opponent TransCanada was increasingly bogged down—literally and figuratively—on both sides of the border. By 2014 the company's workers and equipment were stuck in limbo, and its communication strategy didn't appear to be gaining traction with the public. In a bid to find an alternative to the stalling Keystone XL project, the company introduced a pipeline proposal that would travel west to east across Canada instead of a North American north–south route. Called Energy East, it would not only have an operational impact for TransCanada by rerouting oil and natural gas to different refineries (this time on Canada's East Coast); it would also bring its own public relations value to the broader pipeline and energy debates in North America. That's because Energy East emerged as a symbolic and real replacement for Keystone XL. U.S. lawmakers, faced with the prospect of losing pipeline construction jobs and tax revenues to Canada, might conceivably be pressured into approving the Keystone XL pipeline's construction sooner. This was no mere publicity stunt on the part of TransCanada. The company was intent on delivering Alberta bitumen to refineries on the Atlantic coast.

However, even as TransCanada bought up real estate across its home country for the project, Canadians were proving to be just as resistant to a pipeline traveling across their prairies, forests, farmlands, and tribal territories. This opposition was not lost on TransCanada's public relations agency at the time, Edelman, one of the world's most powerful and influential agencies. The global PR firm set out to win over support for a pipeline by appealing to many of the same publics who figured prominently in the Nebraska pipeline story, including those living in rural communities. But a strategist who was delegated to lead TransCanada's Energy East account went too far and scandalized, ironically, his own global reputation agency.

As 2014 drew to a close, Greenpeace shocked the public and made headlines across the world when it leaked planning documents Edelman had created for TransCanada to deal with mounting activism and opposition to Energy East in Canada. The communication proposal not only laid out the emerging pipeline debate within Canada as a war to be won at any cost; it privately proposed manipulative practices in a bid to undermine the public and to deal a lethal blow to the same green advocates who had turned Keystone XL into a contended environmental symbol. "The opposition is headed north," declared the Edelman-authored Grassroots Advocacy Vision Document. "Unfortunately, the impact that ENGOs [environmental nongovernmental organizations] have had on energy policy in the U.S. has clearly encouraged these groups to migrate those efforts and expertise into the Canadian policy arena." Among the document's chief recommendations was the creation of a "grassroots" advocacy program which would attract union members, pro-energy citizenry, economic boosters, and supportive communities associated with the pipeline. But what exactly was the "grassroots" that had become such a coveted objective of this public relations campaign? To understand the word is to revisit its place in American history and its particular connection to the Great Plains.

In the fall of 1903, the United States was gearing up for another presidential election. Theodore Roosevelt had held the highest office in the land for two years as a Republican, but his reelection was far from certain, especially as the Democrats charged Roosevelt's party with being influenced by corporate donations. On September 8 of that same year, the *Kansas City Journal* reported from Topeka that A. W. Smith, the department commander of the Kansas Grand Army of the Republic, had just returned from San Francisco, where he had attended the organization's national meeting. The Grand Army of the Republic was a fraternal organization comprised of American Civil War veterans from the Union Army, Navy, Marine Corps, and Revenue Cutter Service. As soldiers who had fought for their country's very survival, they rightfully wanted a say in the nation's political future and specifically who would be Roosevelt's running mate for the 1904 election.

The name that emerged from their national assembly was General Eli Torrance of Minnesota, a former commander in chief of the Grand Army of the Republic who had fought in the Pennsylvania regiment during the Civil War. Torrance was a lawyer and strong orator—he authored a speech called "Citizen Soldier" that reputedly received highest praise from President Roosevelt. Most importantly, according to A. W. Smith, Torrance was seen as a leader who got things done for his fellow veterans: he had "accomplished more things for the benefit of the old soldier than any other commander-in-chief before or since." To get Torrance on the ticket, however, would require a movement across the West to pressure the president and the party to consider their choice for vice president nominee. "It is up for the old soldiers of each state to work up sentiment for Torrance for vice president," said Smith in his exchange with the *Kansas City Journal*. "Roosevelt and Torrance clubs will be organized in every locality. We will begin at the grass roots" (*Salt Lake Herald* 1903).

On the record, at least, the term "grass roots" had been invoked in American life for the first time to describe state-based advocacy by and for the people—Civil War veterans, no less—at a time when citizens of the heartland and the West were demanding democratic representation and a greater stake in national life. The same term was further parsed out in 1912 by Indiana Senator Albert Jeremiah Beveridge, another ally and supporter of Roosevelt, who articulated it as a metaphorical outgrowth of rural life. Describing the reform-minded Progressive Party founded by Roosevelt, he quipped, "This party has come from the grass roots. It has grown from the soil of people's hard necessities."

The term grassroots, therefore, comes to define a movement championed by people who are literally on (or of) the ground in the places where politicians, business leaders, and other elites generally speaking are not. Which is why something was off about Edelman's use of the term. Rather, the word that actually describes what they were proposing is *astroturfing*. *Astroturfing* has come to describe the usage of front groups to enable corporations to take part in public debates and lobby governments behind the guise of grassroots coalitions or community concern (Beder 1998). Sports fans know Astroturf as the brand name for the industrial product that emulates real grass, a popular playing surface for participants in professional football, soccer, and baseball. Bluntly put, it is fake grass. Astroturfing, therefore, represents the antithesis of the kind of organic communication that is implied by the term *grassroots*. Astroturfing produces the perception that an idea or organization has grassroots support when it does not, by intentionally falsifying both sources and authenticity of a message (Cox et al. 2008). As a communication practice, it is disparaged as "lazy, misleading and potentially illegal"; it can be damaging for parties and raises many serious ethical questions (Jacobs 2012). It can be effective, however. Previous research shows that astroturf initiatives can be successful in creating uncertainty among publics in global warming debates, in turn undermining the legitimacy of real grassroots organizations and promoting business interests over environmental protection (Cho et al. 2011).

As an internal planning document, the Grassroots Advocacy Vision Document leaked by Greenpeace to the media was never intended for public consumption. As a result, it revealed even more than what outsiders might presume about how environmental activists are considered in the corporate boardroom. Not surprisingly, lessons learned in the American heartland provided a key template for organizing in Canada. It noted the success of the American Petroleum Institute in using "digital grassroots tools to mobilize industry employees and other concerned Americans" in support of Keystone XL. It also highlighted a related effort in support of hydraulic fracturing: The American Fuel and Petrochemical Manufacturers had assembled more than 150,000 activists who in turn submitted more than 15,000 comments to an Environmental Protection Agency hearing. But garnering support from association groups wasn't enough. The Energy East pipeline needed to address "the new realities of designing, building, and operating a major pipeline project in North America." A pipeline supporter progression model was proposed where individuals with interest in the issue would, through recruitment, mobilization, and direct appeals "to an individual's trigger points," eventually become fervent participants. The idea was for the company to actively manage and encourage a pro-pipeline movement. As the document noted, in somewhat chilling fashion, "Not every advocate will do everything we ask of him or her, and not every advocate will have the willingness or ability to become a true champion. Accordingly, we must track and monitor how individuals behave and perform so that we can provide them with the materials calls to action that best align with where they are and what they are able to offer—while always pushing them to do just a bit more." All of this and more found its way into the pages of the *Guardian* and *New York Times*, which undoubtedly embarrassed TransCanada and set back its pipeline aspirations on both sides of the border.

In November of 2014, shortly after the publication of the leaked strategy document, TransCanada announced that it would not be renewing its contract with Edelman. The public relations agency issued a surprisingly curt news release after the parting of ways, describing its strategy as a desire "to drive an active public discussion that gives Canadians reason to affirmatively support the project." According to the firm, the conversation about Edelman's efforts had distracted from the conversation about the project: "We stand by our strategy. It was both ethical and moral, and any suggestion to the contrary is untrue." But the hasty parting of ways between TransCanada and Edelman, and the scandalous treatment of the Energy East document by the international press, spoke volumes about the trajectory of pipeline debates in North America, the desperation of some lobbyists to get oil pipelines built, and the power of the grassroots in Nebraska that had caused Edelman to cross a public relations line in shocking fashion up in Canada.

Scholars of public interest communication often advocate for the concepts of mutuality and compromise in standoffs that feature institutions fending off aggrieved publics. The idea is that by engaging in honest and legitimately two-way dialogue, an outcome can be brokered that is acceptable to both parties, and arguably meets the expectations or aspirations of a wider public. Perhaps to the chagrin of proponents of normative dialogism in public affairs, this never occurred during the years-long battle between TransCanada and Bold Nebraska over the construction of the Keystone XL Pipeline. There would be no acceptable compromise more than a decade after the pipeline proposal was brought to the attention of government officials. In many ways, Bold Nebraska's communication fed off the idea of an epic pipeline battle raging across the Great Plains. A move toward mutuality would not only have been a strategic mistake; it would have taken the wind out of the populist, coalition-driven narrative that inspired thousands of website and social media missives, feature stories in the national media, and hundreds of real-time engagements. Besides this fact, Bold Nebraska and TransCanada were so far apart in terms of their eco-philosophies that finding any kind of common ground would have proven extraordinarily difficult. Kleeb became convinced of this reality—of two separate, virtually impenetrable paradigms—when she saw an image of TransCanada CEO Russ Girling in a media story about the pipeline. Girling, photographed at his desk, was backdropped by a painting depicting what she described as a "beautiful, rolling landscape—with pieces of pipe getting ready to go into the trench." That visual, romanticizing encroaching industrialization in the natural world, depicted an ecological outlook that was anathema to Bold Nebraska's worldview. "That was a huge lightbulb moment for me," she said. There could be no compromise between the two organizations.

Toward a Grassroots Civic Environmental Persuasion

Apart from the Grassroots Advocacy Vision Document and many tit-for-tat publicity squabbles with Bold Nebraska, TransCanada's implementation of communication and public relations strategies is not a central focus of this book. Rather, I have set out to assess the communication strategies of Bold Nebraska amid a recalibration of environmental politics in America. Looking back at Bold Nebraska's strategic advocacy shows that very little of its environmental appeals consisted of dialogue or engagement with TransCanada, even though a vast majority of communication missives were *about* TransCanada and its Keystone XL pipeline effort. The plentiful dialogue in Bold Nebraska's communication was driven by conversations with Nebraskan farmers, ranchers, landowners, tribal members, and more generally the Nebraska public. Bold Nebraska had little incentive to sit down with the company because, outside of early routing concerns, the pipeline became an all-or-nothing scenario, symbolic at once of the future of America's hinterlands but also of a global ecological challenge. To this end, TransCanada provided the perfect foil for Bold Nebraska's rural environmentalism: a foreign corporation serving the interests of "big oil" and perpetuating a cycle of global fossil fuels addiction and unsustainable carbon emissions. Any serious degree of mutual engagement would have distracted from Bold Nebraska's establishment of TransCanada as the perpetual antagonist or "other." To do so might provide a means for TransCanada to better tell its story and to amplify its corporate social responsibility message, one that included its thousands of well-paid employees in Canada but also the United States; its contributions of millions of dollars to thousands of nonprofit organizations across North America; and its own investments in protecting biodiversity, improving environmental stewardship, and reducing greenhouse gas emissions. There is more gray area to these disputes than mainstream media narratives might account for. But Bold Nebraska's mission from the very beginning was to win "hearts and minds," not to reach mutual understanding nor to provide TransCanada with an even tepid endorsement. This goes against the view that the mutually satisfactory outcome better serves society's interests, even when it forces compromise or co-optation.

Such a dynamic for public communicators conjures up the German philosopher Jürgen Habermas's (1993, 31) discourse ethics, emphasizing the importance of equitable societal participation in communication procedures that are different from institutional arrangements—ones that "that obligate specific groups of people to engage in argumentation," including corporate meetings, government hearings, and university seminars. The discourse ethics tenet of the ideal speech situation, which provides opportunity for all to participate and for participants to be themselves, is manifested in the pipeline activism through the prolific usage of public events, social media conversations, and action items leading to political impact. By encouraging hyperlocal grassroots participation both symbolically and in practice, it also provided what Habermas explains as the opportunity for participants to have the equal ability to influence each other. It is through this lens that Bold Nebraska's strategic communication can be best understood as a vehicle for civic action and social change. Bold Nebraska's activism underpins the views that public relations as applied action is a means to coalition-building and by extension strengthening democratic institutions (Sommerfeldt 2013). When infused with civic engagement, it situates audiences less as formalized "stakeholders" and more as the "neighbors, friends, families, co-workers" who play such a crucial role in a spiral of advocacy (Mundy 2013).

A good example of this comes from Bold Nebraska's usage of the call to action tactic, which was embedded in nearly half of the organization's website strategic communication output measured in this study. In marketing parlance, calls to action are intended to provoke an immediate response or engagement by imploring audiences to "call now," "find out more," or "visit a store today" (Guillory 2015). Labeled by Bold Nebraska as "action items," they were a recurring part of the organization's messaging. They implored their audience to go beyond merely elaborating upon Bold Nebraska's ideas. They asked members and readers to engage in real-time: to fundraise, attend lawmaker meetings and court sessions, participate in demonstrations, sign petitions, spend time with their family members at community events, and write to politicians and lawmakers. In other words, they were generators of civic engagement and action at every level and opportunity. This was the furthest thing from the "armchair activism" that is regularly derided by some commentators. Such civic engagement communication is concurrent with the assessment of movement framing as a catalyst for ameliorative action, as well as the role of frame alignment in creating linkages between otherwise disparate groups or individuals (Snow and Benford 1998; Snow et al. 1986).

Bold Nebraska's calls to action reinforced the powerful combination of public communication and member activation within activist movements. A movement's audience and membership serve as a means to broadly diffusing ideas and action across a network of connected individuals (McAdam 1982). In Bold Nebraska's case, this network was the rural citizenry of Nebraska. It is worth noting also that these action items were numerous in some stories. For example, an October 25, 2011, missive written by Jane Kleeb implored supporters to write to President Obama, call their state senator, write a letter to the editor, post pictures of the I Stand with Randy land rights campaign to the social media site Flickr, and sign a Nebraska anti-pipeline petition along with a similar petition at the White House. These are examples of the "micromobilization processes" used to align a movement's organizational goals and ideology with the values and beliefs of targeted individuals (Snow et al. 1986).

With a notable exception of its participation in a major climate rally in Washington DC and a handful of national media opportunities, Bold Nebraska's events were almost exclusively located in the state of Nebraska. Unsurprisingly, such calls for audience engagement enjoyed a statistically significant association with the issue frame of farming and ranching. The confluence of the farming/ranching issue frame with action items provided a hyperlocalization, rooting Bold Nebraska in a specific time and place. Here, farmers and ranchers emerged as the state-based grassroots advocates described in the spiral of advocacy, helping Bold Nebraska's mantra resonate with a local constituency before advancing to state and national lawmakers (Mundy 2013). Their key

Fig. 26. Rancher and landowner Randy Thompson, who sued the governor and legislature of Nebraska (*Thompson v. Heineman*) over the constitutionality of the proposed pipeline route, became one of the faces of Bold Nebraska's activism thanks to the I Stand with Randy campaign. Photo by Alex Matzke (matzke.photo). Photo courtesy of Bold Nebraska.

involvement also conjured up memories of Nebraska's century-old tradition of agrarian collective populism.

Calls to action provide a feedback mechanism for the host organization as well. Membership action is in part predicated on enthusiasm and support for the overarching cause (and sub-causes). In farming and ranching, Bold Nebraska found a particularly rich area for building on-the-ground support and for leveraging this support into direct political action. While this engagement through action also existed in other issue frames, other issues did not garner a significant association with this engagement in the way that farming and ranching did. Here, Bold Nebraska played to its strengths and its region's character. As part of the state's cultural and economic fabric, the topic of farming and ranching naturally resonated with Nebraskans, paving the way for tangible political results.

There is one caveat here: climate change, which continues to be a leading environmental topic in the United States as well as a catalyst for the general public's participation in environmental action and discourse, did not emerge as a primary focal point for this civic engagement. Instead, it was represented as an issue indirectly through the issues of sustainable farming, clean energy, and the ecological value of the Sandhills and Ogallala Aquifer. This can be attributed in part to other state, national, and international organizations also focusing (with greater expertise) on the topic, rendering some of Bold Nebraska's attempts to engage with the topic directly somewhat redundant. Many other environmental groups have taken up the climate change cause and have engaged with politicians and publics on the topic. For Bold Nebraska to have duplicated the efforts of its environmental allies across the state and country might have risked diminishing interest and fostering a diluted activism. At the same time, climate change—as a national political issue—remains topically more vulnerable to political partisanship than regionalized environmental concerns like agricultural land and water. To focus exclusively on climate change would have hampered Bold Nebraska's ability to develop and navigate a delicate bipartisan coalition, and specifically to bring Republican ranchers and farmers into its progressive-populist fold.

Ultimately, Bold Nebraska's communication toggled between activism against TransCanada's Keystone XL pipeline and advocacy for the rural citizenry of Nebraska. Such advocacy took on several forms, including raising collective awareness of climate change impacts on the state's ecology, empowering its audiences to engage with alternatives to fossil fuels such as solar and wind power, and placing the pipeline fight in a broader context that situated Nebraska's agricultural industries as necessarily intertwined with a healthy ecology. Here, discourse ethics situates this advocacy as facilitating an exchange of ideas in civic and community contexts. Environmental activism directed against the pipeline provided Bold Nebraska with its organizational raison d'être and drove its narrative for the better part of a decade. Yet it was the work of community- and regional-level advocates who facilitated the viability and power of this activism through their ability to forge coalitions and long-term civic engagements that were foundational to the pipeline fight.

Habermas's utopian model of discourse, alongside emerging considerations of public relations as a practice that props up civic life instead of institutional objectives, does not exist in a communication vacuum, however. Bold Nebraska's arrival at a narrative-driven grassroots communication style was built upon powerful rhetorical devices and the activation of the innate core values of its audience. This communication strategy hearkens back to the legacy of public relations pioneer Edward Bernays, the nephew of Sigmund Freud, whose early twentieth-century PR campaigns integrated charged emotional appeals and extravagant visual displays and events to sway public opinion in matters of consumerism, health, politics, and U.S. foreign policy. While he is sometimes considered the originator of modern public relations and is well known to undergraduate students interested in public relations, psychology, and political communication, his legacy has fallen out of favor in some scholarly circles. This is because his ability to singlehandedly construct events as news, garner third-party endorsements of his ideas, and pull the levers of human emotion to sell consumer products and political ideologies has been described as everything from unethical manipulation to dangerous propaganda. The ability to influence and change public discourse in a democracy is a responsibility not to be taken lightly, and less-than-flattering reconsiderations of Bernays's legacy by critical scholars bear this hard reality out.

Yet Bernays was not the first communicator to infuse acts of persuasion into civic dialogue in the United States. Environmentalist John Muir, an early advocate of wilderness preservation in the country, is considered "one of the patron saints of twentieth-century American environmental activity" for his prolific writings and media missives about wild landscapes, which helped ordinary Americans rethink their relationship with nature (Holmes 1999). Such preservation efforts led to the establishment of Yosemite National Park, among other nationally protected geographies. Muir also cofounded in 1892 an environmental group known today for its wide-ranging green advocacy and activism across the United States: the Sierra Club, one of Bold Nebraska's key allies in the fight against Keystone XL. Bold Nebraska's foray into rhetorically charged environmental appeals merely continued an American tradition dating back to the 1800s. But it did so with the recognition that a globalized, polarized, and resources-hungry world requires an attunement to established and emergent communication strategies in the public sphere.

The integration of environmental populist appeals into civic discourses creates what I refer to here as a *civic environmental persuasion*—contingent upon the building blocks of hyperlocalization, narrative, civic engagement, and bipartisan populism. It emphasizes both the ability of the communicator to gain legitimacy through contextual factors (localization, personal interaction, appeals to community, culture, and heritage) and the willingness of the audience to embrace such activisms or advocacies as part of their broader cultural and individual narratives. This environmental advocacy is underpinned by a hyperlocalization that recognizes environmental and societal challenges contextually, whether they take the form of affected family farms, local lakes and streams, or community air quality. It also positions local advocacy as a form of social engagement, fostering civic action as a virtual but also face-to-face endeavor. Environmental master frames are energized by a narrative fidelity that tells the hopeful story of American communities, celebrates their cultural heritage, and bridges gaps between different social groups and political affiliations. This ethos-driven bipartisanship fosters a populist coalition politics where groups work together for a social good and are ideally positioned to press for changes in public policy. This counters some conventional wisdoms about green policy today. In Nebraska, rigid environmental mandates drawn up by government or corporate institutions were not parachuted into communities. Rather, the solutions to combating environmental degradation materialized and grew from the ground up and reflected the voices of the collective local citizenry.

Bold Nebraska's years-long campaign against the TransCanada Keystone XL petroleum pipeline is but one case of strategic environmental communication and as such is not necessarily generalizable to the many other environmental protest movements that exist globally or have transpired in the past decade. Even today, new pipeline battles are breaking out in jurisdictions far from Nebraska. However, in setting out to understand the unique attributes of contemporary environmental activism as a form of strategic communication, the case of Bold Nebraska and its pipeline fight sheds new light on the potential prominence of communication and media amid a growing global ecological crisis. Nebraska's pipeline opposition highlighted the effectiveness of strategic advocacy framing, with specific framing elements constructing meaning and persuasive messaging to achieve specific environmental goals. These elements—including contextual, metaphorical, and visual appeals—can and do coexist. That is, framing elements do not exist in a discursive vacuum. Rather, they can complement one another in projecting more robust and inclusive environmental messages and propping up bipartisan and coalition-driven activism. An overwhelming majority of Bold Nebraska's website articles featured multiple framing elements, and some of these elements enjoyed significant associations with one another. For example, the strategic framing element of context was linked with elements such as metaphors and populism. In combination, these elements provided the necessary links between ecological fact and narrative, information and persuasion, community impact and personal attitudes.

Furthermore, multiple framing elements existed in conjunction with specific environmental issue frames. Communication vehicles such as populism and regional and historical context, for example, were particularly prominent in Bold Nebraska's stories dealing with agriculture, land rights, and globalization. The deployment of environmental issue frames attracts and mobilizes supporters, even though they dilute the potential power of any one single frame (Reber and Berger 2005). Green activists, however, can control the degree to which these issue frames are utilized, thus intentionally giving greater power to some frames over others. For example, climate change and global warming were a significant part of Bold Nebraska's messaging, but they did not supersede the even more salient issues of farming, land rights, or environmental threats, all of which had a more contextualized and local dimension.

There is a feedback loop here involving stakeholders and larger audiences that deserves further scrutiny. Successful social movement organizations are results-driven entities dependent on strategic pitches that resonate with specific publics (Bob 2001). Bold Nebraska was especially masterful at feeling out and cultivating environmental issues that resonated with Nebraskans. Such a connection between activism and strategy may seem obvious from the perspective of mass and public communication scholarship, but it challenges understandings of social movements from other scholarly domains that minimize the impact of strategy, or dismiss public relations approaches to social or environmental change as being anathema to movement purity. This also applies to the construction of the messages themselves. While Bold Nebraska's ultimate objective of stopping the pipeline never wavered, its pitches to publics and the media were malleable and dynamic, evidenced by the variety of framing devices employed and a changing array of framing issues over time. When land rights and eminent domain became a key issue for Nebraska landowners on the pipeline's proposed path, so Bold Nebraska was able to leverage the prominence of this issue with appropriate messaging. Thus, people power derived from the grassroots *was* driving Bold Nebraska's trajectory and not the other way around.

When Indigenous communities voiced their opposition to Keystone XL, Bold Nebraska was well positioned to integrate their perspective, including a Cowboy and Indian Alliance, within the organization's environmental activism. Coalition politics presented new opportunities and challenges, but ultimately transformed the understanding of prairie environmentalism. To this end, these activists were able to reach different publics based on the construction of their messaging and an especially acute understanding of their immediate environments and publics. Far from impure, this communication was rooted in local, historic, and bipartisan ecological concerns. Environmental movements are therefore wise to evolve alongside the changing circumstances of both the local (civic affairs) and the material (ecological conditions)—

not only to serve as conduits for effective change, but also to secure further resources and to persuade supporters, policymakers, and the general public. Such a trajectory of activism fulfills a civic vision for the role of public interest communication in a democracy by cultivating relationships based on common goals and facilitating public dialogue and participation.

Bold Nebraska campaigned against the Keystone XL pipeline using a multitude of pitches and appeals. Some of these proved more prolific or effective than others, but all of them contributed to what ultimately became the metanarrative of anti-pipeline populism. This was demonstrated through one of Bold Nebraska's highest-profile moments, the staging of the Harvest the Hope concert. The event, with its incorporation of historical symbols and narrative imagery, helped attendees and audiences make sense of both the organization and the movement. Harvest the Hope fostered a much-needed narrative fidelity for coalition-based environmentalism through rhetorical performance. By bringing non-Native rural and Indigenous communities together, it justified Bold Nebraska's broader pipeline activism and helped audiences see the issue through a new worldview—one that disrupts established narratives and ideologies of environmentalism and of the West. It also fulfilled the vision of the iconic music festival as a creator of mythology (Cunha 1988) and as a catalyst for collective rethinking of social issues (Peterson 1973). For strategic and environmental communication scholars, Harvest the Hope is an important reminder that persuasive appeals within activism and public interest communication are effective when steeped in narrative, storytelling, and performance. Even if this perspective is evidenced in explanations such as "culture jamming" (Harold 2004) and "carnivalesque activism" (Weaver 2010), it has been mostly overlooked even within communication scholarship.

Central also to Bold Nebraska's success during this timeframe was media coverage of the organization and the pipeline issue. The five-year analysis of media coverage showed Bold Nebraska to be a source of news, a messenger of anti-Keystone XL activism, and a counterpoint to pro-pipeline perspectives. As with Bold Nebraska's own website communication, national media stories tended to include multiple strategic framing elements, which often carried over from Bold Nebraska's original communication. The most prominently used elements—such as aggrieved rural spokespersons or prairie metaphors—moved from Bold Nebraska's communication into the domain of national news. Strategic framing approaches again played an outsized role—providing ready-made angles for media coverage about an environmental topic (such as messengers or statistics) that helped garner sought-after and highly influential media coverage. Such coverage is also shown to help impart a media narrative about the organization that is reflective of how the organization sees itself. Bold Nebraska was actively managing its coverage in the news. As public interest communicators, activists do not control media coverage, but through deliberate framing choices they can wield significant influence in how journalistic decisions are made and how discourses about organizations and issues are shaped. At the very least, they can ensure that they are part of mainstream news narratives that often fail to account for voices from the periphery or the heartland.

The pipeline fight provided a communication terrain rich in symbolic- and values-laden messaging, which helped to drive Bold Nebraska's activism and strategic communication. This idealism—asserting the mental and spiritual conceptions of ecology—enjoys a long-standing tradition in environmental communication. Yet also encountered was a style of communication borne of the natural world itself, centering the soil, water, plants, animals, and wider rural ecology on the Great Plains. Such materialism emphasized the role of natural matter and its role in shaping phenomena and human consciousness.

What was revealed ultimately was a communicative approach that toggled between these philosophies of ecological idealism and materialism. A hyper-localized, contextually rich environment became symbolic for the history, heritage, and values of these prairie residents. Hopes for cleaner energy sources were made manifest in the renewable energy barn, built in the path of the pipeline. The importance of agricultural crops and tribal tradition was represented through the sacred Ponca corn planting—the so-called seeds of resistance, planted at the Tanderup farm in Neligh. One rancher's fight against the pipeline's intrusion onto his land became a symbol for individual rights and a formidable rallying cry: "Stand with Randy." In other words, the strategic communication deployed by Bold Nebraska did not emerge in a vacuum. It was directly connected to the environmental elements and prairie ecosystems the organization sought to protect—linking lofty ideas about ecology to the raw materials that underpinned its ecological discourse.

What is also remarkable about these discursive appeals is that they were rooted in a historic mythology about the West—starting with the Cowboy and Indian Alliance but also extending to Bold Nebraska's numerous grassroots campaigns. They mirrored what Nelson (2018) describes as cowboy politics, providing a distinct form of pathos that connects the heroic cowboys to the lands they seek to protect. In other words, the aesthetics of the West are predicated on the land—including its lakes, rivers, grasslands, and mountains. The grand ecologies of the frontier stand in for not only a landscape to be protected but one that represents the cowboy's aspirations for individual and community virtues: "The lands create character as much or more through their lessons in beauty. The soul who fails to open to the peculiar beauties of western lands—from the high plains and scraggly shrubs to the barren buttes and wild flowers or the rocky deserts and tumbling weeds—is a soul who finds no home in the West. . . . The lands nurture character as much through opportunities of beauty as through tests of will, intelligence, or judgement" (Nelson 2018, 113). It is through this lens that the strategic inclusion of the Nebraska Sandhills, the Ogallala Aquifer, and the Platte River watershed became especially important. They imbued Bold Nebraska's myth-making with an enduring land ethic and a set of ready-made appeals that communicated the alarming challenges facing the American hinterland.

The Canadian communication theorist Harold Innis famously argued that natural resources extractive processes helped explain not only the growth of civilizations, but the attributes of their societies, including their communication and media functions. Innis was the rare scholar who rightly connected the global communication landscape to an ecological political economy that underpinned a limitless demand for raw materials. To this end, oil and gas pipelines have emerged as the railroads of the twenty-first century, crisscrossing and networking the North American continent as they transport one of the world's most sought after commodities—and ushering in a new era of profit, protest, and associated news coverage. To paraphrase his University of Toronto colleague Marshall McLuhan, who further articulated Innis's deterministic vision within media scholarship, the environment *is* the message. Bold Nebraska's activism—embedded in a specific rural history and geography and connected to Nebraska soil and water, was a grassroots undertaking in the most literal sense. Such a ground-up advocacy approach, as a civic environmental persuasion, underscores not only the materiality of communication but also the foundational role of the environment to our democratic processes and institutions. The grassroots activists who are successful in fighting the construction of new pipelines through precious wilderness areas, productive family farms, and sacred tribal territories rightfully recognize the linkage of their strategic communication to their sense of place, their connection to communities, and their existence within the natural world.

Epilogue

After Nebraska

On March 31, 2020, the company now known as TC Energy announced it was moving forward with the construction of Keystone XL. It again noted the pipeline's potential benefits: "Thousands of new jobs, billions in economic stimulus and enhanced North American energy security" (Nasdaq.com). Less than a year later, just hours after being inaugurated as the forty-sixth president of the United States, Joseph Biden canceled the pipeline permit. But the pipeline's fate was hardly settled. Within weeks, a coalition of attorneys from twenty-one states sued Biden and his administration for rescinding the permit. And so the pipeline saga would continue with seemingly no end in sight and another massive rift between America's red and blue states in the making.

The complex legacy of partisan national politics and Biden's presidential predecessors looms large over the trajectories of Bold Nebraska and the Keystone XL pipeline. During his tenure as president, Donald Trump emerged as a vocal proponent of the oil and gas industry and the construction of Keystone XL in particular. The pipeline's future appeared to be as important to the president as it was to the oil sands' most vocal critics. During his tenure Trump set the stage for Keystone XL to continue its standing as one of the most contested environmental symbols in modern American history. In order to understand the significance of Trump's presidency as it relates to the pipeline, however, one must go back in time—by one year and three days exactly—before his historic and surprising election-day victory in 2016.

On November 6, 2015, Trump's presidential predecessor, Barack Obama, provided what was thought to be final closure to the Keystone

XL pipeline saga by rejecting TransCanada's permit on the grounds that it was not in the national interest of the United States. Bold Nebraska hailed the decision as a "historic victory for farmers, ranchers, Tribal Nations and the unlikely alliance that formed" in Nebraska to fight a battle that lasted well over a half-decade. The threat of the pipeline was rendered dead. To mark its victory, Bold Nebraska set out in 2016 as the Bold Alliance to bring its message to three new states—Iowa, Oklahoma, and Louisiana—to focus on fighting other fossil fuel projects and outlaw eminent domain for private enterprise (Duggan 2016). It provided expertise and consulting to anti-pipeline activists in West Virginia, Virginia, Minnesota, and Wisconsin. In this sense, it doubled down on its focus on state-based advocacy while expanding the footprint of the original Bold Nebraska communication strategy. The alliance described itself as "a network of small and mighty groups in rural states. . . . We fight fossil fuel projects, protect landowners against eminent domain abuse, and work for clean energy solutions while building an engaged base of citizens who care about the land, water and climate change." The degree to which the Bold Alliance aspired to emulate the original Bold Nebraska advocacy recipe was striking. The fight against Keystone XL served meaningfully as a template for fights ahead across rural America—against fracking, offshore drilling, and other petroleum pipelines.

The emergence of the Bold Alliance also underscored the potential evolution of social movement organizations in the environmental arena. Through strategic communication and public engagement, these groups could coalesce with different organizations and publics on different issues. Saliency with publics situated Keystone XL as the defining issue for Bold Nebraska, which was once described by a media pundit as a movement in search of a cause until the pipeline arrived. In turn, Bold Nebraska's communication elevated the pipeline debate to a symbolic fight over the energy economy, climate change, and the ecological future of America's hinterlands. This wasn't just a battle for the soul of Nebraska—it was a proxy for the national environmental debate, with international repercussions. Rural dwellers in other states would inevitably look to Bold Nebraska for direction in their own environmental battles, giving way to the emergence of a Bold Alliance. Even as this ambitious undertaking brought Bold Nebraska's strategic activism to new jurisdictions, leader Jane Kleeb remained politically active in her home state, and was elected as chair of the Nebraska Democratic Party during the summer of 2016. At the time, the pipeline issue appeared to be settled. Key organizers embarked on new endeavors and environmental fights were shifting to different parts of the country.

Meanwhile, two well-publicized national environmental events during 2016 evoked memories of Bold Nebraska's hinterlands activism. During the summer and fall, Native American protests against the Dakota Access Pipeline emerged as a much larger rallying cry across the United States for Indigenous rights and environmental justice. Like Keystone, what became known as the Standing Rock protests emerged as a focal point for discourse about energy consumption, fossil fuels, and the rights of Native Americans. With supporters like the Bold Alliance and 350.org and a national profile, the Dakota Access Pipeline protests were even dubbed at one point "the new Keystone" (McKibben 2016)—minus the Nebraska-specific mythology but arguably with a larger national profile.

While it is tempting to contrast the two movements given their obvious similarities and Great Plains identities, there are some key distinctions that limit such comparison and therefore warrant careful analysis. First, the protests against Dakota Access Pipeline were led by the Standing Rock Sioux Tribe, who successfully transformed the events in North Dakota into a much larger conversation about Native American rights. Second, the protests drew Native Americans from across the region and the country (as well as Indigenous support worldwide). But they also drew committed environmentalists, divestment activists, and university students from across the country as well. In turn, eventful DAPL protests occurred not just at Standing Rock but in major cities and college towns across the country. This situated the DAPL protests as a national event. Finally, in what may be the most important diversion between the two activisms, the DAPL protests were less about persuasion and more about direct action through peaceful demonstration. Yet the Standing Rock standoff between police and demonstrators is also remembered for its acrimony. While both movements were effective and raised public consciousness, they took on very different trajectories in terms of function and form. Perhaps only when the ultimate fates of both pipelines are known will scholars be able to fully and fairly compare these two movements and assess their final environmental and political impacts.

Earlier in 2016, in the high desert of eastern Oregon, a very different kind of protest saw armed ranchers, militants, and self-styled patriots from across the American West seize the Malheur National Wildlife Refuge, citing grievances over the federal government's management of public land. The refuge occupiers came under heavy criticism from environmentalists and Oregon's tribal communities for this act, which set off fierce debate about their aggressive protest tactics. Yet in the wake of a not-guilty verdict on federal charges related to the stand-off later in the year, some of these protesters called for sympathy and alliance-building with the Standing Rock Sioux fighting the Dakota Access Pipeline (Brosseau 2016, para. 2). Such overtures, while largely rejected by Dakota pipeline protesters, did underscore shifting values in rural America that ultimately situated contemporary grassroots environmentalism as a historic resistance against unfriendly government policy and corporate intrusion. At the same time, these rural conflicts in the West underscored the renewed significance of the hinterland to national politics in the United States. These were not isolated incidents. Rather, they became contemporary touchstones for long-simmering debates over land rights, climate change, energy policy, and the widening cultural and political divides between rural and urban America. It was only a matter of time before these political storms became part of a much larger national conversation.

Yet both of these historic moments were mere opening acts for the year's main political event. The election of Donald Trump on November 9, 2016, was nothing short of a national political earthquake, ushering in a dramatically new civic era in the United States. The aftershocks from that event—the heightened political polarization and the more obvious divide between rural and urban voters—continued to reverberate in American political life. Regardless of whether they supported or opposed the 2016 election outcome, the day lives on in the memory of most Americans. For Bold Nebraska, Trump's election was a pivotal and confusing moment in the organization's trajectory. Unlike his political opponents from either the Democratic or Republican parties, Trump neither waffled on his pro-pipeline stance nor diminished its significance as a political wedge issue. In other words, he embraced its symbolism and its status as a political flashpoint. And his popularity with working-class and rural voters across the state and the country made his position more salient and persuasive than other pipeline proponents. He actively campaigned in support of the construction of the Keystone XL campaign not in spite of its environmental ramifications but because of them; this was his shot across the bow, and the traditional institutions of the environmental movement took it personally.

Upon Trump's election, his advisers quickly went to work looking for ways to reverse Obama's earlier decision in a bid to jumpstart infrastructure development and deliver on Trump's campaign promise of green-lighting the pipeline in particular (Dlouhy 2016). Trump's immediate selection of Rex Tillerson, the chair and CEO of Exxon Mobil, to the secretary of state position further emphasized the inevitability of a revived showdown over the pipeline's future. That showdown commenced within minutes of Trump's taking office on January 24, 2017, when he issued a presidential executive action to advance the pipeline's approval. Keystone XL was such a visible focus of Trump's first day in office that even those activists who played significant roles in the years-long pipeline debate were caught off-guard.

During her interview for this research, Jane Kleeb was frank about both the disruption and cognitive dissonance the events of 2016 created. "It was a gut punch," she said, remembering the moment the president signed the Keystone XL executive action. "Because you had just worked eight years on stopping the pipeline, and to have a victory [Obama's earlier rejection], and then to have that reversed with a stroke of a pen. We went into defense mode, defending at the local and state level." But that wouldn't be easy in Nebraska, where Trump enjoyed strong support. For observers from academia, government, and Wall Street, it was easy to dismiss the president on account of his rough demeanor, disagreeable social media communication, and hardline policy positions. However, Trump enjoyed broad appeal with farmers and ranchers, predicated on a unique personal style but also his articulation of substantive grievances over agricultural and trade policies. His brand of economic populism created a unique conundrum for environmentalists in the heartland, Bold Nebraska included.

What drove his support with Nebraskans and agricultural workers in particular? For the outsider, it might seem difficult to marry anti-pipeline advocacy with support for a politician who consistently carried the torch for pipeline construction at every turn. Yet some impacted farmers and ranchers might have tuned out Trump's pro-pipeline rhetoric in the hope that it represented grandstanding more than hard policy. And there were certainly many other Nebraskans who had supported the pipeline's construction all along. Unlike the majority of politicians at the national level, Trump spoke directly to farmers and other working-class Americans during his rallies and channeled their grievances into campaign promises. Apathy might also have played a role in this disconnect. Some Nebraskans, like many of their fellow Americans, had grown tired of the bickering and extreme political partisanship on a number of national issues, including Keystone XL. Many citizens, including farmers, were ready to move on. Finally, there were those citizens who voted not so much for Trump as against the Democratic Party, which took little to no interest in farmers specifically or in rural environmental affairs more broadly during the 2016 election. Trump's election was indeed a wake-up call for both parties about the political discontent within the working-class American electorate. No matter how one rationalizes it, Trump's election and subsequent executive action on Keystone XL represented a demoralizing moment for Bold Nebraska and a complicated milestone for rural environmentalism.

Jane Kleeb herself acknowledged this during her 2018 interview. "The vast majority of our farmers and ranchers are disappointed in Trump," said Kleeb. But, she said, "it doesn't mean they didn't vote for him." That's not only because his Republican brand ushered in the usual election votes but also because Trump actually *did* pay notice to them. Trump's raw rhetoric—in stump speeches, during television interviews, and on Twitter—regularly folded the plight of farmers into his trade promises and threats. "Trump has had this ability to talk about farmers and ranchers at the national level, but his policies hurt ranchers and farmers," said Kleeb. "He's a showman, and he is really good at communications and keeping his base solidified."

The challenge of keeping a bipartisan environmental coalition intact therefore became a growing concern. As the chair of the Democratic Party in Nebraska, Kleeb provided an important counterperspective here—and she was critical of her own party's ability to make those rural connections at the national level. Unlike Republicans, she argued, her party blew its chance to connect with Americans living in the hinterland, especially farmers and ranchers, during the 2016 election. "The Democrats are at fault on so many levels, and the environmental and climate community, because they didn't spend enough time on the rural," she said.

It's a biting criticism coming from someone so close to the heart of the environmental movement in flyover country. In some ways, Kleeb's assessment echoed a key critique of the environmental movement: it is too often removed from the life experiences of working Americans in the heartland, including the farming, ranching, and Indigenous communities who factored so large in Bold Nebraska's activism. Environmental progressives, climate activists, and national news media who report about green causes would be wise to extract themselves from the coastal and metropolitan regions and spend more time in the places where petroleum infrastructure and other resources projects are being built. They might also spend more time engaging with the people who live in these places and better understand their complicated relationship with the land but also with America's history and government systems. Ironically enough, this critique could extend to Kleeb's own venture to British Columbia's Cortes Island, where she was implored by national and blue state environmentalists to play nice with Canada—big oil politics notwithstanding. The harsh juxtaposition of environmentalists hobnobbing at a coastal institute like Hollyhock, with its French intensive garden and organic vegetarian fare, against a Donald Trump rally attended by working-class Nebraskans at a state fairgrounds or airport tarmac, is not necessarily fair. But the cosmopolitanism-populism contrast does exist in some quarters of the public imagination, and it will grow as long as the rift between urban and rural Americans does.

Trump's efforts in reinvigorating the pipeline proposal during his presidency were also notable for succeeding where TransCanada's well-financed but relatively cautious and often clumsy public relations efforts had failed to gain traction with Nebraskans. Like Bold Nebraska, Trump had a knack for attacking the status quo, deploying emotional and metaphorical language, and building epic narratives and dramatic conflict to support his argument. His communication approach, ironically, was much closer to Bold Nebraska's grounded rhetorical style than the 2016 Democratic candidate Hillary Clinton or former president Barack Obama. In Trump, Bold Nebraska was dealing with a much more formidable communication foe who transformed the makeup of both national parties. The arrival of Trumpism as a national political phenomenon fusing politics and culture, even more than Trump the individual, represented a defining milestone for prairie politics and environmentalism in the decades ahead.

Even as the big picture for energy policy remains unsettled in an increasingly polarized United States, the real and symbolic skirmishes on the ground between pipeline proponents and foes have continued. Over the course of the last decade, the Bold Nebraska–versus–TransCanada saga has not been without its strange and quirky moments owing to this conflict. The dust-up over pipeline advertising at Cornhuskers football games—culminating in TransCanada receiving a thumbs down from coaching legend Tom Osborne—certainly was one. There were the games of kick-the-can outside the governor's mansion and other staged publicity events. Other curious stories emerged from the Harvest the Hope rock concert, which involved a convergence of celebrities, their handlers, environmental activists, music fans, and Antelope County locals—but also area politicians, first responders, and event workers.

The missing beer money scandal, for example, provided a stark reminder that hosting a rock festival fundraiser is not without its financial risks. And organizers even contended that a former TransCanada employee had infiltrated the ranks of concert security before he was found out and asked to leave the Tanderup farm, thus contributing a somewhat conspiratorial footnote to Bold Nebraska's most prominent event. For better or worse, these anecdotes helped to further grow the Nebraska pipeline fight metanarrative.

In the years between 2010 and 2021, Bold Nebraska and TransCanada sparred in the mainstream media, on social media, and at public events—all in a quest to win hearts and minds and convince policymakers of the correctness of their point of view. In 2019 another eyebrow-raising story crossed the desks of business editors in Canada and the United States: TransCanada was changing its name. No longer would the Calgary-based company be identified with its home country—the nation that had fed Bold Nebraska's globalization narrative and hundreds of populist appeals over the course of a decade, thanks simply to a name. Instead, it would be known generically as TC Energy. Just like that, the company had vanquished its symbolic affiliation with the oil-producing nation to the north, at least by formal identification. And as one north-of-the-border pundit mused in the *National Post*, TransCanada appeared to be looking for recognition outside of pipelines. "It is easy to understand why its shareholders and agents wanted to work 'Energy' into a new name," wrote the *Post*'s Colby Cosh (2019). "TransCanada now does a fair amount of stuff that is not pipelines, although they are still the overwhelming majority of its business, and it is in some respects becoming a true energy provider, as opposed to merely an energy mover."

The name change was also notable for how it displaced a company from its home country and situated it as a global enterprise. Large multinational banks that have moved across national boundaries or overseas to expand their business services come to mind, such as RBC (Royal Bank of Canada), HSBC (Hongkong and Shanghai Banking Corporation), and UBS (Union Bank of Switzerland). The *National Post* conjured up a comparative example from the fast food industry: KFC, the acronym for Kentucky Fried Chicken. The name change ostensibly moved the consumer conversation about the company away from fried chicken and the company's home state of Kentucky at a time when it was expanding aggressively outside of North America—effectively distancing itself from its regional identity and hostile health narratives about fried food and factory farmed poultry. Yet, as Cosh wrote, all companies come from someplace. And so do their products. Petroleum infrastructure is no exception.

For over a decade, Bold Nebraska's powerful blend of persuasion and public events reminded Nebraskans that TransCanada was not from the American heartland and that Alberta's oil sands were a far cry from Texas crude. Of course, both organizations featured geography in their names—a fact that proved advantageous for one organization and a reputational challenge for the other. In every headline and press release that featured the two names, audiences were reminded that this was not just a battle between two ecological philosophies. Rather, it was a clash that pitted one region of the continent against the other, as distasteful as that prospect might have been for those environmentalists who wanted Bold Nebraska to tone down its rhetoric against America's neighbors to the north. As for the new moniker? A name change for TransCanada might help the organization recalibrate its reputation in unfamiliar markets, but Bold Nebraska's relentless communication (including thousands of communication missives) has meant that within Nebraska, at least, the name change to TC Energy represents window dressing as opposed to substantive reputational change. Besides, the change may have been a moot point when the company announced the pipeline's advancement in 2020. The COVID-19 pandemic swept the Keystone XL saga and Bold Nebraska's protests to the sidelines of public consciousness, at least temporarily, as Americans were preoccupied with a much more immediate existential threat.

As TC Energy launched Nebraska into a new era of contentious pipeline politics in 2020, it was a fair time to ask a question of its long-time pipeline foe. Did Bold Nebraska achieve its objective of stopping the pipeline while transforming Nebraska's political landscape? The answer to this question is contingent upon who is being asked. Within its communication, Bold Nebraska was not shy about celebrating or taking credit for political developments that aligned with its mission of slowing the pipeline's progress. However, the battle over pipelines is far from over in the state and will likely continue indefinitely. Furthermore, Nebraska's political landscape remains mostly unchanged. After a decade of campaigning against TransCanada's pipeline, this would appear to be a discouraging result for Bold Nebraska.

Yet through a lens of persuasion, the organization's accomplishments emerge as more successful. Strategic communication should amplify a message but also foster behavioral and opinion change—emphasizing mediation but also face-to-face communication, relationships, and involvement. To this end, Bold Nebraska deployed thousands of media messages to people in Nebraska and beyond. Its strategic outreach also resulted in hundreds of newspaper articles and television stories, reaching Nebraska's population of 1.9 million residents. Such coverage also garnered millions of views nationally and internationally through outlets like the *New York Times* and the *Washington Post*. Thus, Bold Nebraska's message was certainly amplified.

Yet by the aforementioned benchmarks of behavioral change and interpersonal engagement, of equal if not greater significance were the hundreds of engagement opportunities embedded within the civic communication, themselves a natural outgrowth of Bold Nebraska's activism and involving Nebraskans from all walks of life. Individuals such as Randy Thompson, the Republican rancher who steered clear of politics previously, came to embody the opportunities for bipartisan engagement on the part of citizens outside of the political establishment. The mediation of Bold Nebraska through public and media relations, then, was always with a larger purpose: to enable the civic engagement necessary for Nebraskans to have a collective voice in regional and national affairs. Website and media discourses gave way to community gatherings, fundraisers, information sessions, political actions, and an iconic event like Harvest the Hope—all of which influenced the way thousands of participating Nebraskans previously viewed Keystone XL, itself a symbol of a contested political, economic, and environmental future.

By such a measure, then, Bold Nebraska's ambitious objective of transforming politics in Nebraska was realized—not through one grand political gesture but instead through hundreds, even thousands, of engagements and micromobilizations. Such a transformation was not reached strictly through the influencing of state and national policy but through the ongoing projection of a localized environmental metanarrative and the nonmediated engagement of thousands of Nebraskans from across the state who normally might not have participated in such politics. The ultimate fate of Keystone XL remains a critical outcome by which Bold Nebraska will be measured in the long run, but the organization's legacy rests upon much more than the potential construction of one pipeline. Its activation of rural community members from across the political divide as vocal, visible participants in the public sphere may be its most important achievement.

Both the vastness of the American heartland and its natural riches mean it will continue to be the sight of environmental conflict and exploitation. As pointed out by historian Gretchen Heefner (2012), who traced the burial of one thousand intercontinental ballistic missiles across the American prairie a half-century ago, "we are still meant to overlook the plains." Heartland environmentalists, then, have no choice but to remain vigilant. Ironically, the ongoing volatility in the price of crude oil made Alberta's oil sands projects much less solvent, and the province's petroleum economy has been beset by job layoffs, declining investment, and a global economic uncertainty exacerbated by the COVID-19 pandemic. That fiscal trajectory has inevitably raised questions about the economic viability of the pipeline, even as the province of Alberta continues to strongly advocate for its construction. Yet for both its supporters and opponents, Keystone XL remains more than just resource infrastructure or economic catalyst; it is a symbol of how humanity will choose to interface with the natural world in the century ahead. However, even as debates over Keystone continue—as viable oil project or once-rejected symbol of the climate dialogue—such discussions are likely to be overwhelmed by new proposals for mining, fracking, and other extraction projects. But, as Kleeb herself noted, nothing energizes environmental politics and brings out concerned citizens like "a raging pipeline fight."

The longevity of Nebraska's activists relative to other pipeline opponents in the United States does raise questions about state specificity. Other jurisdictions in the path of the same pipeline similarly lay claim to unique ecologies, not to mention aggrieved landowners in the pathway of other projects. Few states rival South Dakota's landscapes and cultural history, and fewer yet enjoy the nationwide agricultural heritage of Kansas. Yet neither state has enjoyed near the prominence in slowing down the project as the pipeline fighters from across its state borders. Nebraska proved to be TransCanada's weakest link, if not its Waterloo. Art and Helen Tanderup realized their home state was playing an outsized role in the national debate when they attended a pipeline meeting in Great Falls, Montana, where half of the meeting's discussion was focused on what was happening in Nebraska. For Art Tanderup, the success of Nebraska's activists started with the simple act of joining forces instead of citizens acting alone. "We organized," he said. "From the South Dakota border to the Kansas border, there were only one hundred of us landowners that stood up and said 'no' out of I don't know how many. That small group is across the political spectrum and includes Native Americans."

Nebraska's connection to the land became a dominant theme in any discussion about the pipeline's impact, and a driving emotional force for environmental activists. "Most [pipeline opponents] are in the Sandhills and where the aquifer is," said Tanderup. "This has become about the water, and the number of irrigation wells that the pipeline comes close to, the number of rivers and streams that it crosses, and the wildlife, the whooping cranes, the Sandhill cranes. All these things come into play." That sentiment, about an enduring regional land ethic fueling a protection of the local environment, is shared by Kleeb. "The farmers and ranchers in Nebraska go back generations, and continue to run family farm operations," she said. "The tie to the land is much more tied to the identity of the people here. In Nebraska, there was the tradition of homesteaders, and embracing Native Americans. There was a sense of community with each other."

The powerful combination of collective action, community engagement, and some prairie stubbornness ensured that Keystone XL has left, perhaps counterintuitively, a legacy of renewed civic environmentalism in Nebraska. "It's the persistence of people saying this is wrong, we are not going to lie down and let this happen," said Tanderup. "We have boots and moccasins on the ground. We work together because we feel we are protecting water, we are protecting the earth." Only half joking, he recognizes his personal evolution and the change for many of his fellow farmers in all of this: "We are becoming those environmentalists you know!"

Yet such a journey shouldn't come as a surprise. The American hinterland will undoubtedly continue to be the site of localized ecological exploitation—whether the root cause is mining, manufacturing, industrial agriculture, or, yes, energy production. Other farmers are bound to follow the Tanderups' lead in the face of looming ecological threat and a present climate challenge. Such degradation emerges as a proxy for the social, economic, and environmental injustices facing hinterland populations in the United States and globally. Bold Nebraska's nuanced framing of Keystone XL provided the means to achieve success with its short-term strategic objective of stopping the pipeline, but it also set the stage for the organization to expand its footprint and tackle future contentious extraction projects beyond Nebraska through bipartisan, localized, and culturally resonant appeals. An embrace of strategic communication and engagement fostered Bold Nebraska's ability to sustain collective action and member beliefs. It also helped attract new supporters, garner national media coverage and public attention, and affect policy change at the state and national levels. Unlike TransCanada's identity crisis, Bold Nebraska never wavered from being a steadfast reflection of its home state's people, its land and water, and its agrarian and Native American traditions and beliefs. It is a reminder to the environmental movement that key to winning hearts and minds is prioritizing people and place over politics and power, alongside a vision for a sustainable future over the stark implications of the ecological status quo.

REFERENCES

Abourezk, Kevin. 2011. "Huskers Cut Off Deal with TransCanada." *Lincoln Journal Star*. https://journalstar.com/news/local/huskers-cut-off-deal-with -transcanada/article_039e8c32-65e9-51ba-8463-34b6de3234bc.html.

Alinsky, Saul David. 1989. *Rules for Radicals: A Practical Primer for Realistic Radicals*. New York: Vintage.

Anderson, Benedict. 2006. *Imagined Communities: Reflections on the Origin and Spread of Nationalism*. Brooklyn NY: Verso.

Anderson, Deborah S. 1992. "Identifying and Responding to Activist Publics: A Case Study." *Journal of Public Relations Research* 4, no. 3: 151–65.

Arias-Maldonado, Manuel. 2020. "Sustainability in the Anthropocene: Between Extinction and Populism." *Sustainability* 12, no. 6: 2538.

Arnold, Elizabeth. 2018. "Doom and Gloom: The Role of the Media in Public Disengagement on Climate Change." Harvard Kennedy School Shorenstein Center on Media, Politics, and Public Policy. May 29, 2018. https://shorensteincenter .org/media-disengagement-climate-change/.

Ausmus, William A. 1998. "Pragmatic Uses of Metaphor: Models and Metaphor in the Nuclear Winter Scenario." *Communications Monographs* 65, no. 2: 67–82.

Bales, Susan Nall, and Franklin D. Gilliam Jr. 2009. "Lessons from the Story of Early Child Development: Domain Decisions and Framing Youth Development." *New Directions for Youth Development* 124 (Winter): 119–34.

Bales, Susan Nall, Franklin D. Gilliam Jr., P. Patrizi, K. Sherwood, and A. Spector. 2004. *Communications for Social Good*. Washington DC: Foundation Center. https://foundationcenter.issuelab.org/resources/24963/24963.pdf.

Barnett, Clive. 2003. "Media Transformation and New Practices of Citizenship: The Example of Environmental Activism in Post-Apartheid Durban." *Transformation: Critical Perspectives on Southern Africa* 51, no. 1: 1–24.

Bataille, Gretchen M., ed. 2001. *Native American Representations: First Encounters, Distorted Images, and Literary Appropriations*. Lincoln: University of Nebraska Press.

Bauer, Martin W. 2000. "Classical Content Analysis: A Review." In *Qualitative Researching with Text, Image and Sound*, edited by Martin W. Bauer and George Gaskell, 131–51. London: Sage.

Baysha, Olga, and Kirk Hallahan. 2004. "Media Framing of the Ukrainian Political Crisis, 2000–2001." *Journalism Studies* 5, no. 2: 233–46.

Beder, Sharon. 1998. "Public Relations' Role in Manufacturing Artificial Grass Roots Coalitions." *Public Relations Quarterly* 43, no. 2: 21–23.

Beeson, Mark. 2019. "Conclusion: The Unsustainable Status Quo." In *Environmental Populism: The Politics of Survival in the Anthropocene*, by Mark Beeson, 111–21. Singapore: Palgrave Macmillan.

Benford, Robert D. 1997. "An Insider's Critique of the Social Movement Framing Perspective." *Sociological Inquiry* 67, no. 4: 409–30. doi:10.1111/j.1475-682X.1997. tb00445.x.

Benford, Robert D., and David A. Snow. 2000. "Framing Processes and Social Movements: An Overview and Assessment." *Annual Review of Sociology* 26: 611–39.

Berkenkotter, Carol, and Thomas N. Huckin. 1995. *Genre Knowledge in Disciplinary Communication: Cognition/Culture/Power*. New York: Routledge.

Biello, David. 2014. "Keystone Pipeline Will Impact Climate Change, State Department Reports." *Scientific American Blog Network*. January 31, 2014. http://blogs.scientificamerican.com/observations/2014/01/31/keystone-pipeline-will -impact-climate-change-state-department-reports/.

Bitzer, Lloyd F. 1968. "The Rhetorical Situation." *Philosophy & Rhetoric* 1, no. 1: 1–14.

Black, Jason Edward. 2002. "The 'Mascotting' of Native America: Construction, Commodity, and Assimilation." *American Indian Quarterly* 26, no. 4: 605–22.

Blumer, Herbert. 1971. "Social Problems as Collective Behavior." *Social Problems* 18, no. 3: 298–306.

Bob, Clifford. 2001. "Marketing Rebellion: Insurgent Groups, International Media, and NGO Support." *International Politics* 38, no. 3: 311–34.

Bogojević, Sanja. 2019. "The Erosion of the Rule of Law: How Populism Threatens Environmental Protection." *Journal of Environmental Law*: 389–93. doi:10.1093/jel/eqz030.

Bold Nebraska. 2010. "Protect Our Economic Activity, Put the Brakes on the Pipeline." http://boldnebraska.org/protect-our-economic-activity-put-the -brakes-on-the-pipeline/.

———. 2011. "Huskers Sack TransCanada." https://boldnebraska.org/huskers -sack-transcanada/.

———. 2012. "Nebraska 18 Invites Pres. Obama for Beer Beef Summit." https://boldnebraska.org/nebraska-18-invites-pres-obama-for-beer-beef-summit/.

———. 2014. "Neil Young's 'Who's Gonna Stand Up' at Harvest the Hope #NoKXL Concert." YouTube. https://www.youtube.com/watch?v=iGacvlk__IU.

———. 2016. "Our Mission." http://boldnebraska.org/about/.

Boos, Robert. 2015. "Native American Tribes Unite to Fight the Keystone Pipeline and 'Government Disrespect.'" *The World*. https://theworld.org/stories/2015-02-19/native-american-tribes-unite-fight-keystone-pipeline-and-government-disrespect.

Bowe, Brian J., Taj W. Makki. 2015. "Muslim Neighbors or an Islamic Threat? A Constructionist Framing Analysis of Newspaper Coverage of Mosque Controversies." *Media, Culture & Society*, 0163443715613639.

Boykoff, Jules, and Eulialie Laschever. 2011. "The Tea Party Movement, Framing, and the Us Media." *Social Movement Studies* 10, no. 4: 341–66.

Boykoff, Maxwell T. 2007. "Flogging a Dead Norm? Newspaper Coverage of Anthropogenic Climate Change in the United States and United Kingdom from 2003 to 2006." *Area* 39, no. 4: 470–81.

Braroe, Niels Winther. 1975. *Indian and White: Self-Image and Interaction in a Canadian Plains Community*. Stanford University Press.

Bridger, Jeffrey C. 1996. "Community Imagery and the Built Environment." *Sociological Quarterly* 37, no. 3: 353–74.

Bronstein, Carolyn. 2005. "Representing the Third Wave: Mainstream Print Media Framing of a New Feminist Movement." *Journalism & Mass Communication Quarterly* 82, no. 4: 783–803.

Broom, Glen M., Shawna Casey, and James Ritchey. 1997. "Toward a Concept and Theory of Organization-Public Relationships." *Journal of Public Relations Research* 9, no. 2: 83–98.

Brosseau, Carli. 2016. "After Malheur, Patriot Groups Claim Common Cause with Other Protest Movements." *The Oregonian*. https://www.oregonlive.com/oregon-standoff/2016/10/after_malheur_patriot_groups_s.html.

Brubaker, Rogers. 2004. "In the Name of the Nation: Reflections on Nationalism and Patriotism." *Citizenship Studies* 8, no. 2: 115–27.

Brulle, Robert J. 1996. "Environmental Discourse and Social Movement Organizations: A Historical and Rhetorical Perspective on the Development of US Environmental Organizations." *Sociological Inquiry* 66, no. 1: 58–83.

Brysk, Alison. 1996. "Turning Weakness into Strength: The Internationalization of Indian Rights." *Latin American Perspectives* 23, no. 2: 38–57.

Burke, Kenneth. 1969. *A Rhetoric of Motives*. Berkeley: University of California Press.

———. 1989. *On Symbols and Society*. Chicago: University of Chicago Press.

Chang, Chun-Tuan, and Yu-Kang Lee. 2009. "Framing Charity Advertising: Influences of Message Framing, Image Valence, and Temporal Framing on a Charitable Appeal 1." *Journal of Applied Social Psychology* 39, no. 12: 2910–35.

Charland, Maurice. 1987. "Constitutive Rhetoric: The Case of the Peuple Quebecois." *Quarterly Journal of Speech* 73, no. 2: 133–50.

Cheney, George. 1983. "The Rhetoric of Identification and the Study of Organizational Communication." *Quarterly Journal of Speech* 69, no. 2: 143–58.

Cho, Charles H., Martin L. Martens, Hakkyun Kim, and Michelle Rodrigue. 2011. "Astroturfing Global Warming: It Isn't Always Greener on the Other Side of the Fence." *Journal of Business Ethics* 104, no. 4: 571–87.

Chong, Dennis. 2012. "Framing of Economic and Social Rights in the United States." In *Media, Mobilization and Human Rights: Mediating Suffering*, edited by Tristan Anne Borer, 122–42. New York: Zed Books.

Clark, Jill K., Kristen Lowitt, Charles Z. Levkoe, and Peter Andrée. 2021. "The Power to Convene: Making Sense of the Power of Food Movement Organizations in Governance Processes in the Global North." *Agriculture and Human Values* 38, no. 1: 175–91.

Collins, Gail. 2014. "Republicans (Heart) Pipeline." *New York Times*, November 7, 2014. http://www.nytimes.com/2014/11/08/opinion/gail-collins-republicans -heart-pipeline.html.

Conner, Alana, and Keith Epstein. 2007. "Harnessing Purity and Pragmatism." *Stanford Social Innovation Review* 5, no. 4: 61–65.

Cosh, Colby. 2019. "With Name Change, TransCanada Is Running from Its Own History." *National Post*. https://nationalpost.com/opinion/colby-cosh-with -name-change-transcanada-is-running-from-its-own-history.

Cox, Joshua L., Eric R. Martinez, and Kevin B. Quinlan. 2008. "Blogs and the Corporation: Managing the Risk, Reaping the Benefits." *Journal of Business Strategy* 29, no. 3: 4–12.

Cox, Robert. 2012. *Environmental Communication and the Public Sphere*. New York: Sage.

Cozen, Brian. 2013. "Mobilizing Artists: Green Patriot Posters, Visual Metaphors, and Climate Change Activism." *Environmental Communication: A Journal of Nature and Culture* 7, no. 2: 297–314.

Creswell, John W., and Vicki L. Plano Clark. 2017. *Designing and Conducting Mixed Methods Research*. London: Sage.

Cronon, William. 2009. *Nature's Metropolis: Chicago and the Great West*. W. W. Norton.

Cunha, Victoria. 1988. "The Medium Is the (Rock) Message: A Mythic Comparison of Woodstock and Live Aid." Annual Meeting of the Speech Communication Association, November 3–6, 1988, New Orleans LA.

Dale, Stephen. 1996. *McLuhan's Children: The Greenpeace Message and the Media.* Toronto: Between the Lines.

D'Angelo, Paul, and Jim A. Kuypers, eds. 2010. *Doing News Framing Analysis: Empirical and Theoretical Perspectives.* New York: Routledge.

Davies, William. 2020. "Green Populism? Action and Mortality in the Anthropocene." *Environmental Values* 29, no. 6: 647–68.

Della Porta, Donatella. 2020. "Building Bridges: Social Movements and Civil Society in Times of Crisis." *VOLUNTAS: International Journal of Voluntary and Nonprofit Organizations* 31: 938–48.

DeLuca, Kevin Michael. 2005. *Image Politics: The New Rhetoric of Environmental Activism.* Mahwah NJ: Lawrence Erlbaum Associates.

Demeritt, David. 1994. "The Nature of Metaphors in Cultural Geography and Environmental History." *Progress in Human Geography* 18, no. 2: 163–85.

Demirdöğen, Ülkü D. 2010. "The Roots of Research in (Political) Persuasion: Ethos, Pathos, Logos and the Yale Studies of Persuasive Communications." *International Journal of Social Inquiry* 3, no. 1: 189–201.

De Waal, Alex. 2016. "Designer Activism and Post-Democracy." *Transformation.* https://www.opendemocracy.net/transformation/alex-de-waal/designer-activism-and-post-democracy.

Dieter, Heribert, and Rajiv Kumar. 2008. "The Downside of Celebrity Diplomacy: The Neglected Complexity of Development." *Global Governance* 14, no. 3: 259–64.

Dimitrova, Daniela V., Lynda Lee Kaid, Andrew Paul Williams, and Kaye D. Trammell. 2005. "War on the Web: The Immediate News Framing of Gulf War II." *International Journal of Press/Politics* 10, no. 1: 22–44.

Dlouhy, Jennifer. 2016. "Trump Aides Eye Reviving Keystone by Rescinding LBJ's Order." *Bloomberg Markets,* November 23, 2016. https://www.bloomberg.com/news/articles/2016-11-23/trump-aides-eye-reviving-keystone-by-rescinding-lbj-s-order.

Duggan, Joe. 2016. "Bold Nebraska Leader to Run Umbrella Group, Bold Alliance." *Omaha World-Journal.* https://omaha.com/state-and-regional/bold-nebraska-leader-to-run-umbrella-group-bold-alliance-with-chapters-in-three-other-states/article_e05ee2a2-e551-51d2-a430-498d6d7a204c.html.

Dunaway, Finis. 2008. *Natural Visions: The Power of Images in American Environmental Reform.* Chicago: University of Chicago Press.

Edwards, Lee. 2016. "The Role of Public Relations in Deliberative Systems." *Journal of Communication* 66, no. 1: 60–81.

Edelman.com. 2015. "About Us." http://www.edelman.com/who-we-are/about-us/.

Elbein, Saul. 2014. "Jane Kleeb vs. the Keystone Pipeline." *New York Times*. https://www.nytimes.com/2014/05/18/magazine/jane-kleeb-vs-the-keystone-pipeline.html.

Entman, Robert M. 1993. "Framing: Toward Clarification of a Fractured Paradigm." *Journal of Communication* 43, no. 4: 51–58.

———. 2007. "Framing Bias: Media in the Distribution of Power." *Journal of Communication* 57, no. 1: 163–73.

———. 2008. "Theorizing Mediated Public Diplomacy: The Us Case." *International Journal of Press/Politics* 13, no. 2: 87–102.

Entman, Robert M., and Andrew Rojecki. 1993. "Freezing Out the Public: Elite and Media Framing of the US Anti-nuclear Movement." *Political Communication* 10: 155–73.

Etter, Michael, and Oana Brindusa Albu. 2020. "Activists in the Dark: Social Media Algorithms and Collective Action in Two Social Movement Organizations." *Organization*, 1350508420961532.

Finnegan, Cara A. 2004. "Doing Rhetorical History of the Visual: The Photograph and the Archive." In *Defining Visual Rhetorics*, edited by Charles A. Hill and Marguerite Helmers, 195–214. Mahwah NJ: Lawrence Erlbaum Associates.

Fisher, Walter R. 1987. *Human Communication as Narration: Toward a Philosophy of Reason, Value, and Action*. Columbia: University of South Carolina Press.

Flusberg, Stephen J., Teenie Matlock, and Paul H. Thibodeau. 2017. "Metaphors for the War (or Race) against Climate Change." *Environmental Communication* 11, no. 6: 769–83.

Foss, Sonya K. 2004. "Framing the Study of Visual Rhetoric: Toward a Transformation of Rhetorical Theory." In *Defining Visual Rhetorics*, edited by Charles A. Hill and Marguerite Helmers, 303–31. Mahwah NJ: Lawrence Erlbaum Associates.

Foss, Sonya K., Karen A. Foss, and Robert Trapp. 2014. *Contemporary Perspectives on Rhetoric*. Long Grove IL: Waveland Press.

Foster, John Bellamy, and Brett Clark. 2015. "Crossing the River of Fire: The Liberal Attack on Naomi Klein and This Changes Everything." *Monthly Review* 66, no. 9: 1.

Frank, Thomas. 2020. *The People, No: A Brief History of Anti-populism*. New York: Metropolitan.

Gallicano, Tiffany Derville. 2009. "Personal Relationship Strategies and Outcomes in a Membership Organization." *Journal of Communication Management* 13, no. 4: 310–28.

Gamson, William, and G. Wolsfeld. 1993. "Media and Movements: A Transactional Analysis." *Annals of the American Journal of Political and Social Science* 528: 114–25.

Gamson, William A., Bruce Fireman, and Steven Rytina. 1982. *Encounters with Unjust Authority*. Homewood IL: Dorsey Press.

Gamson, William A., and Andre Modigliani. 1989. "Media Discourse and Public Opinion on Nuclear Power: A Constructionist Approach." *American Journal of Sociology* 95, no. 1: 1–37.

Garofalo, Reebee. 1993. "Understanding Mega-Events." *Peace Review* 5, no. 2: 189–98.

Gellner, Ernest. 2008. *Nations and Nationalism*. Ithaca NY: Cornell University Press.

Gilliam, Franklin D., Jr. 2006. "A New Dominant Frame: The Imperiled Child." E-Zine 22, Frameworks Institute. http://www.frameworksinstitute.org.

Gilliam, Franklin D., Jr., and Susan Nall Bales. 2001. "Strategic Frame Analysis: Reframing America's Youth." *Social Policy Report* 15, no. 3: 3–14.

Gilliam, Franklin D., Jr., and Susan N. Bales. 2002. "Strategic Frame Analysis and Youth Development: How Communications Research Engages the Public." In *Handbook of Applied Developmental Science: Applying Developmental Science for Youth and Families: Historical and Theoretical Foundations*, edited by Richard M. Lerner, Francine Jacobs, and Donald Wertlieb, 421–36. Thousand Oaks CA: Sage.

Gitlin, Todd. 1979. "Prime Time Ideology: The Hegemonic Process in Television Entertainment." *Social Problems* 26, no. 3: 251–66.

———. 1980. *The Whole World Is Watching: Mass Media in the Making and Unmaking of the New Left*. Berkeley: University of California Press.

Gomm, Roger, Martyn Hammersley, and Peter Foster, eds. 2000. *Case Study Method: Key Issues, Key Texts*. Thousand Oaks CA: Sage.

Greenberg, Josh, and Graham Knight. 2004. "Framing Sweatshops: Nike, Global Production, and the American News Media." *Communication and Critical/Cultural Studies* 1, no. 2: 151–75.

Grunig, James E. 1989. "Sierra Club Study Shows Who Become Activists." *Public Relations Review* 15, no. 3: 3–24. doi:10.1016/S0363-8111(89)80001-3.

———. 2000. "Collectivism, Collaboration, and Societal Corporatism as Core Professional Values in Public Relations." *Journal of Public Relations Research* 12, no. 1: 23–48.

———. 2006. "Furnishing the Edifice: Ongoing Research on Public Relations as a Strategic Management Function." *Journal of Public Relations Research* 18, no. 2: 151–76.

References

Grunig, James E., and L. A. Grunig. 2008. "Excellence Theory in Public Relations: Past, Present, and Future." In *Public Relations Research: European and International Perspectives and Innovations*, edited by Ansgar Zerfass, Betteke van Ruler and Krishnamurthy Sriramesh, 327–47. Berlin: Springer Science+Business Media.

Grunig, James E., and Todd Hunt. 1984. *Managing Public Relations*. New York: Holt, Rinehart and Winston.

Grunig, Larissa A. 1986. "Activism and Organizational Response: Contemporary Cases of Collective Behavior." *Association for Education in Journalism and Mass Communication Annual Conference: Public Relations Division*.

———. 1989. *Environmental Activism Revisited: The Changing Nature of Communication through Organizational Public Relations, Special Interest Groups and the Mass Media*. Troy OH: North American Association for Environmental Education.

Guillory, Susan. 2015. "How's Your Press Release Call to Action?" *Cision*. http://www.cision.com/us/2015/05/hows-your-press-release-call-to-action/.

Guiniven, John E. 2002. "Dealing with Activism in Canada: An Ideal Cultural Fit for the Two-Way Symmetrical Public Relations Model." *Public Relations Review* 28, no. 4: 393–402. doi:10.1016/S0363-8111(02)00162-5.

Gulliver, Robyn, Kelly S. Fielding, and Winnifred Louis. 2020. "The Characteristics, Activities and Goals of Environmental Organizations Engaged in Advocacy within the Australian Environmental Movement." *Environmental Communication* 14, no. 5: 614–27.

Gusfield, Joseph R. 1994. "The Reflexivity of Social Movements: Collective Behavior and Mass Society Theory Revisited." In *New Social Movements: From Ideology to Identity*, edited by Enrique Laraña, Hank Johnston, and Joseph Gusfield, 58–78. Philadelphia: Temple University Press.

Guttman, Nurit. 2000. *Public Health Communication Interventions: Values and Ethical Dilemmas*. Thousand Oaks CA: Sage.

Habermas, Jürgen. 1993. *Justification and Application*. Translated by Ciarin Cronin. Cambridge MA: MIT Press.

Hallahan, Kirk. 1999. "Seven Models of Framing: Implications for Public Relations." *Journal of Public Relations Research* 11, no. 3: 205–42. doi:10.1207/s1532754xjprr1103_02.

———. 2001. "The Dynamics of Issues Activation and Response: An Issues Processes Model." *Journal of Public Relations Research* 13, no. 1: 27–59.

Haller, Beth. 1998. "Crawling toward Civil Rights: News Media Coverage of Disability Activism." In *Cultural Diversity and the US Media*, edited by Yahya R. Kamalipour and Theresa Carilli, 89–98. Albany: SUNY Press.

Hansen, Anders. 2011. "Communication, Media and Environment: Towards Reconnecting Research on the Production, Content and Social Implications of Environmental Communication." *International Communication Gazette* 73, no. 1–2: 7–25.

Hansen, James. 2012. "It's Game Over for the Climate." *New York Times*, May 9, 2012. http://www.nytimes.com/2012/05/10/opinion/game-over-for-the-climate .html.

Harold, Christine. 2004. "Pranking Rhetoric: "Culture Jamming" as Media Activism." *Critical Studies in Media Communication* 21, no. 3: 189–211.

Hausdoerffer, John. 2009. *Catlin's Lament: Indians, Manifest Destiny, and the Ethics of Nature*. Lawrence: University Press of Kansas.

Hayter, Roger. 2003. "'The War in the Woods': Post-Fordist Restructuring, Globalization, and the Contested Remapping of British Columbia's Forest Economy." *Annals of the Association of American Geographers* 93, no. 3: 706–29.

Heath, Robert L. 2000. "A Rhetorical Perspective on the Values of Public Relations: Crossroads and Pathways toward Concurrence." *Journal of Public Relations Research* 12, no. 1: 69–91.

Heefner, Gretchen. 2012. "Minutemen Missiles: Hidden in the Heartland." *Huffington Post*, September 20, 2012. http://www.huffingtonpost.com/2012/09/20 /minuteman-missiles-hidden-silos-america_n_1897913.html.

Hefflinger, M. 2014. "Help Farm the Ponca Sacred Corn and No KXL Crop Art." *Bold Nebraska*. http://boldnebraska.org/help-farm-the-ponca-sacred-corn -and-no-kxl-crop-art/.

Heller, Agnes. 1985. "The Discourse Ethics of Habermas: Critique and Appraisal." *Thesis Eleven* 10, no. 1: 5–17.

Helvarg, David. 1998. "Alabama's Eco-bulldogs." *Sports Afield*, September.

Henderson, Alison. 2005. "Activism in 'Paradise': Identity Management in a Public Relations Campaign against Genetic Engineering." *Journal of Public Relations Research* 17, no. 2: 117–37.

The Hill. 2014. "How Blue or Red Is Your State?" October 24, 2014. http://thehill .com/blogs/ballot-box/house-races/221721-how-red-or-blue-is-your-state.

Hilton, Steve. 2018. *Positive Populism: Revolutionary Ideas to Rebuild Economic Security, Family, and Community in America*. New York: Crown Forum.

Hoenisch, Steve. 2005. "Habermas' Theory of Discourse Ethics." *Criticism.com*. http://www.criticism.com/philosophy/habermas-ethics.html.

Holmes, Steven Jon. 1999. *The Young John Muir: An Environmental Biography*. Madison: University of Wisconsin Press.

Hon, Linda Childers, and James E. Grunig. 1999. "Guidelines for Measuring Relationships in Public Relations." Institute for Public Relations. https://www

.instituteforpr.org/wp-content/uploads/Guidelines_Measuring_Relationships .pdf.

IBIS World. 2020. "Global Oil and Gas Exploration and Production Industry Trends (2015–2020)." https://www.ibisworld.com/global/market-research -reports/global-oil-gas-exploration-production-industry/.

Iyengar, Shanto. 1990. "Framing Responsibility for Political Issues: The Case of Poverty." *Political Behavior* 12, no. 1: 19–40.

Jacobs, Joanne. 2012. "Faking It: How to Kill a Business through Astroturfing on Social Media." *Keeping Good Companies* 64, no. 9: 567–70.

Jansen, Robert S. 2011. "Populist Mobilization: A New Theoretical Approach to Populism." *Sociological Theory* 29, no. 2: 75–96.

Jarvis, Brooke. 2013. "Keystone XL: State Department Dodges the Big Questions." *Rolling Stone*, March 13, 2013. http://www.rollingstone.com/politics /news/keystone-xl-state-department-dodges-the-big-questions-20130313.

Jasper, James M. 1997. *The Art of Moral Protest: Culture, Creativity and Biography in Social Movements.* Chicago: University of Chicago Press.

Jenkins, Joseph, and Charles Perrow. 1977. "Insurgency of the Powerless: Farm Worker Movements (1946–1972)." *American Sociological Review* 42, no. 2: 249–68.

Johnson, Davi. 2007. "Martin Luther King Jr.'s 1963 Birmingham Campaign as Image Event." *Rhetoric & Public Affairs* 10, no. 1: 1–25.

Johnson, R. Burke, and Anthony J. Onwuegbuzie. 2004. "Mixed Methods Research: A Research Paradigm Whose Time Has Come." *Educational Researcher* 33, no. 7: 14–26.

Juris, Jeffrey S. 2005. "Violence Performed and Imagined Militant Action, the Black Bloc and the Mass Media in Genoa." *Critique of Anthropology* 25, no. 4: 413–32.

Karlberg, M. 1996. "Remembering the Public in Public Relations Research: From Theoretical to Operational Symmetry." *Journal of Public Relations Research* 8, no. 4: 263–78. doi:10.1207/s1532754xjprr0804_03.

Katz, Bruce, and Jeremy Nowak. 2018. *The New Localism: How Cities Can Thrive in the Age of Populism.* Washington DC: Brookings Institution Press.

Katz, Elihu. 2006. "Rediscovering Gabriel Tarde." *Political Communication* 23, no. 3: 263–70.

Katz, Elihu, and Paul F. Lazarsfeld. 2017. *Personal Influence: The Part Played by People in the Flow of Mass Communications.* New York: Routledge.

Kazin, M. 1998. *The Populist Persuasion: An American History.* Ithaca NY: Cornell University Press.

Kemerling, J. 2019. "Justin Kemerling Design Co." https://www.justinkemerling .com/hello/.

Kensicki, L. J. 2001. "Deaf President Now! Positive Media Framing of a Social Movement within a Hegemonic Political Environment." *Journal of Communication Inquiry* 25, no. 2: 147–66.

Kent, Michael L., and Maureen Taylor. 1998. "Building Dialogic Relationships through the World Wide Web." *Public Relations Review* 24, no. 3: 321–34.

———. 2002. "Toward a Dialogic Theory of Public Relations." *Public Relations Review* 28, no. 1: 21–37.

Keystone-XL.com. 2015. XL Pipeline Maps and Information. https://web.archive .org/web/20150702031052/http://keystone-xl.com/about/the-keystone-xl-oil -pipeline-project/.

———. 2017. "Five Years, 1 Billion Barrels, and 10 More Cool Facts about the Keystone XL Pipeline." https://web.archive.org/web/20170628071206/http:// www.keystone-xl.com/five-years-one-billion-barrels-and-ten-more-cool-facts -about-the-keystone-system/.

Klandermans, Bert. 1992. "The Social Construction of Protest and Multiorganizational Fields." In *Frontiers in Social Movement Theory*, edited by Aldon D. Morris and Carol McClurg Mueller, 77–103. Madison: University of Wisconsin Press.

Klein, Naomi. 2013. "Time for Big Green to Go Fossil Free." *The Nation*, May 1, 2013. http://www.thenation.com/article/174143/time-big-green-go-fossil-free.

Klumpp, James F. 1973. "Challenge of Radical Rhetoric: Radicalization at Columbia." *Western Journal of Communication* 37, no. 3: 146–56.

Koenig, Thomas. 2004. "On Frames and Framing." International Association for Media and Communication Research Annual Meeting, Porto Alegre, Brazil.

Kohn, Sally. 2014. "GOP, Climate Change Is Not Partisan Football." CNN, November 14, 2014. http://www.cnn.com/2014/11/14/opinion/kohn-climate-change /index.html.

Koontz, John. 2003. "Etymology: What Is the Origin of the Word Nebraska?" *Siouan Languages*. https://web.archive.org/web/20171208120202/http://spot .colorado.edu/~koontz/default.htm.

Kowalchuk, Lisa. 2009. "Can Movement Tactics Influence Media Coverage? Health-Care Struggle in the Salvadoran News." *Latin American Research Review* 44, no. 2: 109–35.

Krämer, Benjamin. 2014. "Media Populism: A Conceptual Clarification and Some Theses on Its Effects." *Communication Theory* 24, no. 1: 42–60. http://doi.org /10.1111/comt.12029.

Kruse, Corwin R. 2001. "The Movement and the Media: Framing the Debate over Animal Experimentation." *Political Communication* 18, no. 1: 67–87.

Kutz-Flamenbaum, Rachel V., Suzanne Staggenborg, and Brittany Duncan. 2012. "Media Framing of the Pittsburgh G-20 Protests." *Research in Social Movements, Conflicts and Change* 33: 109–35.

Kuypers, Jim A. 2010. "Framing Analysis from a Rhetorical Perspective." In *Doing News Framing Analysis: Empirical and Theoretical Perspectives*, edited by Paul D'Angelo and Jim A. Kuypers, 286–311. New York: Routledge.

Lakoff, George. 2010. "Why It Matters How We Frame the Environment." *Environmental Communication* 4, no. 1: 70–81.

———. 2014. *The All New Don't Think of an Elephant! Know Your Values and Frame the Debate*. White River Junction VT: Chelsea Green.

Landsman, Gail H. 1987. "Indian Activism and the Press: Coverage of the Conflict at Ganienkeh." *Anthropological Quarterly* 60, no. 3: 101–13.

Larson, Brendon. 2009. "Should Scientists Advocate? The Case of Promotional Metaphors in Environmental Science." In *Communicating Biological Sciences: Ethical and Metaphorical Dimensions*, edited by Brigitte Nerlich, Richard Elliott, and Brendon Larson, 145–52. Surrey: Ashgate.

Larson, Robert W. 1974. *New Mexico Populism: A Study of Radical Protest in a Western Territory*. Louisville: Colorado Associated University Press.

Laycock, David H. 1990. *Populism and Democratic Thought in the Canadian Prairies, 1910–1945*. Toronto: University of Toronto Press.

Leber, Rebecca. 2015. "Stephen Harper Turned Canada into a Climate Villain. The Election Won't Change That." *New Republic*. September 9, 2015. https://newrepublic.com/article/122724/stephen-harper-turned-canada-climate-villain.

Lester, Marilyn. 1980. "Generating Newsworthiness: The Interpretive Construction of Public Events." *American Sociological Review* 45, no. 6: 984–94.

Liebler, Carol M., and Jacob Bendix. 1996. "Old-Growth Forests on Network News: News Sources and the Framing of an Environmental Controversy." *Journalism & Mass Communication Quarterly* 73, no. 1: 53–65.

Lim, Merlyna. 2013. "Framing Bouazizi: 'White Lies,' Hybrid Network, and Collective/Connective Action in the 2010–11 Tunisian Uprising." *Journalism* 14, no. 7: 921–41.

Lundgren, Anna Sofia, and Karin Ljuslinder. 2011. "'The Baby-Boom Is Over and the Ageing Shock Awaits': Populist Media Imagery in News Press Representations of Population Ageing." *International Journal of Ageing and Later Life* 6, no. 2: 39–71.

Mahtesian, Charlie. 2020. "How Trump Rewired the Electoral Map." *Politico*, February 7, 2020. https://www.politico.com/news/magazine/2020/02/07/election-2020-new-electoral-map-110496.

Mann, Charlie Riborg, and George Ransom Twiss. 1910. *Physics*. Chicago: Scott, Foresman.

Martinez, Daniel E., and David J. Cooper. 2017. "Assembling International Development: Accountability and the Disarticulation of a Social Movement." *Accounting, Organizations and Society* 63: 6–20.

Matthes, Jorg. 2009. "What's in a Frame? A Content Analysis of Media Framing Studies in the World's Leading Communication Journals, 1990–2005." *Journalism & Mass Communication Quarterly* 86, no. 2: 349–67.

McAdam, Doug. 1982. *Political Process and the Development of Black Insurgency, 1930–1970*. Chicago: University of Chicago Press.

McCracken, Grant. 1988. *The Long Interview*. Newbury Park CA: Sage.

McCurdy, Patrick. 2013. "Mediation, Practice and Lay Theories of News Media." In *Mediation and Protest Movements*, edited by Bart Cammaerts, Alice Mattoni, and Patrick McCurdy, 57–74. Bristol: Intellect.

McGee, Michael Calvin. 1980. "The 'Ideograph': A Link between Rhetoric and Ideology." *Quarterly Journal of Speech* 66, no. 1: 1–16.

McKee, Robert, and Bronwyn Fryer. 2003. "Storytelling That Moves People." *Harvard Business Review* 81, no. 6: 51–55.

McKibben, Bill. 2016. "Why Dakota Is the New Keystone." *New York Times*. https://www.nytimes.com/2016/10/29/opinion/why-dakota-is-the-new-keystone.html.

Merrill, Karen R. 2002. *Public Lands and Political Meaning: Ranchers, the Government, and the Property between Them*. Berkeley: University of California Press.

Mundy, Dean E. 2013. "The Spiral of Advocacy: How State-Based LGBT Advocacy Organizations Use Ground-up Public Communication Strategies in Their Campaigns for the 'Equality Agenda.'" *Public Relations Review* 39, no. 4: 387–90.

Nadasdy, Paul. 2005. "Transcending the Debate over the Ecologically Noble Indian: Indigenous Peoples and Environmentalism." *Ethnohistory* 52, no. 2: 291–331.

Nasdaq.com. 2020. "TC Energy to Build Keystone XL Pipeline." March 31, 2020. https://www.nasdaq.com/press-release/tc-energy-to-build-keystone-xl-pipeline-2020-03-31.

National Park Service. 2021. "National Natural Landmarks: Nebraska Sand Hills." https://www.nps.gov/subjects/nnlandmarks/site.htm?Site=NESA-NE.

National Resource Defense Council. 2015. "Stop the Keystone XL Pipeline." https://web.archive.org/web/20151207050225/http://www.nrdc.org/energy/keystone-pipeline/.

Nelson, John. 2018. *Cowboy Politics: Myths and Discourses in Popular Westerns from "The Virginian" to "Unforgiven" and "Deadwood."* Lanham MD: Lexington Press.

Nerlich, Brigitte. 2010. "'Climategate': Paradoxical Metaphors and Political Paralysis." *Environmental Values* 19, no. 4: 419–42.

———. 2012. "'Low Carbon' Metals, Markets and Metaphors: The Creation of Economic Expectations about Climate Change Mitigation." *Climatic Change* 110, no. 1–2: 31–51.

Nerlich, Brigitte, and Nelya Koteyko. 2009. "Carbon Reduction Activism in the UK: Lexical Creativity and Lexical Framing in the Context of Climate Change." *Environmental Communication* 3, no. 2: 206–23.

Neumeier, Marty. 2005. *The Brand Gap.* Berkeley CA: Peachpit.

Ostler, Jeffrey. 1992. "Why the Populist Party Was Strong in Kansas and Nebraska but Weak in Iowa." *Western Historical Quarterly* 23, no. 4: 451–74.

———. 1993. *Prairie Populism: The Fate of Agrarian Radicalism in Kansas, Nebraska, and Iowa, 1880–1892.* Lawrence: University Press of Kansas.

Pan, Zhongdang, and Gerald M. Kosicki. 1993. "Framing Analysis: An Approach to News Discourse." *Political Communication* 10, no. 1: 55–75.

Patterson, Graeme. 1990. *History and Communications: Harold Innis, Marshall McLuhan, the Interpretation of History.* Toronto: University of Toronto Press.

Pearson, Ron. 1989. "Business Ethics as Communication Ethics: Public Relations Practice and the Idea of Dialogue." *Public Relations Theory* 27, no. 2: 111–31.

Peterson, Richard A. 1973. "The Unnatural History of Rock Festivals: An Instance of Media Facilitation." *Popular Music & Society* 2, no. 2: 97–123.

Pholi, Kerryn. 2014. "Recognize What?" *The Spectator—Australia.* https://www.spectator.com.au/2014/06/recognise-what/.

Piven, Frances Fox, and Richard Cloward. 1978. *Poor People's Movements: Why They Succeed, How They Fail.* New York: Vintage.

Poli, Corrado. 2015. "Populism and Environmentalism." In *Environmental Politics: New Geographical and Social Constituencies*, by Corrado Poli, 39–44. Cham: Springer.

Rademacher, Heidi E. 2020. "Transnational Social Movement Organizations and Gender Mainstreaming Bureaucracies: An Event History Analysis, 1981–1998." *International Journal of Sociology* 50, no. 6: 445–72.

Reber, Bryan H., and Bruce K. Berger. 2005. "Framing Analysis of Activist Rhetoric: How the Sierra Club Succeeds or Fails at Creating Salient Messages." *Public Relations Review* 31, no. 2: 185–95. doi:10.1016/j.pubrev.2005.02.020.

Redford, Kent H. 1991. "The Ecologically Noble Savage." *Cultural Survival Quarterly* 15, no. 1: 46–48.

Reese, Stephen. D. 2001. "Prologue: Framing Public Life." In *Framing Public Life: Perspectives on Media and Our Understanding of the Social World*, edited by S. Reese, O. Gandy, and A. Grant. Mahwah NJ: Lawrence Erlbaum Associates.

Renzi, Barbara Gabriella, Matthew Cotton, Guilio Napolitano, and Ralf Barkemeyer. 2017. "Rebirth, Devastation and Sickness: Analyzing the Role of Metaphor in Media Discourses of Nuclear Power." *Environmental Communication* 11, no. 5: 624–40.

Riffe, Daniel, Stephen Lacy, and Frederick Fico. 2014. *Analyzing Media Messages: Using Quantitative Content Analysis in Research*. New York: Routledge.

Rogers, Everett M. 2010. *Diffusion of Innovations*. New York: Simon and Schuster.

Rohler, Lloyd. 1999. "Conservative Appeals to the People: George Wallace's Populist Rhetoric." *Southern Communication Journal* 64, no. 4: 316–22.

Rolfe, Mark. 2016. *Reinvention of Populist Rhetoric in the Digital Age*. London: Palgrave Macmillan.

Rooduijn, Matthijs, and Teun Pauwels. 2011. "Measuring Populism: Comparing Two Methods of Content Analysis." *West European Politics* 34, no. 6: 1272–83.

Rotstein, Abraham. 1977. "Innis: The Alchemy of Fur and Wheat." *Journal of Canadian Studies* 12, no. 5: 6–31.

Russill, Chris. 2009. "Whale Wars: A Deeper Shade of Green on the Public Screen." FlowTV. http://flowtv.org/?p3465.

Ryan, Charlotte, Kevin M. Carragee, and William Meinhofer. 2001. "Theory into Practice: Framing, the News Media, and Collective Action." *Journal of Broadcasting & Electronic Media* 45, no. 1: 175–82.

Ryan, Charlotte M., Karen Jeffreys, Jim Ryczek, and Janelle Diaz. 2014. "Building Public Will: The Battle for Affordable—and Supportive—Housing." *Journal of Poverty* 18, no. 3: 335–54.

Saldana, Dave. 2014. "Willie Nelson and Neil Young Come to the Aid of Bold Nebraska." Center for Media and Democracy's PR Watch. http://www.prwatch.org/news/2014/08/12580/willie-nelson-neil-young-come-aid-bold-nebraska.

Salt Lake Herald. 1903. "Boom for Gen. Torrance." September 25, 1903. https://chroniclingamerica.loc.gov/lccn/sn85058130/1903-09-25/ed-1/seq-6/.

Seguin, Chantal, Luc G. Pelletier, and John Hunsley. 1998. "Toward a Model of Environmental Activism." *Environment and Behavior* 30, no. 5: 628–52.

Seidman, Gay W. 2000. "Adjusting the Lens: What Do Globalizations, Transnationalism, and the anti-Apartheid Movement Mean for Social Movement Theory." In *Globalizations and Social Movements: Culture, Power, and the Transnational Public Sphere*, edited by John Guidry, Michael D. Kennedy, and Mayer Zald, 339–58. Ann Arbor: University of Michigan Press.

Semetko, Holli A., and Patti M. Valkenburg. 2000. "Framing European Politics: A Content Analysis of Press and Television News." *Journal of Communication* 50, no. 2: 93–109.

Semino, Elena, and Michela Masci. 1996. "Politics Is Football: Metaphor in the Discourse of Silvio Berlusconi in Italy." *Discourse & Society* 7, no. 2: 243–69.

Seo, Hyunjin, Ji Young Kim, and Sung-Un Yang. 2009. "Global Activism and New Media: A Study of Transnational NGOs' Online Public Relations." *Public Relations Review* 35, no. 2: 123–26. doi:10.1016/j.pubrev.2009.02.002.

Shaw, Christopher, and Brigitte Nerlich. 2015. "Metaphor as a Mechanism of Global Climate Change Governance: A Study of International Policies, 1992–2012." *Ecological Economics* 109, 34–40.

Simmons, Terry Allan. 1974. "The Damnation of a Dam: The High Ross Dam Controversy." Master's thesis, Simon Fraser University, 1974.

Smith, Ronald D. 2013. *Strategic Planning for Public Relations*. New York: Routledge.

Snow, D. A., R. Vliegenthart, and P. Ketelaars. 2018. "The Framing Perspective on Social Movements: Its Conceptual Roots and Architecture." In *The Wiley Blackwell Companion to Social Movements*, 392–410. Oxford: Wiley Blackwell.

Snow, David A., and Robert D. Benford. 1988. "Ideology, Frame Resonance, and Participant Mobilization." *International Social Movement Research* 1, no. 1: 197–217.

———. 1992. "Master Frames and Cycles of Protest." In *Frontiers in Social Movement Theory*, edited by Aldon D. Morris and Carol McClurg Mueller, 133–55. New Haven: Yale University Press.

———. 2000. "Clarifying the Relationship between Framing and Ideology in the Study of Social Movements: A Comment on Oliver and Johnston." *Mobilization* 5, no. 2: 55–60.

Snow, David A., E. Burke Rochford Jr., Steven K. Worden, and Robert D. Benford. 1986. "Frame Alignment Processes, Micromobilization, and Movement Participation." *American Sociological Review* 51, no. 4: 464–81.

Sobkowicz, Pawel, Michael Kaschesky, and Guillaume Bouchard. 2012. "Opinion Mining in Social Media: Modeling, Simulating, and Forecasting Political Opinions in the Web." *Government Information Quarterly* 29, no. 4: 470–79.

Sommerfeldt, Erich J. 2013. "The Civility of Social Capital: Public Relations in the Public Sphere, Civil Society, and Democracy." *Public Relations Review* 39, no. 4: 280–89.

Stake, Robert E. 1978. "The Case Study Method in Social Inquiry." *Educational Researcher* 7, no. 2: 5–8.

Stanley, Ben. 2008. "The Thin Ideology of Populism." *Journal of Political Ideologies* 13, no. 1, 95–110. http://doi.org/10.1080/13569310701822289.

Steinert, Heinz. 2003. "The Indispensable Metaphor of War: On Populist Politics and the Contradictions of the State's Monopoly of Force." *Theoretical Criminology* 7, no. 3: 265–91.

Steinmetz, George. 1992. "Reflections on the Role of Social Narratives in Working-Class Formation: Narrative Theory in the Social Sciences." *Social Science History* 16, no. 3: 489–516.

Stephens, John, and Robyn McCallum. 1998. *Retelling Stories, Framing Culture: Traditional Story and Metanarratives in Children's Literature*. New York: Garland.

Stokes, Ashli Q. 2005. "Metabolife's Meaning: A Call for the Constitutive Study of Public Relations." *Public Relations Review* 31, no. 4: 556–65.

———. 2013. "You Are What You Eat: Slow Food USA's Constitutive Public Relations." *Journal of Public Relations Research* 25, no. 1: 68–90.

Stokes, Ashli Q., and Donald Rubin. 2009. "Activism and the Limits of Symmetry: The Public Relations Battle between Colorado GASP and Philip Morris." *Journal of Public Relations Research* 22, no. 1: 26–48.

Suddaby, Roy, and Royston Greenwood. 2005. "Rhetorical Strategies of Legitimacy." *Administrative Science Quarterly* 50, no. 1: 35–67.

Sweetser, Kay D., Guy J. Golan, and Wayne Wanta. 2008. "Intermedia Agenda Setting in Television, Advertising, and Blogs during the 2004 Election." *Mass Communication & Society* 11, no. 2: 197–216.

Szasz, Andrew. 1994. *Ecopopulism: Toxic Waste and the Movement for Environmental Justice*. Minneapolis: University of Minnesota Press.

Ten Eyck, Toby A., and Melissa Williment. 2003. "The National Media and Things Genetic Coverage in the *New York Times* (1971–2001) and the *Washington Post* (1977–2001)." *Science Communication* 25, no. 2: 129–52.

Terkildsen, Nayda, and Frauke Schnell. 1997. "How Media Frames Move Public Opinion: An Analysis of the Women's Movement." *Political Research Quarterly* 50, no. 4: 879–900.

Thompson, Paul B. 1997. *Food Biotechnology in Ethical Perspective*. London: Blackie.

Tierney, Kathleen, Christine Bevc, and Erica Kuligowski. 2006. "Metaphors Matter: Disaster Myths, Media Frames, and Their Consequences in Hurricane Katrina." *Annals of the American Academy of Political and Social Science* 604, no. 1: 57–81.

TransCanada. 2017. "Stronger Together—Celebrating One Year Anniversary of CPG Acquisition." https://www.tcenergy.com/stories/business-and-economy/stronger-together--celebrating-one-year-anniversary-of-cpg-acquisition/.

Tsatsanis, Emannouil. 2011. "Hellenism under Siege: The National-Populist Logic of Antiglobalization Rhetoric in Greece." *Journal of Political Ideologies* 16, no. 1: 11–31.

Tuchman, Gaye. 1978. *Making News: A Study in the Construction of Reality.* New York: Free Press.

Tufekci, Zeynep. 2013. "'Not This One': Social Movements, the Attention Economy, and Microcelebrity Networked Activism." *American Behavioral Scientist* 57, no. 7: 848–70.

U.S. Census Bureau. 2019. Nebraska Quick Facts. https://www.census.gov /quickfacts/fact/table/NE#.

U.S. Energy Information Administration. 2020. "Petroleum and Other Liquids Imports by Country of Origin." https://www.eia.gov/dnav/pet/pet_move _impcus_a2_nus_epc0_im0_mbblpd_a.htm.

U.S. Geological Survey. 2009. "Water Quality in the High Plains Aquifer, Colorado, Kansas, Nebraska, New Mexico, Oklahoma, South Dakota, Texas, and Wyoming, 1999–2004." Available at https://pubs.usgs.gov/circ/1337/pdf/C1337 .pdf.

Väliverronen, Esa. 1998. "Biodiversity and the Power of Metaphor in Environmental Discourse." *Science & Technology Studies* 11, no. 1: 19–34.

Van Dyke, Nella, and Bryan Amos. 2017. "Social Movement Coalitions: Formation, Longevity, and Success." *Sociology Compass* 11, no. 7: e12489.

Vollaire, Rich. 2019. "Logo Design: Cowboy and Indian Alliance." https://www .richvollaire.com/#/cowboy-indian-alliance/.

Walsh, Edward J. 1981. "Resource Mobilization and Citizen Protest in Communities around Three Mile Island." *Social Problems* 29, no.1: 1–21.

Walton, Bryan K., and Conner Bailey. 2005. "Framing Wilderness: Populism and Cultural Heritage as Organizing Principles." *Society and Natural Resources* 18, no. 2: 119–34.

Watson, Bruce. 2002. "George Catlin's Obsession." *Smithsonian Magazine.* http:// www.smithsonianmag.com/arts-culture/george-catlins-obsession-72840046/.

Weaver, C. Kay. 2010. "Carnivalesque Activism as a Public Relations Genre: A Case Study of the New Zealand Group Mothers against Genetic Engineering." *Public Relations Review* 36, no. 1: 35–41.

Wellock, Thomas R. 1998. *Critical Masses: Opposition to Nuclear Power in California, 1958–1978.* Madison: University of Wisconsin Press.

Widener, Patricia. 2007. "Benefits and Burdens of Transnational Campaigns: A Comparison of Four Oil Struggles in Ecuador." *Mobilization: An International Quarterly* 12, no. 1: 21–36.

Wiktorowicz, Quintan. 2004. *Islamic Activism: A Social Movement Theory Approach*. Bloomington: Indiana University Press.

Wilkinson, Katharine K. 2012. *Between God and Green: How Evangelicals Are Cultivating a Middle Ground on Climate Change*. Oxford, UK: Oxford University Press.

Willow, Anna. 2010. "Images of American Indians in Environmental Education: Anthropological Reflections on the Politics and History of Cultural Representation." *American Indian Culture and Research Journal* 34, no. 1: 67–88.

Wilson, Robert M. 2017. "Faces of the Climate Movement." *Environmental History* 22, no. 1: 128–39.

Wodak, Ruth. 2015. *The Politics of Fear: What Right-Wing Populist Discourses Mean*. London: Sage.

Wodak, Ruth, Majid Khosravinik, and Brigitte Mral. 2013. *Right-Wing Populism in Europe: Politics and Discourse*. London: A&C Black.

Wolfgang, Ben. 2015. "A Republican President in 2017 Could Revive Debate over Keystone Pipeline." *Washington Times*, November 9, 2015. http://www.washingtontimes.com/news/2015/nov/9/keystone-oil-pipeline-debate-could-rise-again-with/?page=all.

Worster, Donald. 2004. *Dust Bowl: The Southern Plains in the 1930s*. Oxford, UK: Oxford University Press.

Youngdale, James M. 1975. *Populism: A Psychohistorical Perspective*. Port Washington NY: Kennikat Press.

Zilber, Tammar B., Rivka Tuval-Mashiach, and Amia Lieblich. 2008. "The Embedded Narrative: Navigating through Multiple Contexts." *Qualitative Inquiry* 14, no. 6: 1047–69.

INDEX

Page locators in italics indicate illustrations.

CPSIA information can be obtained
at www.ICGtesting.com
Printed in the USA
LVHW101808251022
731529LV00002B/77

9 781496 208392